# Dynamite Gloves

# Dynamite Gloves

## The Fighting Lives of Boxing's Big Punchers

### John Jarrett

'The puncher always has a chance. Give me the guy who can punch, to manage, to bet on, or just to watch.'

Jimmy Johnston, *The Bog Bandit*, 1935

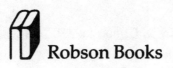 Robson Books

First published in Great Britain in 2001 by Robson Books,
10 Blenheim Court, Brewery Road, London N7 9NT

A member of the Chrysalis Group plc

All photographs are from the author's private collection.

The author and the publishers have made every reasonable effort to
contact all copyright holders. Any errors that may have occurred are
inadvertent and anyone who for any reason has not been contacted
is invited to write to the publishers so that a full acknowledgement
may be made in subsequent editions of this work.

0857193361

British Library Cataloguing in Publication Data
A catalogue record for this title is available from the British Library

ISBN 1 86105 409 2

Typeset by SX Composing DTP, Rayleigh, Essex
Printed by Mackays of Chatham plc, Chatham, Kent

I wish to dedicate this book to my wife Mary
for always being in my corner

| | |
|---|---|
| CPP | CLN |
| CBA | CLO |
| CFU | CMI |
| CIN 5/02 | CPE |
| CKI 12/02 | CRI |
| CLE | CSA |
| CLH 11/01 | CSH |
| CLHH | |

# Acknowledgements

I wish to place on record my sincere thanks and appreciation to Bernard Hart of Lonsdale Sports and Jeremy Robson of Robson Books for their encouragement and support in getting this thing airborne. I hope it flies okay.

John Jarrett
February 2001

# Contents

# Introduction

I suppose we all like to finish work early, and boxers are no different. They don't fight more than twelve rounds these days but if they can get it over with in round one, so much the better. Former WBA welterweight champion Jose 'Pipino' Cuevas used to say, 'I come for a knockout whenever I fight. I have to end it as soon as possible because I know the other guy is trying to do the same thing to me.'

All fight fans love the thrill of a knockout, whether it comes in the first round or the last. It brings them to their feet with a roar in their throats and gives them something to talk about until next time. As old-time fight manager and promoter Jimmy Johnston would say, 'The puncher always has a chance. Give me the guy who can punch, to manage, to bet on, or just to watch.'

In the following pages you will meet some of the best punchers in the business, some of my favourites anyway. From tiny tearaways like Terrible Terry McGovern and Jimmy Wilde to murderous middleweights like Stanley Ketchel, Sugar Ray Robinson, and Rocky

Graziano, to heavyweight hitters like Jack Dempsey, Joe Louis, and Rocky Marciano. Some of them had little or no education, but they knew the shortest distance between two points was a straight right, and that added up to money in the bank! The dynamite in their fists blasted them out of the gutter, out of dead-end jobs, off the unemployment lines, to a permanent place in boxing's hall of fame. This book tells you how they got there. Seconds out!

# The Brooklyn Terror

# 1

For a skinny little fellow, Terry McGovern was a deadly puncher. Just how deadly was perhaps best attested by a story told by veteran New York sports columnist Frank Graham.

'One night, Jimmy Johnston, then a fighter, was looking at some bouts at the old Polo Athletic Club in New York, when the match-maker came to him and asked him to go in as a substitute. "Against who?" demanded Jimmy. "Terry McGovern," he was told. "Not me!" said Jimmy, shaking his head. A fighter named Charley Roden was sitting next to Johnston and he offered to take on Terrible Terry. So he went in with McGovern. Roden was only about 5ft 4in tall, and McGovern hit him so hard on the top of his head that he never grew another inch!'

Sam Taub was associated with boxing for over sixty years. A sports writer and editor for the *New York Morning Telegraph*, he pioneered live blow-by-blow announcing of fights on the radio and reckoned he had seen almost 12,000 fights and broadcast 7,500 of them. 'No matter how long a man may be associated with boxing,' he said in 1974, 'he will have his heroes. My first idol was Terry McGovern, the Brooklyn Madcap, who became the bantamweight and later feather-weight champion of the world. Terry was a fury in the ring and never put up a bad performance in his entire career.'

In his 1958 autobiography, Nat Fleischer wrote, 'In 1899 I saw my first professional fight, a contest in which Terry McGovern was pitted against Pedlar Palmer, the British champion. I've lived that fight over and over again. For me that was the thrill of thrills . . . to be twelve years old and present at one of the most talked-about bouts in American pugilism!

'My home was but a few doors away from the Brace Memorial School for newsboys, an organization opposite St Bridget's Church on the corner of Avenue A and Eighth Street in New York City. I did chores after school for Superintendent Walter Grosvenor and Grove Dale, the athletic director. The walls of Dale's room were decorated with photographs of famous athletes, and McGovern was among his favourites. I had completed dusting when Dale, pointing to McGovern, remarked, "There's a great little fighter. I'm going to see him box for the championship tomorrow. Mr Grosvenor was to accompany me, but he can't make it. If you can get permission from your mother, I'll take you along." I was delighted at the invitation but needless to say, I didn't ask my mother, knowing her answer would be "No!" Instead, I rushed out of the building, waited a while, then returned to tell Mr Dale that permission had been granted. The impression that fight left me with patterned my future.'

Fleischer went on to become a journalist and sports editor and in 1922 founded *The Ring* magazine, which he published and edited until his death in 1972. In his all-time rankings of the world's best fighters, he always rated Terry McGovern the number one featherweight. Many years later, in his 1943 biography of McGovern, Fleischer would recall, 'A bright and dazzling light of the roped arena was the great little champion, Joseph Terrence McGovern, the pride of Brooklyn. "Terrible Terry" they called him, and truly terrible he was to the majority of the opponents he encountered during his fistic career. No bantamweight or featherweight ever packed a more dangerous punch than did Terry. No fighter of his weight piled up such a consistent record for tearing pell-mell into his adversaries and smothering them with wicked jolts, hooks, uppercuts, and vicious swings. In every sense of the phrase, he was a pugilistic marvel . . . During McGovern's brief, but startlingly spectacular reign of two years, he rolled up a bigger knockout record than was amassed by John L. Sullivan in the latter's entire career.'

Terry McGovern, the fighter they called The Brooklyn Terror, was actually born in Jamestown, Pennsylvania, in 1880, a week short of St Patrick's Day. He was still a babe in arms when the family moved to New York City and settled in South Brooklyn. The area around Court Street, where the McGoverns lived, was a predominantly Irish working-class neighbourhood and fist-fighting was a way of life for the kids who ran the streets. And young Joseph Terrence McGovern was a kid who loved to fight just for the hell of it.

Yet it was baseball, Terry's second love, that led him into a career as a professional fighter. Still in his teens when his father died, the boy worked in a local lumber yard and organized their baseball team. In a dispute with a rival team captain, Terry put the gloves on with the other young fellow and they were still slugging each other when darkness came and their pals pulled them apart. By that time, the gloves were torn to shreds and the boys didn't look much better.

Young McGovern's boss at the lumber yard, Charley Mayhood, was a boxing nut and he saw potential in the wild Irish slugger. With former welterweight Harry Fisher training him, Terry was entered in a local amateur competition at 105 pounds. He was a sensation, his dynamite fists knocking out four opponents on the first night, three the next day, and four more on finals night to clinch the title. Terry McGovern was the talk of the town as he knocked out 21 of his 31 amateur foes and Charley Mayhood signed him for his first professional fight at Dan Jackson's club in April 1897. Jack Shea was belted out inside the first round and Terry's end of the purse came to $25.

Terry always credited Billy Newman with giving him his start on the championship ladder. Billy ran fight shows at the old Polo Athletic Club at 155th Street and Eighth Avenue and was the first promoter to realize the possibilities of cheap boxing in New York. Newman ran weekly shows on a Saturday night and the young Irish kid from Brooklyn soon became a regular headliner. When Newman ran fights at the Waverley Club in Yonkers, one of his best attractions was Terry McGovern. The first of his three fights with George Munroe took place there in May 1898, twenty rounds at 112 pounds. This was a tremendous scrap that finished up all square, and Munroe demanded a return bout over twenty-five rounds. That was George's big mistake. Holding his own after twenty rounds, Munroe was tiring and, coming out for the twenty-fourth session, he was an easy target for McGovern's savage assault. A crashing right to the head floored Munroe for a count of nine and no sooner was he upright than he was smashed to the canvas again. Just beating the count, George was defenceless and Terry's final right to the chin dropped him on his face to be counted out.

The sensational victory put McGovern in the fistic headlines. It also had a far-reaching effect on his career. George Munroe's manager was a young Jewish fellow named Sam Harris and as he viewed the wreckage of his meal ticket that night in Yonkers, he figured it wouldn't be a bad idea to have a few words with this McGovern boy.

So he took Charley Mayhood and his tiger for a bite of supper and things worked out very nicely. 'Mayhood,' wrote Fleischer, 'accepted Harris's offer to manage the boy with the stipulation that he (Mayhood) should attend to Terry's training. It was a wise move, for the Harris-McGovern-Mayhood combination was slated to turn out a very successful one. Under its astute workings, Terry McGovern was to become internationally famous as the prize ring's greatest sensation.'

Oddly enough, in his first fight for his new manager, McGovern was beaten for the first time as a professional. It was also odd that Harris agreed to the conditions laid down by Tim Callahan's cagey manager Billy Roche, that there would be a clean break and no hitting in the clinches, exactly the type of warfare in which Terry excelled. Callahan was a good boxer and after seven rounds he was leading on points. He was also tiring as young McGovern forced him around the ring. Back in the corner after the tenth round, manager Roche whispered some advice in Tim's ear.

At that time there existed an organization known as the American Protective Association, a somewhat fanatical body opposed to the Roman Catholic Church. McGovern was a staunch Roman Catholic, as indeed was Callahan, but that didn't stop him baiting Terry as they got to grips in round eleven. 'You're nothing but an APA rat!' he said to Terry in a clinch, 'and I never saw one of them I couldn't lick.'

McGovern's Irish temper flared immediately and, grabbing Callahan around the neck with one glove, he smashed his other fist into his face several times before the referee pulled them apart and sent Terry to his corner, disqualified. Callahan returned to his corner to be met by a smiling Billy Roche, who had gambled on McGovern losing his temper and breaking the rules, thus losing a fight he was winning.

That fight was in July 1898 and Terry McGovern would not be beaten again until November 1901. He fought 41 times, and those hammering fists sent 33 of his victims home early. He strung 18 consecutive knockouts together in one ten-month stretch, taking out some of the biggest names in the business, men like Pedlar Palmer, George Dixon, Harry Forbes, Patsy Haley, Eddie Santry and Oscar Gardner. It was awesome power for a little guy who weighed 115 pounds soaking wet!

In his first fight with Harry Forbes, McGovern was in at the deep end, for the Chicago battler was not only a fine boxer but possessed of a knockout punch, and Windy City fans were already acclaiming him the natural successor to their own Jimmy Barry as world bantamweight champion. Having cleaned up the best in the west, Forbes was ready for the best in the east, and that meant Terry McGovern. The Brooklyn Terror at least had the advantage of fighting on home turf, for the match was secured by veteran Johnny Reagan, the bareknuckle scrapper who went forty-five rounds with Nonpareil Jack Dempsey in a famous battle for the middleweight title. Reagan staged the fight at the Pelican Athletic Club at Bay Ridge, Brooklyn, the winner to receive $200 against $100 to the loser, twenty rounds or less.

As recorded by Nat Fleischer many years later, McGovern 'smashed into Forbes at high speed, trying for a quick knockout, but the Chicagoan ducked, sidestepped, and blocked like a miniature Jim Corbett, and for several rounds he completely baffled McGovern. But these terrific onslaughts began to worry Forbes, who found himself so busy trying to dodge wicked punches that he couldn't retaliate in kind and was forced to fall back on strictly defensive tactics. Yet the Chicago lad rallied, brought all his science to bear on the situation and repeatedly took the upper hand by dint of clever, effective jabbing, and fast footwork that constantly carried him safely out of the danger zone.

'As the fifteenth round opened . . . the Chicagoan came out of his corner swiftly and met McGovern halfway, risking a slugging match with the dynamic Brooklynite. They were mixing like wildcats, when suddenly McGovern dropped his guard and backed away. Forbes, thinking his opponent had weakened, rushed him. Terry let go a flashing right that landed clean on the jawpoint. Forbes stiffened, fell forward on his face and was counted out. The Chicago lad had stepped into a trap and the teeth had closed on him. The incident was remarkable in that Terry had never been known to 'pull a stall' in that fashion . . . But on this occasion, at least, he outfoxed a really clever boxer.'

Austin Rice had a reputation as an iron man of the ring and had never been knocked out when he faced McGovern at the Pelican Club in December 1898. He brought a big crowd with him from Connecticut and their wagers were readily covered by the sporting citizens of Brooklyn. Booked for twenty-five rounds, this was a good fight for ten heats with Rice giving as good as he received, and in the eleventh he had Terry reeling from a terrific right to the jaw. But the boy they were already calling Terrible Terry came storming back at his man and in the fourteenth, with their man being hammered from pillar to post, Rice's seconds threw the towel in. As Fleischer recalled, 'Austin's legendary armour of proof had cracked under the hammer assaults of the Brooklyn socker!'

A month later McGovern's growing legion of supporters jammed the Greenwood Club in Brooklyn to see him fight Casper Leon, the Sicilian-born veteran and idol of New York's Italian-American fans. Leon could box and he could punch, but he had been around the block a couple of times and Terrible Terry was a solid two-to-one on favourite by the time the first bell rang to send them on their twenty-five rounds journey. Casper made it to halfway, almost. He was gradually worn down by the tireless aggression of the kid from Brooklyn and was in bad shape answering the bell for round twelve. McGovern now launched a savage body attack that drove Leon back to the ropes where he was rocked to his toenails by a vicious left hook. He tried to clinch but Terry shook him off and smashed a terrific left to the jaw that dropped Leon to the canvas for the full count.

McGovern and Leon would fight again but it didn't make the record books. In his autobiography *50 Years At Ringside*, Nat Fleischer would recall, 'It was at the Howard Athletic Club in New York City in 1912 that I saw the greatest all-out Donnybrook ever staged outside Ireland. The three McGoverns, the famous Terry and his brothers Hughie and Phil, engaged the three Leons, Casper, Jack and Benny, in a family affair. In this sensational bout, Phil McGovern was fighting Benny Leon. Terry and Hughie McGovern were handling Phil in his corner, while Casper and Jack were looking after Benny. It was a marvellous scrap and eventually Benny knocked Phil flat with a right cross. Terry McGovern, tricky as ever, reached for the arm of the time-keeper to prevent him from counting Phil out.

'Casper Leon took in the situation in a flash and rushed towards Terry. The audience stood on its feet yelling as these two ex-monarchs of the ring tore into each other. Before anybody knew what was happening, Hughie McGovern had dashed over to Terry's aid and encountered Jack Leon en route. In an instant the crowd forgot all about the fight between Phil and Benny . . . To deafening cheers, the battling brothers went at it like infuriated terriers. The fighting blood of the Italians and the Irish was at boiling point and it was streaming down the faces of the contestants. Some of the spectators dashed into the fray and then a full-dress riot began. It raged for best part of half-an-hour and was quelled when Captain Reynolds and his police reserves rushed to the scene . . . They were accustomed to being called out to subdue the riotous McGoverns, who spent the greater part of their time beating up the New York bluecoats!'

When he had just turned nineteen, however, Terry McGovern was more interested in beating up his fellow man in the boxing ring, and for his birthday in March 1899 they gave him Patsy Haley at the Lenox Club in New York City. From Buffalo, Haley was a brilliant boxer and his dazzling left hand and speedy footwork kept him out of the danger zone for eight rounds. But from round nine a veritable rain of blows threatened to wash Haley clear out of the ring. McGovern's body punches took all the steam out of Patsy and in the eighteenth round he was felled by a tremendous right to the jaw. When he got up it was all over.

By that summer of '99, efforts were being made on both sides of the Atlantic for a contest between the British bantamweight champion Pedlar Palmer and George Dixon, the world featherweight titleholder. On a hurried visit to New York in January 1896, Pedlar had boxed a six-round draw with the heavier man, and both London and New York wanted them to box for Dixon's title. With neither side able to reach agreement, Sam Harris stepped in and made a firm offer to Palmer's manager Peggy Bettinson for Pedlar to meet McGovern for the world's bantamweight title at Tuckahoe, New York, on 12 September. Thinking McGovern an easier fight than Dixon, Bettinson accepted.

In his 1956 history of the National Sporting Club, *Noble and Manly*, author Guy Deghy wrote, 'The startling novelty about Pedlar Palmer in the ring was that he made it all seem so easy. The elegance of battling without ever having to resort to an evident reserve of energy had already impressed the Club in Peter Jackson's style, but here was a little man who ducked fast blows and dodged well-placed punches with the grace of a ballet dancer, and bobbed up again taunting and mocking his adversary with his playful, smiling, cheeky alertness. Here at last was the first of the National Sporting Club's own stars.'

By the time he stepped into the ring at that wooden arena at Tuckahoe outside New York to face McGovern, Palmer had beaten Billy Plimmer to become British champion and racked up notable victories over visiting American stars like Johnny Murphy, Eddie

Stanton, Dave Sullivan and Billy Rotchford. He was unbeaten as a money fighter, with only the draw with George Dixon spoiling his perfect record. He was anxious to meet Dixon again for his title, but first there was this Irish fellow from Brooklyn . . .

In his previous fight, Terry had annihilated Johnny Ritchie inside three rounds of a fight set for twenty-five rounds at 118 pounds and described by the *New York Herald* as being for the American bantamweight title. Now he was to meet Palmer for the world championship vacated by Jimmy Barry, with the limit set at 116 pounds. Terry was half-a-pound inside, with the Cockney from Canning Town two pounds lighter. The contest had aroused tremendous interest and a crowd of 10,000 arrived in special trains. Around the ring sat such prominent pugs as the mighty John L Sullivan, Jim Corbett, Kid McCoy, Jack McAuliffe, Bob Fitzsimmons and Tom Sharkey. When they were introduced from the ring, Sullivan received the biggest cheer – he was still their favourite, him and this little fellow called Terrible Terry McGovern, the Brooklyn Terror.

From an upstairs window of a house overlooking the arena, Terry's young wife Grace watched and waited, holding their two-month-old son, Joey, and she felt better when Terry managed to wave a glove from his corner before timekeeper Johnny Pollock sent them on their way. Palmer tried two left jabs which were short of the target and, as McGovern stepped back, Pedlar lost his balance and fell to his knees. Back on his feet, the Englishman was suddenly in trouble. McGovern unleashed a furious attack and Palmer was driven to the ropes, his efforts at retaliation brushed aside by the savage fury of the American's flying fists.

'McGovern had smiled once,' wrote Fleischer in his 1943 biography, 'when the battle began. Then his mouth had shut like a steel trap as he stalked his prey like a fighting pit terrier, his jaws set in bulldog viciousness . . . his speed increased, his battering swings grew faster and more furious, and Palmer was wilting under the punishment. The little Englishman couldn't escape by footwork. Terry had him cornered. But there came a momentary respite for the hapless visiting boxer, for suddenly the bell rang and McGovern checked his rain of blows. It was an accident. Johnny Pollock had let the hammer slip, giving a false signal. Referee Siler realized quickly that a mistake had been made and sent the fighters back into action again.

'Terry sailed in again. One headlong rush and he had Palmer pinned against the ropes . . . A flush left hook right on the jaw sent Palmer down. He was badly dazed and horribly bewildered, so much so that he only took six seconds of the count before slowly rising . . . Terry was on him like a flash, shooting in rips to the body. Palmer clinched and McGovern beat him loose from the grip. Terry closed in, pounded the Englishman's body again with devastating punches. Palmer's knees bent. Terry hooked a stiff left to the stomach and followed with a stunning overhand right on the jaw. Palmer dropped in a stricken heap. Siler began the count. Palmer was in pain. He writhed and turned partly over on his side. He attempted to get off the canvas but could not raise his weakened body even with the help of his hands. His eyes were glazed, but no blood was visible on his face. Siler counted the fatal "Ten!" Palmer still lay prostrate. His seconds hurried through the ropes and carried him to his corner. The crowd was momentarily stunned by the sudden finish but after a second or two of silence, exploded in a roaring chorus of cheers that shook the plank seats of the arena.'

In seventy-five sensational seconds, Terry McGovern had become bantamweight champion of the world at the tender age of nineteen. Everyone wanted to see the new champion, and manager Sam Harris accepted a unique offer from Chicago promoter Lou Houseman to fight two men in one night at his Tattersall fight club. But when opponents Billy Smith and Patsy Haley held out for more money, McGovern found himself facing Billy Rotchford in the Chicago ring, though not for long. The Brooklyn Terror bounced Billy off the canvas five times in the first round and Rotchford's second, the old heavyweight Joe Choynski, threw the sponge in to save his tiger getting killed. The Windy City fans wanted more of McGovern and Houseman finally agreed terms with Smith and Haley for 18 November 1899, each man to go six rounds with the champion.

Patsy Haley was first into the ring. He had gone eighteen rounds with Terry eight months previously in New York by virtue of some clever fast boxing, but this night he was on his way back to the dressing room before the first round had run its course. Patsy put aside his boxing and met the Terror head on – not a wise move. Terry smashed a right to the chin and Haley hit the deck. Up at the count of seven, Patsy was forced across the ring to the ropes as McGovern unleashed a barrage of punches, culminating in a savage right to the jaw, and Haley was out before he hit the floor.

Billy Smith had his fight all worked out before he stepped into the ring. He was a crafty boxer in more ways than one. A bookmaker had promised Billy $500 if he could last four rounds with McGovern, and the Philadelphia lad figured he could. He ran like a thief in the first round, much to Terry's annoyance. In round two, the champ managed to corner Smith enough to knock him down seven times, but Billy got up seven times. He wanted that $500. Alas, he didn't make it through round three. Warned by the referee to make a fight of it, Billy hit Terry but when Terry hit him back with a left hook Smith crashed to the canvas. Still groggy when he arose at nine, Billy was pounced upon by McGovern who promptly knocked him spark out with two smashes to the jaw.

The little champion was the talk of the town and the manager of a vaudeville house offered him a two-week engagement to box four rounds on the stage, every night and two matinees. Sam Harris was not so happy when the signs outside the theatre billed McGovern as 'meeting all comers!' McGovern was a champion now, not just another pug, but Terry talked Harris around, saying, 'Let it go for the all-comers gag. I can take care of these local lugs, Sam, it'll be good practice.' As good as his word, Terry stopped nine men during the fortnight on the boards and the $25 offered by Harris to anyone lasting four rounds with his tiger went unclaimed. Joe Humphreys, the famous ring announcer, had joined Harris in handling McGovern, and Joe found that Terry had slipped each of his opponents five bucks to ease their pain.

By the end of the year McGovern had fought himself out of bantamweight opposition and Harris went after the featherweight title held by the great black Canadian George Dixon. Like McGovern, Dixon had won the bantamweight title by knocking out a Briton, Nunc Wallace, before stepping up a division to take the featherweight championship, in 1891. But now it was January 1900 and Dixon was pushing thirty, neglecting training and keeping bad company. Tom O'Rourke, who had discovered Dixon and managed his career, had warned his champion, 'You're not in shape, and you're no kid. One night you'll run into somebody tough and it will be too much for you unless you're ready.'

O'Rourke's words would ring true that night at the Broadway Athletic Club, which occupied a building opposite John Wanamaker's department store near Astor Place. For the first four rounds George Dixon was the Little Chocolate of old and the big crowd was electrified by his brilliant showing. In the fifth, a sizzling left hook sent McGovern to the canvas but Terry jumped straight up and was fighting back at the bell. From then on it was the kid's fight, his hammering fists breaking down the body of the veteran and then breaking his spirit.

This was Fleischer's description of the eighth round, in his 1938

*Black Dynamite* series: 'Both men were jaded. Dixon's lip and eye bleeding as they came to the front. In a rush and a whirlwind, Dixon slipped to his knees at the north ropes. McGovern helped him up. Another McGovern onslaught and Dixon went to the floor in McGovern's corner. He arose groggy. They fought back to Dixon's corner, and with lightning blows McGovern knocked Dixon under the ropes thrice in quick succession in the south-west corner. It was a brave dying. The coloured boy's face was streaming blood. Again he staggered across the ring and went down hard in McGovern's corner. One more fall, a last appealing look from Dixon, and the latter's manager, merciful on his coloured boy's behalf, threw up the sponge after the bell sounded, and a new title holder was crowned.'

With the Broadway club anxious to stage Terry's first title defence, Sam Harris went looking for a challenger. He went to Chicago and booked McGovern to box six rounds there with local star Eddie Santry, a good boxer with dynamite in his right fist. Eddie had knocked out British champion Ben Jordan, who had defeated George Dixon, and Santry figured to give the Brooklyn Terror a stiff workout. Before their Chicago bout, however, Harris got together with Santry's manager, Sam Pooler, and they agreed their boys would box the six rounds to No Decision, setting up a fight for the championship in New York. If McGovern kayoed Santry inside the six rounds, the New York fight would no longer be an attraction.

Which was fine, until Eddie Santry got the idea he could land a sneak punch and knock the world champion out. That was his second mistake. His first was even thinking about it! Round one passed over peacefully, but in the second, Eddie saw an opening and smashed a right to Terry's jaw, sending him reeling across the ring. McGovern recovered and when he got back to his corner, he whispered to Harris, 'This fellow is trying to cross me!' Sam's answer was short and to the point: 'Cut loose and knock him out!'

His Irish temper rising by the second, McGovern tore after his man through rounds three and four and Santry had his work cut out just staying alive. The end came in the fifth as Terry's savage body punishment took its toll and Santry was brought to his knees by a left swing that landed behind his ear. He struggled in vain to beat the count but his dream of a title fight in New York died there on the dirty canvas where the champion had dropped him.

With Santry out of the picture, the Broadway club matched McGovern with Oscar Gardner in a championship match over twenty-five rounds at 122 pounds. They called Gardner The Omaha Kid and he was one of the best in the west, where he had knocked out men like Dave Sullivan and Sammy Kelly in racking up eighty-one fights. He feared no man, and Terrible Terry McGovern was just another fighter. At the opening bell that night in March 1900, Oscar met the champion's rush with his own lethal fists and the spectators were soon on their feet as the two smashed punches from all angles. Then it happened. Gardner beat McGovern to the punch with a thudding left hook to the jaw and Terry crashed to the canvas, badly hurt. Referee Charlie White, hand-picked by Harris, began to count slowly as McGovern focused his eyes on Gardner, who was standing over him. With a huge effort, the stricken champion grabbed Gardner's right leg and hung on like a drowning man clutching at driftwood. Protesting loudly to the referee, Oscar tried to shake McGovern free of his leg. The referee then stopped his count and warned McGovern to stop holding. With Terry's head clearing by the second, he was back on his feet and back in the fight. Gardner's corner reckoned nineteen seconds had passed before the champion was on his feet ready to continue.

Gardner was unable to repeat his success as McGovern smashed him all over the ring in the second round and he was in bad shape at the bell. In his McGovern biography, Fleischer would write, 'Gardner was strictly on the defensive when the third round began . . . Terry, on the contrary, was alive with hot energy, out for revenge, aflame with the lust of battle. He lit on top of the Omaha Kid as nimbly and ferociously as a lynx leaps from a treetop to a hunter's shoulders, in a clawing onset . . . McGovern brought over his left with slashing force plumb on the point of the Kid's jowl. It was a killing punch and laid out the boy from Omaha as cold as the proverbial canned oyster . . . Even though the "long count" incident was a bit off colour, no doubt remained in the minds of those who witnessed the battle that the better man had won.'

In July 1900, Terry McGovern completed the third leg of a remarkable treble. At Madison Square Garden, he entered the ring to face Frank Erne, lightweight champion of the world by virtue of his victory over Kid Lavigne. Terry was sure he could whip Erne at the lightweight limit of 133 pounds. Sam Harris was not so sure. He persuaded Erne to fight Terry at 128 pounds and take the loser's share of the purse if he failed to stop McGovern within ten rounds! In that fight alone, Sam Harris proved his worth as a manager. In reducing to 128 pounds, the lightweight champion went through agony, his face breaking out in fever blisters, his skin drawn tightly over his cheek-bones, and he thirsted for a drink he dare not take. On fight day, he looked ready for a sanatorium, not a fight with the Brooklyn Terror.

Frank knew he was in no condition to go too many rounds and he gambled everything on a beautiful left hook as McGovern rushed him in the opening round. The punch nailed Terry on the button and he went down in a heap, the crowd erupting at the sight of their favourite scrambling on the canvas. As the count reached nine, however, Terry was on his feet and he chased Erne around the ring, those dynamite gloves of his exploding in Frank's face. At the bell the lightweight champion staggered to his corner, his nose broken, mouth torn and bleeding.

Coming up for the second round, Erne tried to get behind his jab, but McGovern swept him aside with a ferocious assault and the boy from Buffalo was glad to hear the bell. But the respite lasted a mere sixty seconds before he was back on the firing line and a tremendous right to the head sent Erne crashing to the floor. Badly hurt, he struggled to his feet only to be smashed down again. Gamely he hauled himself off the canvas once more to face his tormentor but before McGovern could hit him again the sponge came hurtling into the ring and Frank Erne was finished for the night.

In less than twelve months, Terrible Terry McGovern had knocked out Pedlar Palmer to win the bantamweight crown, stopped George Dixon to win the featherweight title, and hammered lightweight champion Frank Erne to bloody defeat inside three rounds, albeit in a non-title bout. The Brooklyn Terror was the fistic idol of America, his popularity rivalled only by the mighty John L Sullivan, and the former heavyweight champion was a great supporter of McGovern. Joe Humphreys recalled a story of a drunken Sullivan visiting Terry's training camp and trying to pry open a cage in which Terry kept a pet wildcat so that he could fight the creature. John L finally gave up and threw the cage with the screeching feline out of a window.

In December 1900, McGovern was involved in a fight which killed the sport in Chicago for a number of years, although he was absolved of all blame in a somewhat tawdry affair. Former lightweight champion Joe Gans, Terry's opponent that cold night, was one of the greatest fighters in the history of the glove game, but he brought shame to his name when he offered no resistance to McGovern's hammer fists and folded up in the second round after being knocked down four times. Rumours of a 'fix' were rife before the bout and the finger pointed at Joe's manager, gambler Al Herford. The booing of the sell-out crowd of 17,000 rattled the walls of the Tattersalls arena as the brilliant Gans stumbled before McGovern's flailing fists. When questioned by reporters next day, referee George Siler said, 'I do not wish to accuse any fighter of faking, but if Gans was trying to win last night, I do not know much about this game.'

Bristling with indignation, Al Herford claimed he had lost $5,000 in bets on the fight and said Gans had been hurt by a solar plexus punch in the first minute, 'the first crack out of the box,' he said. 'It completely upset him. It is taking credit from Terry McGovern to use those fake remarks. He won from Gans and he won fairly.' But some five years later, the rumours were more or less confirmed in a *Chicago Tribune* story by George Siler, who quoted Gans as saying he and his manager 'expected to reap a harvest but that his share of the ill-gotten proceeds fell well below expectations'.

The finger of suspicion was levelled at McGovern himself when he fought Aurelio Herrera at Mechanic's Pavilion in San Francisco in May 1901. A couple of newspapermen accused Terry of allowing Herrera to stay over four rounds to accommodate gamblers who had bet on the Mexican doing so. 'The truth of the matter was,' Fleischer would write, 'that Terry found Herrera a mighty tough proposition, did his best to stop him, was nearly stopped himself in the fourth round, and finally accomplished the trick by making a desperate rally in the fifth, when the Mexican was hammered into submission.'

The great lightweight champion Battling Nelson wrote in his autobiography, 'Aurelio Herrera was the greatest whirlwind fighter that ever lived. He could hit like a trip hammer and he was so fast that his arms worked like the piston rods on the New York Central *Twentieth Century Limited* engine going at the rate of 100 miles an hour. When least expected, his fist would shoot out like the head of a snake and down you would go . . . I shall never forget how surprised Terry McGovern was when he hit him a right-hand swing on the jaw in the first round at 'Frisco. "Why, he didn't budge an inch," said McGovern. "I landed a beaut on the point of his jaw and it was just like hitting a

Marvin safe. My mitt bounded off like a pebble and he came right back at me."'

It was in the fourth that Herrera fired a dynamic right to McGovern's jaw and knocked him senseless. Terry should have fallen but he didn't; out on his feet, only instinct allowed him to survive to the bell. In the corner, as always, his marvellous recuperative powers sent him out for the fifth and savage blows had the Mexican down three times. He only got up twice.

Like a lot of fighters of his time, Terry was a mass of superstitions. Joe Humphreys told Fleischer, 'Nat, there was probably never a fighter who believed more in lucky omens than Terry. I'll never forget the day he fought Herrera in San Francisco. He climbed into the ring all smiles, greeted his friends at ringside and then sat down to await the instructions of the referee. Suddenly, one of the spectators signalled to Sam Harris, Terry's manager, and pointed to McGovern's left shoe. It was unlaced. This was one of Terry's deepest super-stitions. During the preliminary work, between the time that McGovern entered the ring and went to the middle for instructions, the trainers had purposely neglected to tie the lace. When the referee motioned the fighters to the middle of the ring, Terry took off the unlaced shoe, spat in it for good luck, put it on again and told one of his handlers to lace it.'

The young Irish slugger had a fiery temper, and it contributed to his downfall as a champion when he fought Young Corbett in November 1901. 'Dumb Dan' Morgan remembered, 'McGovern had speed and could box, too. His only shortcoming was his erratic temperament. He could be riled into losing a fight. Young Corbett was as cool as McGovern was hot-headed. He came out of the middle West to meet Terry, who was a one-to-five favourite. On his way to the ringside, the cool kid from Denver pounded on McGovern's dressing-room door, shouting, "Come on out, Terry, and take your beating." McGovern blew up like the battleship *Maine* and Corbett knocked him out in two rounds.

'He repeated the performance sixteen months later, stopping McGovern in eleven rounds. Terry was incensed. The men had fought both times at 126 pounds, instead of at the 122 pound featherweight limit. As Corbett left the ring after the second knockout, McGovern snarled, "You ain't the champion, anyway. You didn't make the weight."

'"That's okay with me," replied Corbett. "I'm satisfied just to be known as the guy who knocked out Terrible Terry McGovern!"'

# The Michigan Assassin 2

Fight manager Dan Morgan was known as 'Dumb Dan' around the American boxing scene because he never stopped talking, but then Dan knew what he was talking about. He knew Stanley Ketchel, who was still middleweight champion of the world when he was shot dead in 1910.

'I've known quite a few Happy Warriors,' recalled Morgan, 'devil-may-care fellows who grinned their way through life, out of the ring. Almost without exception, these happy-go-lucky lads were vicious and ruthless in the ring. Take Stanley Ketchel, for instance. He lived a crowded life. He crammed more living into twenty-four years than most men jam into a full span. He packed more action into one round of fighting than most boxers do in fifteen. Steve, as he was affectionately known to intimates, had the look of a champion and the disposition, out of the ring, of a daring, romantic college kid. He could be gentle and tender, tough and ruthless. He could turn from affability to assassination in a flash.'

In his biography of Ketchel, veteran boxing authority Nat Fleischer, editor and publisher of *Ring Magazine*, wrote, 'The fight game never boasted a greater fighter or a more colourful figure than the Michigan Assassin. The title fitted Steve like a glove. That is just what he was, a rushing, tearing demon of the ring, who made his opponent think all the furies of Hades had been turned loose. I've never seen a fighter who staged such an attack as Ketchel. He got his punches away from all angles, always was "cocked" and in shooting position. If he missed with one hand, he would nail his opponent with the other. He was game as a bulldog and tough as a bronco. There was no stopping him. He always was on top of his man, blazing away with both hands.'

In winning fifty-two of his sixty-four professional fights, Ketchel's hammering fists sent forty-nine of his unfortunate victims home early. As he once said, 'If a fighter hasn't got the punch, he might as well quit the ring.'

This Jekyll and Hyde character of the prize ring was perhaps best summed up in an anecdote about one-time world featherweight champion Abe Attell, told by Dumb Dan Morgan. 'Abe Attell, who has a nose that is splashed all over his face, was asked, "If you were so clever, how come you got that nose?" Stanley Ketchel gave it to me, replied Attell. The record book does not show that Attell and Ketchel ever fought, and Attell was reminded of that fact. "He did it with a brick," said Abe. "He was throwing it at a sparring partner and I walked into the line of fire."'

Playful, yet dangerous. That was Stanley Ketchel, and he was never more dangerous than when the padded mittens were laced on his hands. 'I had heard that Ketchel's dynamic onslaught was such as could not be withstood,' said Philadelphia Jack O'Brien, light-heavyweight champion of the world, before the first of his two fights with Ketchel, 'but I figured I could jab his puss off.' After being smashed to the canvas by Ketchel's blazing fists, Philadelphia Jack recalled Stanley as 'a tumultuously ferocious person'.

Ketchel was a complex character. He once told his great pal Hype Igoe, 'My brain has got to be in the right mood to fight.' They were sitting in the dressing-room one night and it was ten minutes to fight time. 'That lousy ape called my mother a ——!' said Stan in a quivering voice, repeating it over and over. Puzzled, Igoe asked, 'Who did?'

'Him, the guy I'm gonna get in that ring tonight and kill!' answered Stan.

'But you never saw him before in your life,' said Igoe.

'That don't make no difference,' snarled Ketchel. 'That bastard said it and I'm gonna murder him!'

The kid who became the most famous fist fighter of his generation was born Stanislaus Kaicel in Grand Rapids, Michigan, on 14 September 1886, of mixed German and Polish ancestry. The name change came in Chicago, courtesy of an old fighter named Socker Flanagan who ran a lunch counter on the corner of Van Buren Street. Barely into his teens, young Stan had come into the Windy City on a freight train and was befriended by Flanagan, who saw him flatten a local bully in a street fight. Socker gave the kid a job, a place to sleep, all he could eat – and a new name. 'No matter what racket you make up your mind to follow,' he told the wide-eyed boy, 'it'll pay you not to sport a foreign-soundin' moniker. You was born in America, so why carry a foreign brand? Forget the Kaicel layout and cop yourself a new handle. Make it Ketchel. That's got a punch to it and is dead easy to curl your lip around!'

A couple of years later, Steve Ketchel rode the rods as far west as Silver Bow, Montana, where he was tossed off the train by a burly railroad cop. He walked the seven miles into Butte, where he took a job as waiter in The Copper Queen. The feisty kid got into a brawl with the bouncer one day soon afterwards and flattened him with a haymaker of a right hand. The saloon owner promptly gave him the other fellow's job, ten bucks a night.

'Butte was a bona fide dime-novel town in 1902,' wrote John Lardner. 'It was made for Ketchel. Built on what they called the richest hill in the world, it mined half the country's copper. The town looked sooty and grim by day, but it was red and beautiful by night, a patch of fire in the Continental Divide. As the biggest city on the north-west line between Minneapolis and Spokane, it had saloons, theatres, hotels, honky-tonks, and fight clubs by the score. Name actors and name boxers played the town. When Ketchel struck the state, artillery was as common as collar buttons.'

'Ketchel had the heart of a tramp and the soul of a bouncer,' said Dumb Dan Morgan, 'but a bouncer who loved his work.' The boss at the Casino Theatre in the town used to pay Ketchel twenty dollars a week to meet all comers. 'I hit 'em so hard,' Ketchel would say, 'that they used to fall over the footlights and land in the people's laps!'

'If Butte was made for Ketchel,' wrote Lardner, 'so was the fight game. He used to say that he had 250 fights around this time that do not show in the record book. In 1903 he was already a welterweight, well-grown and well-muscled.'

But he wasn't yet well-known, which was why Tommy Ryan readily agreed to meet young Ketchel in a four-round match when he visited Butte on a barnstorming tour. With a hundred-odd bouts behind him, Ryan had been welterweight champion before winning the middle-weight title, and he was still recognized as champion when he slipped through the ropes to face Ketchel. Then the bell rang and Tommy Ryan got the shock of his life as this wild-eyed punk kid flew across the ring, throwing savage blows with fiendish ferocity. Ryan had to call on his vast experience to survive, helped somewhat by manager Jack Curley cutting the rounds short as he realized what his star was up against.

Back in the dressing-room, Ryan exploded. 'What in thunder made you pick that Ketchel guy?' he raged at Curley.

'Well,' said Jack, 'he's only a kid and he looked easy to me. He hasn't any reputation and his name ain't in the record books. Why, nobody ever heard of him!'

'Well, I'm telling you something,' growled Ryan. 'They're goin' to hear plenty about that baby one of these days if he sticks to the punching racket. I never put in a tougher four rounds in my life. Believe it or not, Jack, I had to scrap for all I was worth to keep from hitting the floor in that last round.'

For three years, Stanley Ketchel was the pride of Montana, his savage two-handed attack flattening opponents as fast as they could find them. But he was virtually unknown over the state line – there was no radio or television in those days. They did have newspapers, however, and it was a reporter from the San Francisco *Bulletin*, R A Smith, who advised the young fighter to seek his fortune in the big wide world outside Montana. 'You're too good a fighter to be wasting your time around here,' he told Stanley one night after seeing him rack up a quick knockout in a local club. 'Take my tip, go to the Coast. I know the fight game. I've seen the best of 'em. They don't come any better than you, kid, and you'll never get anywhere hanging around the sticks.'

Smith gave Stan a letter of introduction to a promoter in Sacramento and next day Ketchel was on his way. At that time, May 1907, George Brown was a big name around the California city, a black middleweight who had beaten some top guys and was being lined up to meet Joe Thomas in Marysville on a Fourth of July show. This new kid Ketchel would be an ideal warm-up for the fight with Thomas, who was already being hailed as the successor to Tommy Ryan since the latter's retirement as middleweight champion. Thomas was a clever boxer with a knockout punch and George Brown would do well to improve on the draw in their first fight. But first, there was Stanley Ketchel.

On a flat guarantee of $500, the new kid was out to make an impression. He did, on the crowd and, especially, on George Brown. For two rounds Brown couldn't put a glove wrong as he jabbed the wild-swinging hobo fighter who was trying to chase him out of the ring. Then came round three, and sensation. A terrific right hand smashed against Brown's dusky chin, followed by a tremendous uppercut that lifted him clear of the canvas. Landing on his back, Brown was out for ten minutes and the Golden State had a new fistic hero.

'It may be just as well that Brown got trimmed and fell down on us,' promoter Lou Trevor told his backers, 'because this brash youngster that whaled him is a sure enough fightin' fool, a real slugging devil if ever I saw one. Of course, I don't think he can lick Joe Thomas; for that matter, I don't know anyone in the game that can. But he'll give him a hot tussle while it lasts and he'll go down fighting.'

Young Ketchel didn't see it quite that way. 'I'm twenty-one,' he told Trevor, 'old enough to know I can lick any guy near my weight in the world. If you want to make some easy dough, have a bet on me. This Thomas bird ain't any tougher than plenty of other bimbos I've sent to the cleaners. A champion's only a wonder until some fellow comes along and belts him down. Watch me do some fancy belting on the Fourth!'

'The result of that battle electrified the sporting world,' Nat Fleischer would write. 'It was declared a draw by the referee but the cold truth was that Thomas only escaped being knocked out by a hair's breadth. It seemed incredible to the boxing critics that Joe Thomas, famed from coast to coast as a perfect scientist and deadly two-handed puncher, could have been held even by an unknown youngster who was handicapped both in weight and by experience.

'Yet the youngster had done better than hold him even. When Thomas was knocked through the ropes in the eleventh round by an uppercut to the chin, only the clang of the gong saved him from being counted out. He rallied and fought desperately, gamely, as became a champion. But Ketchel maintained his lead to the final round. Stanley was not awarded the decision he had justly earned, but nonetheless he had triumphed. The world of pugilism rang with his name. He could no longer be ignored.'

Veteran referee Billy Roche was the matchmaker for promoter James W Coffroth's fight club in Colma, a small town south of San Francisco, and when he heard that some unknown kid had not only held Joe Thomas to a draw over twenty rounds but should have been declared the victor, he lost no time offering the boys a return bout on a Labour Day show. They would split fifty per cent of the gate for a fight over forty-five rounds. In his memoirs, Billy Roche would recall, 'They posted $250 forfeit each, guaranteeing themselves to weigh no more than 150 pounds. After the weigh-in – Ketchel 150, Thomas 149 – Ketchel bet the $250 on himself. Later that afternoon, he talked promoter Jim Coffroth into giving him an advance on his purse. It amounted to $4,500 which he also bet on himself.

'It was the first time I ever saw Ketchel. He looked wild, like an animal, and his body looked like it had been chiselled out of granite. From the first round he dug those terrific hooks into Thomas's guts and I, who had been hanging around fighters all my life, had to look away every time I heard that hollow thud of his fist sinking into Joey's middle. Thomas, a brave kid and wonderful boxer, fought back gamely. But his jabs were as effective as a rowboat against a battleship. He'd stick one out, Ketchel would stick out his mug and take it. Then he'd sneer and uncork a hook into Joe's belly. Although Thomas wasn't cut externally he was throwing up blood from the fifth round on. I had the feeling that Ketchel was carrying Thomas, that he didn't want to knock him out because he was having too much fun tearing him apart.

'Then something very strange happened, or at least it was strange to me. Thomas somehow figured out how to step away from Ketchel's dynamite and at the same time counter with stinging rights to the chin. Inwardly, I egged him on. I hate to admit it, but I found myself doing things now and then which favoured Joe. As Ketchel came steamrolling out of his corner for the twenty-ninth round, Thomas set himself and put every drop of strength left in his body behind a right to the chin. It landed with a booming thud and there was Ketchel flat on his back. I didn't give him a chance to get up, but he fooled me. At seven he was on one knee, clutching at the ropes. Just as I was about to call "ten", he was up. I was astonished. It was Joe's last hope of victory. In the thirty-second round Ketchel slugged him with a left to the stomach and a right to the temple and it was over. I went to Jimmy Coffroth in the rear of the arena and told him there wasn't a middleweight, or for that matter a light-heavyweight, in the world who could lick this crazy man, Stanley Ketchel. Never in my ring experience had I seen two men go at such a terrific clip over as long a distance, and never before or since have I seen a man able to hit as hard a blow as the two Ketchel landed after thirty-two rounds of cyclonic milling. Ketchel carried his punch longer than any man that ever breathed.'

The supporters of Joe Thomas were still not convinced that Ketchel was his master and found Stanley only too eager to oblige when approached about a third meeting with the Californian. 'I'm willing to lick him every night in the week,' said Stan cheerfully, 'if they'll ante up the dough for my trouble.'

Three months after their titanic thirty-two-round battle, Stanley Ketchel met Joe Thomas for the third time, in a huge circus tent pitched in the San Francisco baseball park, twenty rounds or less. Dramatic as the fight was that night, with Ketchel winning the decision, it was overshadowed by one of the worst storms to hit the area in living memory. The tent was almost torn down by hurricane force winds, and torrential rain soaked everyone from the fighters to the fans. The electric lighting failed and for the most part the bout was fought in semi-darkness. Yet they never stopped slinging punches.

With Thomas out of the title picture, the main rivals to Ketchel's claim to be top dog in the middleweight division were Jack (Twin) Sullivan, Billy Papke and Hugo Kelly. When Steve threw out a challenge to Jack, the elder Sullivan shook his head. 'Go ahead and fight my brother Mike,' he told Ketchel. 'If you beat him, I'll be willing to take you on.' Mike (Twin) Sullivan had beaten most of the top welterweights in the business but he was no match for the Michigan Assassin. They were matched for twenty rounds at Colma on 22 February 1908. Heading for the dressing-room that night, Ketchel met Sullivan's second carrying a big bag of oranges. Curious, he asked why so much fruit? 'I'm taking them to cut up for Mike,' the fellow said. 'He likes to suck a piece of orange between rounds.' Ketchel grinned broadly. 'Tell Mike for me that he's wasting his dough,' he said. 'He won't need any oranges tonight.'

Nor did he. Mike got home two stinging left jabs to Ketchel's face and Stanley's head snapped back from the impact, but then he shifted his stance and sent a pile-driving right to Sullivan's stomach. As Mike doubled over, a terrific left hook smashed against his jaw and he fell on his face to be counted out. As Jack Sullivan hauled his twin brother back to the corner, he knew he was going to have to fight this fellow Ketchel and redeem the family honour.

Back in the same ring at Colma just ten weeks later, Stanley Ketchel completed the double when he knocked out Jack Sullivan in the twentieth round. A fine boxer, Sullivan outboxed Ketchel in the early rounds of the fight but Steve was as strong as an ox and kept smashing blows in from every angle until Jack could take no more.

'Ketchel crashed a right against Sullivan's left ribs,' wrote Nat Fleischer, 'and followed with a hard right to the pit of the stomach. The last punch was so powerful it caused the Bostonian to curl up and fall in a heap to the canvas. His lips were parted and his eyes rolling, and from the look of distress it seemed that he could not get himself together to continue. He got up, however, just as the timekeeper made the nine count . . . Ketchel then smashed a powerful right under the heart and there was no doubt of the result this time. When Jack fell, his legs were bent under him. When the count of six was reached, he straightened them but couldn't get to his feet. As the count of ten was tolled off, Billy Roche turned to Ketchel, grabbed his hand, and shouted, "You win!"'

Ketchel's sensational victory over Jack (Twin) Sullivan brought him recognition as middleweight champion of the world. He was born for the role. 'There is only one Stanley Ketchel,' wrote Bill Naughton, dean of American sports authorities. 'He's the king of real-life melodrama, unequalled as a dispenser of shock surprises in the world of pugilism.'

Ketchel's meteoric rise from a hobo riding the rods and fighting his way out of the mining camps to the championship of the world was a romance of the ring, a pulp fiction writer's dream. A thousand and one stories were told about him, but as John Lardner wrote in 1954, 'These tall tales weren't necessary. The truth was strong enough. Ketchel was champion of the world, perhaps the best fist fighter of his weight in history, a genuine wild man in private life, a legitimate all-around meteor, who needed no faking of his passport to legend . . . He was the stuff of myth. He entered mythology at a younger age than most of the others, and he still holds stoutly to his place there.'

In a 1961 magazine article, Arthur Ketchel wrote of the older brother he remembered. He recalled 'a warm-hearted, kindly young man, totally different from the murderous renegade some writers tried to make of him . . . Despite stories to the contrary, Stan was a loving son to our mother. He had his first twenty-dollar gold piece made into a necklace for her, and when he became famous he had her sell her home in Detroit and took her to live on a farm he had bought nine miles north of Grand Rapids. He built a training camp on the property and lived there quite a lot in later years. I remember the old place vividly. He had expensive cloth hung on the walls instead of wallpaper, and it was still on the walls when the old place burned down a few years ago. It was there I first met Wilson Mizner, the famous humorist who was supposed to be Stanley's manager. He wasn't. The only men who managed my brother were Willus Britt and Joe O'Connor. Mizner was never more than a close friend.

'There is one thing Stanley didn't do: drink a lot. I have been with him more than once when he tossed a twenty-dollar gold piece on the bar and ordered drinks for the house. But he himself seldom touched a drop. Quite often he would take me along with him on trips to the big towns where he was idolised, often also taking an uncle of ours who would carry Stanley's big diamond ring and the fat bankroll of several hundred dollars so that nobody could pick his pocket. And I don't know why it sticks in my memory but whenever Stanley was out in public he wore big Cuban heels, two-and-a-half inches high. That made him look taller, although he was all of five-feet-nine and weighed 156 pounds.'

In June 1908 Stanley Ketchel stepped into the ring at Milwaukee for the first of his four titanic battles with Billy Papke from Spring Valley. They called Papke the Illinois Thunderbolt and when he faced the champion he was unbeaten in twenty-nine fights with seventeen knockouts. Of German-American parents, Billy was as hard as the coal he had mined alongside his father before becoming a fighter. Stanley Ketchel found that out in their first bout, which he won by decision. Knocked down in the opening round, Papke fought back tigerishly to take the second round and in the fifth he drove Ketchel to one knee with a terrific right to the jaw. Stanley repaid the compliment in the next round and only the bell saved Billy from a knockout. At the final bell both were bloody, but unbowed. They would meet again.

Before the rematch with Papke, Ketchel retained his title twice at San Francisco. He knocked out Hugo Kelly at the Coliseum, the Chicago fighter giving him a rugged time for two rounds before Stan dropped the bomb in round three, a tremendous left hook that put an end to Kelly's interests in the proceedings. Three weeks later Joe Thomas again challenged Ketchel, but by this time Joe's future was all behind him and he was beaten inside two rounds, a murderous barrage of punches ending his title aspirations forever.

'On the night of 7 September 1908,' wrote Fleischer, 'the sport world turned a mental somersault when the startling news was flashed along the wires that in a second battle between Ketchel and Papke at Vernon, California, the middleweight championship had changed hands when Papke knocked out Ketchel in the twelfth round. The general impression was that Papke must have caught Ketchel out of condition. But those who fancied that Stan had neglected training were all wrong. Had he not been in the pink of condition, he could never have stood up for twelve rounds under the severe punishment he absorbed. He lost the fight through a trick.

'At that time it was customary for fighters, after the bell signalled the start of hostilities, to shake hands before getting into action. When the bell for the first round rang, however, and Ketchel extended his right glove for the usual handshake, Papke ignored the gesture and drove a hard left hook to his opponent's unprotected jaw. As Ketchel staggered back, Papke again landed, this time shooting a straight right that caught Stanley between the eyes. Those punches won the battle for Papke. The jaw punch dazed Ketchel and as a result of the second blow his eyes began to close. Papke, who could hit like a steam hammer, was all over Ketchel in the opening round, blasting him from all angles with hooks, swings, and uppercuts. Ketchel was down three times in the first round and once in the sixth. His chief second, Pete Stone, twice had to lance his eyes to reduce the swelling. Still Stanley groped forward, swinging at the antagonist he could no longer see. In the twelfth, Papke dropped Ketchel with a stunning right cross. Referee Jim Jeffries, the former world heavyweight champion, counted eight before Stan rose, to be felled again with another right. This time Jeffries counted nine before he motioned to Ketchel's seconds to take their man to his corner as Ketchel was trying to get to his feet.'

After the fight, a reporter asked the new champion why he had waited until round twelve for the KO. 'When we met in Milwaukee,' said Billy, 'we shook hands in the usual way. Ketchel not only held my hand in a vice-like grip but pulled me towards him and hit me flush in the face with a hard left, breaking a tooth and knocking me down. Right then I decided to get even for that trick. I could have finished Ketchel much sooner, but I figured he deserved an extra dose of punishment.'

The championship reign of William Herman Papke lasted just two months, two weeks and four days. To everyone's surprise, Billy readily agreed to give Ketchel a return fight in San Francisco's old Mission Street arena. This time Ketchel was in superb condition. He felt naked without his title. There would be no handshake this night.

'Manifestly the better man of the two,' wrote Fleischer, 'Ketchel was a fighting demon and in no round of the eleven could it be said that Papke had more than an even break. Ketchel fought the best battle of his career. He boxed well, blocked in a manner that made Papke appear like a novice, landed stiff punches to the body that hurt the defending titleholder and in no way suffered himself from any damage by Papke. The knockout blow was delivered as Papke was backing away from the ropes with guard down. As they separated from a clinch at the command of referee Welch, Papke stepped back with both hands hanging at his sides. Quick as a flash, Ketchel swung a hard left that landed flush on the jaw. Papke dropped but got to his knees as the count got underway and was up at eight. Ketchel was quickly on top of him. The Illinois man made no effort to fight. Staggering about the ring with his gloved hands covering his face as best he could, Papke received a dozen punches on the jaw and body before he finally dropped for the second time. It was evident that Billy was out, but he listened and got to his feet at "eleven", one count too much. There was a look of surprise as referee Welch motioned that Ketchel had won, but Billy had no reason to complain.'

'It was around this time that Willus Britt brought his imagination to bear on Ketchel,' wrote John Lardner. 'That is, he moved in. Willus was a man who lived by piecework. An ex-Yukon pirate, he was San Francisco's leading fight manager and sport, wearing the brightest clothes in town and smoking the biggest cigars . . . Britt won Ketchel over during some tour of San Francisco nightlife by his shining haberdashery and his easy access to champagne and showgirls. In this parlay, champagne ran second with Ketchel. He did drink, some, and the chances are that he smoked a little opium. But he didn't need either, he was one of those people who are born with half a load on. His chief weaknesses were women, bright clothes, sad music, guns, fast cars and candy.'

By this time, the New York sports fraternity were eager to see this savage champion from the West whose ring exploits had already accorded him legendary status. And Willus Britt was just the man to show him off to the Big Apple. 'When Stanley hit Broadway,' wrote Fleischer, 'the astute manager saw to it that he was attired in cowboy garb, from spurs to ten gallon hat. Making daily rounds of the newspaper offices, being introduced at fight clubs, promenading the Great White Way by day and night, dining in the most fashionable restaurants, was the routine . . . Ketchel enjoyed it all immensely. He loved the bright lights, the homage of the crowds, the feeling that he was the centre of attention wherever he appeared in public. The same instinct that urged him to keep moving in his kid hobo days governed his restless spirit now.'

For his first fight in New York, Ketchel was matched with Philadelphia Jack O'Brien, the world light-heavyweight champion, then thirty-one and a veteran of fourteen years in the ring. The contest was staged by the National Athletic Club at the Fiss, Doerr and Carroll horse market on East Twenty-Fourth Street on 26 March 1909, with Ketchel, still only twenty-two, a heavy favourite over Philadelphia Jack.

'In all the years that I have been reporting boxing contests,' wrote Fleischer in 1946, 'I never saw a more vicious bout than the tilt between Jack O'Brien and Stanley Ketchel . . . It was a fight that one sees but once in a lifetime . . . The squared circle never saw a more heroic and lion-hearted stand than O'Brien put up against the annihilating Ketchel, as savage, dynamic and relentless a puncher as the game ever knew. The night the Michigan Assassin crawled through the ropes against the veteran O'Brien, Stanley was tough and hard enough to chew nails and spit tacks. O'Brien's wily old ring head and fighting heart postponed the inevitable for nine scintillating, palpitating rounds. And in the end, the lion-hearted old champion bested Father Time, if not Ketchel, for the final gong rang with O'Brien's tawny thatch in the sawdust box. He had been lifted and dumped there by a left hook from Ketchel that came up with the power there is in a thrust of a steamboat's walking beam, but with referee Tim Hurst's hand coming down at the count of four – the gong saved O'Brien from a certain knockout. That last terrific lash of

Ketchel landing on a man weakened from three previous knockdowns had floored O'Brien stone cold. Tim Hurst could have kept on counting, but the bell saved Jack from the ignominy of a knockout and few who saw the Philadelphia veteran's matchless display of grit, gameness and ring generalship were not glad because of it.'

It was the time of the no-decision era in New York State; if a contest went the scheduled distance, no winner was announced. The newspaper boys covering the fight gave their verdict in print next morning, and that's when all bets were paid off. In his story of the fight for the *New York Press*, Nat Fleischer made O'Brien the winner. Ketchel begged Britt to get him a rematch: 'I don't care how many rounds we are scheduled to fight. I'll knock him out well within the distance this time.'

Stanley got his wish inside three months and was as good as his word. O'Brien was hammered from pillar to post and was saved by the bell in the second round after being dumped three times by vicious body punches. Ketchel wasted no time in the third and Jack was smashed to the canvas twice within forty seconds before the referee called it off. With that dynamic victory over the light-heavyweight champion, Willus Britt dreamed up the big one, a shot at the heavyweight title. The great Jack Johnson was champion at the time and he laughed at the thought of defending his crown against the middleweight titleholder. But Willus Britt talked him into agreeing to a twenty-five-round exhibition with neither man opening up with the artillery. There would be no decision rendered, according to the prevailing law in California, and Johnson would still be champ.

The man they called the Galveston Giant liked the idea of easy money and the match was arranged for 16 October 1909 at Sunny Jim Coffroth's arena in Colma. Just over six feet tall and twenty-five pounds heavier, Johnson more or less toyed with Ketchel for eleven rounds, his gold-toothed smile flashing in the bright sunlight as he boxed the smaller man off. But Stanley Ketchel was becoming frustrated – Johnson was showing him up and he didn't like it. Coming out for the twelfth round, Stanley saw an opening and launched a terrific right-hand shot, and Jack Johnson went down on his backside to a roar from the crowd. Jack didn't stay down. He leaped to his feet, the smile gone as his lips curled into a snarl. Ketchel roared in for the kill and Johnson caught him with a piledriver of a right that lifted him off his feet and left him stretched out on the hot canvas like a starfish. The dream was ended.

'I was nailed on the bone behind my ear,' Johnson would recall. 'It was a terrific shot and it stunned me enough to make me lose my balance. I dropped to the floor, landing on the seat of my trunks. I was more enraged than I was hurt. I don't think I ever hated two people as much as I did Willus Britt and Stanley Ketchel at that particular moment. They tried to double-cross me and steal my championship. I bounced back to my feet and with murder in my heart I watched Ketchel come running at me. I pulled back and shot a right uppercut that almost tore his whole head off. He quivered and then he dropped, spreadeagled on the canvas, dead to the world. His lip had been driven through his teeth with such force that when the gloves were taken off my hands, my second was shocked to find three of Stanley's teeth still embedded in the padding of my right glove.'

The soaring comet that was Stanley Ketchel didn't burn itself out. It was snuffed out just twelve months after that fight with Johnson, by a .22 bullet fired from Steve's own rifle. He was sitting at breakfast on the ranch of his friend Colonel Dickerson in Conway, Missouri, when a farmhand named Walter Dipley shot him in the back, jealous of the attention Stanley was paying to his woman. The bullet entered his body under the shoulder blade and ploughed into a lung. He collapsed and died shortly afterwards from an internal haemorrhage. He was twenty-four years old.

The sports world was shocked at the tragedy and in New York, when Wilson Mizner heard the news, he refused to believe it. 'Start counting,' he said, 'Steve'll get up at nine!' But Steve didn't beat the count this time.

# The Boston Tar Baby 3

A boxing writer once asked Sam Langford how many knockouts he had compiled in his twenty-three years as a professional fighter. A huge grin split his ebony face. 'If I knew they was counting 'em,' he said, 'I'd have knocked 'em all out!'

Sam Langford was that good. In a *Ring Magazine* article a few years ago, writer Mike Silver ranked him number three among boxing's ten greatest punchers of all-time. 'Langford,' wrote Silver, 'mastered every punch. His short hook on the inside and his right cross and uppercut were particularly deadly. His punishing jab was also one of the best. The Boston Tar Baby was effective both at long range and in close; he was a strategist who knew how to manoeuvre, with the ability to explode out of an offensive or defensive position. He could instantly stop when retreating, revert to the offensive, and in the blink of an eye render an opponent unconscious with trip-hammer blows thrown in four and five-punch combinations . . . He understood very well the physics of dynamic punching, timing and distance, speed, balance, leverage, and weight distribution.'

Yet as old Joe Woodman, Sam's manager through most of his career, would recall, 'It's a funny thing but in those early days Sam couldn't break an egg. He won most of his bouts by decision and even when he connected with his best blows nothing happened. It wasn't until 1904, during a fight with Tommy Sullivan in Marlboro, Massachusetts, that he suddenly learned the knack of hitting. I'll never forget that night. Quite by accident, Sam snapped his wrist as he delivered a right to Sullivan's jaw and at the same time leaned into the punch. No one was more surprised than Sam when Sullivan dropped to the deck unconscious. From then on he was a killer when he wanted to be . . . Langford could hurt you terribly with very short punches. I remember the amazement of the reporters the night he stopped Joe Jeannette in ten rounds in Syracuse. They never before had seen such devastating short punches.'

According to *The Boxing Register*, the official record book of the International Boxing Hall of Fame in Canastota, New York, Langford is credited with a total of 293 bouts from 1902 to 1926. Of the 167 victories he racked up, 117 of his victims were either stopped or knocked out.

In an article for *Boxing & Wrestling* magazine in 1954, Stanley Weston quoted several of Langford's knockout victims on Sam's punching prowess. Joe Jeannette recalled, 'He hit me harder than anyone I ever fought, and I was in there with every good fighter of my time, some who weighed as much as 230 pounds.' Big Jim Flynn, the Pueblo Fireman, said, 'The hardest hitter I ever faced was Langford. I fought most of the heavyweights, including Dempsey and Johnson, but Sam could stretch a guy colder than any of them. When Langford hit me, it felt like someone slugged me with a baseball bat. But strangely enough, it didn't hurt; it was like taking ether, you just went to sleep . . . There was a peculiar and kindly thing about him. When he knocked someone out, he always stayed around until the poor bum opened his eyes. Then he'd say, "Ah'm sorry, son, Ah didn't mean to hit you so hard." And, I think he really meant it. He never realized how hard he could punch.'

Harry Wills, the old Black Menace, was another who tabbed Langford the best fighter he ever fought: 'He was a real professional. The kind of fighter you'd like to be but know that no matter how hard you try, you'll never make it. Sam never made a mistake, he always held command, and when he knocked me out in New Orleans in 1916, I thought I had been killed.'

'I interviewed Langford a few years ago,' wrote Weston, 'just before he quit New York and returned to Boston. Naturally, the first question I asked him was, "Who was your toughest opponent?" His reply floored me. "That's easy, Gunboat Smith," he said. "No one who ever seed that Gunner when he was right can say he wasn't tough. That boy was as rough and tough as any white man I ever did fight. And, lawdy me, couldn't he hit with that right hand! In 1913 I wasn't doing much of nothing except hanging around Boston when a promoter asked me if I'd fight Gunboat Smith. And I said, sure, who is he? We fought in Boston and Smith won. Yep, he beat me fair and square and I wasn't kidding no how. But don't forget that the next year I knocked him out in three rounds."'

The old Gunner remembered that fight. Talking to *Ring Magazine* in 1932, he said, 'Man, if old Sam were in his prime today, what he wouldn't do to these heavyweights. There wouldn't be any need of judges or referee, or even timekeeper. He hit me on the top of my head and I thought the roof had caved in. If he landed on the button, it was a quick goodnight.'

Even the legendary Jack Dempsey was quoted as saying, 'The hell I feared no man! There was one man, he was even smaller than I, I wouldn't fight because I knew he would flatten me. I was afraid of Sam Langford!'

To be fair to Dempsey, it was on his first visit to New York as a twenty-one-year-old raw kid that his manager at the time, John Reisler, booked him to fight Langford in Boston. Reisler owned a big barber shop on Broadway, and around New York he was known as John The Barber. He was also a gambler, but young Dempsey was not willing to become a pawn in his game. He was well aware that Sam Langford was one of the best fighters in the world, a veteran of fourteen years fighting the best in the business from lightweight to heavyweight. 'You're wasting your time,' Jack told Reisler. 'I've seen Langford. He'd kill me. I won't fight him. He's too damn good for me.'

Sam Langford was too damn good for his own good. 'Great as he was,' wrote *Ring Magazine* publisher Nat Fleischer, 'Langford never had the good fortune to win and wear a championship crown . . . it was by the merest chance that he never copped a title either as a featherweight, lightweight or welter, although boxing writers were continually predicting his rise to a throne . . . One potent reason was that Langford, just as he appeared to be winning supremacy in a certain division, was sure to outgrow it.'

Yet this giant-killer, who beat some of the finest heavyweights of his era, never grew taller than 5ft 6½in and weighed between 140 and 170 pounds during his prime. He had long arms that gave him a reach of 73in and a deep, powerful chest that measured 44in, with huge shoulders and a broad muscular back. One opponent likened him to 'a human triangle!'

Sam Langford was a sorry sight aged sixteen when he wandered into Joe Woodman's pharmacy near Boston's North Station. His thin body was wrapped in an overcoat three sizes too big for him and tied around the middle with a piece of rope. At his heels trotted a mongrel dog that didn't look much better than the boy. Woodman gave Sam twenty-five cents and sent him off to get something to eat.

'Sam could neither read nor write in those days,' recalled Joe, 'but he was far from dumb. He told me he was born in Weymouth Falls, Nova Scotia, in a house "no bigger than a dog house", and that he had six brothers and seven sisters. He told me he had ants in his pants and liked to see new places and meet new people.'

At that time, Woodman was running boxing shows at the Lenox Athletic Club and he gave young Sam a job as janitor, allowing him and his dog to sleep at the club. The kid loved it, and when his chores were done he would watch the fighters training in the gym, helping out with rubdowns and acting as sparring partner. He could use his fists – he'd had to fight to survive when riding the rods of the freight trains after he ran away from home. Noting his interest, Woodman entered Sam in an amateur tournament and was surprised when he came home with a gold watch, having beaten five opponents, three by KO. 'Sam had the boxing fever in its most virulent form now,' wrote Fleischer in his *Black Dynamite* series, 'and went after the amateurs like a raiding fox after chickens.'

In January 1902 Sam Langford made his professional debut, beating Jack McVickar in three rounds at the Lenox Club, and he made such rapid strides in the glove game that Joe Woodman sold his pharmacy to concentrate on managing Sam's career. It was a partnership that lasted seventeen years and carried Joe and Sam all over the world, from the United States to Canada, England, France, Australia, Panama and Argentina. 'I don't know how many miles of land and water we covered,' said Joe many years later, 'but I can tell you one thing, it was long, often tedious travelling. There were no airplanes, you know, and we had to go by train and ship. We were constantly moving. We didn't stay too long in any one place, just kept going to wherever we could get fights.'

Some measure of Langford's ability can be gained from the fact that he fought four men who are still regarded as among the greatest of all time in their respective weight classes: Joe Gans at lightweight, welterweight Joe Walcott, middleweight Stanley Ketchel and heavyweight Jack Johnson. He beat Gans, got the worst of a draw with Walcott, held the tearaway Ketchel even in a no-decision bout, and was beaten over fifteen rounds by Johnson.

Sam was barely two years into his professional career when he was matched with world lightweight champion Gans, the man they called The Old Master. They clashed at the Criterion Club in Boston in December 1903, fifteen rounds over the weight to protect Joe's title. For the first four rounds Gans fought like the champion he was, his thudding jabs sending Sam's head back on his broad shoulders, left hooks rocking him to his toenails. But from the fifth round, Langford began to come on strong and, more and more, Gans was forced to call upon his defensive wizardry to stay in the fight. At the final bell the referee pointed to Langford as the winner, and the champion ruefully admitted he had underestimated his young opponent.

George 'Elbows' McFadden had been a thorn in the side of Joe Gans on his way to the championship, and Sam Langford was determined to do a better job than Gans when he met McFadden. He did so in spectacular fashion. George stormed across the ring at the opening bell, swinging savage punches as Langford met him with his more accurate blows. A right to the chin staggered McFadden, then back he came with a right uppercut that lifted Sam's head, before Langford smashed home a terrific right hook that brought the blood streaming from McFadden's mouth. A left to the jaw dropped George to his knees, but the bell came to his rescue. It only delayed the inevitable. He was still groggy coming out for work in the second round and Langford set him up with a straight left to the mouth, followed by a short left hook to the jaw, and McFadden was through for the evening. As he rolled across the canvas, his second threw in the towel.

Sam's next fight really established him as a man to reckon with. He was matched with Joe Walcott, the welterweight champion of the world, over fifteen rounds at Manchester, New Hampshire, on 5 September 1904. Editor Arthur Lumley, at ringside for the *New York Illustrated News*, reported, '. . . a vicious fifteen-round draw at the Coliseum . . . The spectators were much displeased by the decision, as the rounds story was one clearly in favour of Langford. He had earned that right and should have gotten the decision . . . After a fine, even opening round, the honours were all in Langford's favour from then on through the seventh . . . In the eighth, Walcott, urged on by his manager Tom O'Rourke, set sail in great style to overcome the handicap . . . Although Walcott carried the fight to Langford from the seventh to the finish, Sam's counter blows counted heavily, and he even outboxed Joe . . . Langford received two hard rights to the chin in the thirteenth round that jarred him, and one under the heart that almost took him off his feet. Those punches were the hardest struck in the fight and had the most telling effect. But Langford came out for the fourteenth round with an abundance of confidence.

'When the bell sounded for the final session, Walcott's anger was still with him, for he refused to shake hands and was razzed for his poor sportsmanship. The round was hectic, with honours about even. Each landed often and hit hard, but Langford's straight lefts had such sting to them that they showed their work when the end of hostilities was announced . . . My personal opinion is that Langford was entitled to the verdict. Watch this well-built Negro, he looks like a sure thing to win either the welterweight or middleweight championship, though he may outgrow both divisions before he reaches his peak.'

Lumley's words were prophetic indeed, for although Sam wasn't growing any taller, his muscular body was filling out and by the end of 1905 he was a middleweight fighting heavyweights – guys like Joe Jeannette, who had held Jack Johnson even in two no-decision bouts and beaten him on a foul. Jeanette had thirty pounds on Langford and was four inches taller when they met, and it was enough to see him through to victory over eight rounds. They would meet again.

In the September 1960 issue of *Ring Magazine*, Ted Carroll wrote, 'With little other competition available to them worthy of the name, Langford, Sam McVey and Joe Jeannette engaged in their own elimination tournament, which never eliminated and lasted for many years. It finally reached the stage where meetings between them were little more than exhibitions between the shadows of what they once were . . . It was not always thus. Back in 1911, 1912 and 1913, McVey, a magnificently proportioned physical specimen with a devastating left hook, and Langford, then one of the greatest fighters of all time, had set the whole continent of Australia agog with series of battles which are still remembered Down Under as momentous contests between superlative fighters . . . They bade farewell to each other, ringwise, in East Chicago on 14 August 1920 in a no-decision travesty of ten rounds. The pair met fifteen times in all.

'In fourteen meetings with Jeannette, Langford found the Hoboken mulatto no pushover. Jeanette, rugged and a clever boxer, gave Sam trouble throughout his career and Langford did not catch up with him until time had warped both men. On 13 May 1916, the Bostonian finally knocked out the capable Jerseyman. The trio picked up an added starter in their private sweepstakes in Harry Wills who, younger than they were, mauled and manhandled them in their waning years as their talents and vitality receded. Wills always insisted he met Langford twenty-two times, but the record showed only eighteen meetings. So instead of a chance at Jack Johnson and the world title, Langford and McVey had to settle for the pantherish and powerful Wills in their declining years.'

It is incredible to note that Langford shared a ring with five men, Joe Jeanette, Harry Wills, Sam McVey, Jim Barry, and Jeff Clark, in a total of seventy-five contests! Like his contemporaries, Sam had great difficulty obtaining meaningful matches with leading white contenders. 'It is a well-established fact,' wrote Bill McCormack, 'that Sam was so good he had to "put on the handcuffs" before any of the big boys would take him on. Langford made L'il Arthur run away and hide. Johnson got the decision, by one means or another, when they fought in Chelsea, Massachusetts, in 1906, but never again could he be lured into the ring with Joe Woodman's squat fighting machine.'

Jack Johnson was two-and-a-half years away from whipping Tommy Burns for the world heavyweight title when he tangled with Langford. In his *Black Dynamite* series, Fleischer wrote, 'This particular battle was to become sort of a thorn in Jack Johnson's side for many a long day to come, although he was declared the winner after fifteen rounds of savage fighting. At the time, Johnson was given full credit for his victory. But years afterwards, when Johnson had beaten Tommy Burns and Sam's manager Woodman was trying to get Sam a shot at Johnson's title, Woodman started a big ballyhoo campaign and sent reams of copy to the newspapers stating that Langford had been robbed of the decision in the Chelsea affair.' In defence of Johnson, the man he rated the greatest heavyweight of all time, Fleischer went on to quote from Langford's autobiography as it appeared in the London *Mirror of Life*: 'In April 1906 I beat Joe Jeannette in fifteen rounds, and in the same ring about three weeks later I met Jack Johnson, and he handed me the only real beating I ever took. I'll take my hat off to Johnson for that victory.'

The story of the fight in the *New York Police Gazette* supported Sam's candid confession, stating, 'With a gameness and capacity for punishment that seemed beyond the powers of a human being, Sam Langford, the coloured fighter, weighing 156 pounds, battled fifteen rounds at the Lincoln Athletic Club of Chelsea with Jack Johnson, who outweighed Sam by about thirty pounds. Johnson gave Langford a terrible beating and was awarded the decision. In the eighth round Johnson wrestled Langford out of a clinch and then drove a terrible left hook to Sam's jaw and Sam went to the mat for a count of nine. He was all in and it looked as though the bout would have to be stopped. Johnson then tried hard to finish him and when he made a vicious swing at Sam, the latter, while trying to get out of the way, fell to the floor from exhaustion. Langford was up in a moment and fought back so hard that Jack was tired when the gong sounded. From then on, Langford showed wonderful blocking and stalling, combined with remarkable gameness. Johnson claimed after the fight that he had broken his left hand in the second round, and an examination by the doctor proved the correctness of his statement.'

In January 1907, after a dispute with Joe Woodman, Sam arranged through Sam Austin, the New York sporting editor, to go to London and fight Tiger Smith at the National Sporting Club, twenty rounds for a purse of $1,500. In their fine book about the NSC, *The Home of Boxing*, A F 'Peggy' Bettinson and B Bennison recorded, 'Tiger Smith had carried all before him while serving in the Army in India as a Hussar . . . he was the type of man who, once in the ring, can only see red; never clever, nothing of a scientist, and, as he stood right foot foremost, an outrage on conventionality, yet a fearless fellow was Smith . . . Against Gunner Moir at the NSC, after two minutes and forty-nine seconds the Tiger was finished. He was beaten hopelessly. Yet Smith held the confidence of his friends to such a degree that some two months later he carried their money in a match with Sam Langford . . . We are familiar with all the best fighters in the world, but few, if any, could have been more formidable than Langford was when in his prime, his lack of inches notwithstanding. Langford was no ordinary man; in a way he was a freak . . . his arms were inordinately long, his craftiness was uncanny, his sense of distance was phenomenal, while his capacity to hit with either hand was tremendous. Tiger Smith was a child in his hands – it was, from the first, ridiculously one-sided. But it was worthwhile to see the coal-black Langford in action.' On Monday of Derby week, Langford was back at the Club to box Geoff Thorne, with Bettinson recalling, 'Langford beat Thorne before we had scarce time to realize that they were in the ring.'

Returning home, Sam again hooked up with his old mentor Joe Woodman. They hit the road again, taking fights wherever they found them, and in May of 1909 Sam found himself back in London, this time with Woodman at his side. The National Sporting Club had obtained a signed promise from Jack Johnson, who had been in London on his worldwide chase of champion Tommy Burns, that should he win the title, he would return to defend it against Langford. Johnson beat Burns for the championship in Sydney but he never did return to the NSC to fight Langford. So the Club matched Sam with Iron Hague for a purse of £1,400 with a sidestake of £200. Bettinson would recall, 'Both Langford and his manager . . . made light of the fact that the Yorkshireman would take the ring nearly three stone heavier, and would stand four inches higher. Langford was a believer in the gospel according to Fitzsimmons: the bigger the man, the easier it is to hit him. Fitzsimmons, then fulfilling a vaudeville engagement in London, was among the large and distinguished company at the ringside, dressed immaculately, a very imposing dandy, and at forty-six he looked the picture of health and physical fitness.

'Iron Hague, as usual, was very much on the large side, and his condition strengthened the opinion which we had previously formed: that training, really conscientious and rigorous training, was not to his liking. Yet in the second round he knocked Langford down with a right hook and we were all genuinely surprised, none more so than Langford. But thereafter it was almost any odds on the black. In the fourth round Langford drove his left to the body, and, following with

49

a right to the chin, caused Hague to be counted out. When seen in his dressing-room, Hague could not understand how a comparatively little man, such as Langford was, could have dropped him. The explanation comes readily. Langford, as we have said before, was no ordinary man. He was a terrible fellow.'

Denied his crack at Johnson for the heavyweight title, the Boston Tar Baby, as one writer had labelled Sam, was within sight of a fight for Stanley 'Steve' Ketchel's middleweight crown in 1910. California promoter Jim Coffroth had offered a purse of $30,000 for a forty-five-round battle between Ketchel and Langford in San Francisco, but first they would cross gloves in a Philadelphia six rounds no-decision bout.

'We wanted the San Francisco fight,' said Joe Woodman, 'with Ketchel's title riding on the line and our hunk of Coffroth's $30,000. Unfortunately, Wilson Mizner and Hype Igoe, who co-managed Ketchel at the time, decided on keeping Coffroth guessing in the hope that he would raise his bid to $40,000, which was the figure they set for a dangerous threat like my Sam. Igoe told me he would take the $30,000 if Coffroth held out, but that he wouldn't accept unless I agreed to the Philadelphia six-rounder. Of course, I was dead against it . . . but I had no alternative, Mizner and Igoe held all the trumps, they had the title. All I had was Sam, the greatest fighting man who ever sucked a breath. Langford never won a world title because he never got the chance. Had not time been wasted fooling around in Philadelphia and Coffroth's proposition accepted immediately, Sam would have been middleweight champion of the world. He could have knocked out Ketchel seven nights a week.'

Sam and the Michigan Assassin agreed to box the six rounds in the Quaker City with nobody getting hurt, and everything was going well for three rounds. But in the fourth, Langford sent over a right with Stanley safely out of distance, only for Ketchel to step into the blow and take it full on the side of the head. He staggered, his arms dropped at his side, and Langford, sizing up the situation, grabbed him and waltzed him around until his head cleared. 'It was like a mother bird teaching her young to fly,' chuckled Woodman as he recalled the incident. 'She doesn't let go until she's sure her baby wouldn't fall and break his neck.'

At the final bell, Sam whispered to Stanley, 'See you in San Francisco, Mr Ketchel.' But the middleweight champion was tragically shot dead a few months later, before they could fight again. When he heard of Ketchel's death, Langford said, 'Poor Steve, he went to his grave thinking he could lick ol' Sam. Ketchel was a friend of Emmett Dalton, the great train robber, and for weeks before the fight Ketchel had me followed by tough guys from Dalton's gang to make sure I wasn't training too seriously. Stanley didn't trust anybody. I felt sorry for him, he had a devil tearing at his insides.'

In February 1911 Sam was back in London, but he would not be performing before the staid National Sporting Club on this occasion. There was a new boy in town, Hugh D McIntosh, a flamboyant Australian promoter who had staged the Johnson-Burns fight in Sydney on Boxing Day 1908. 'When McIntosh came to London,' wrote Guy Deghy in his book *Noble and Manly*, 'he came beating the big drum, and not cap in hand, as the NSC had expected. He was not invited in, not even to take a quick look at the boxing theatre. The snubbed Australian got to work elsewhere. He took a hall at Olympia and there, in February 1911, promoted the sensational fight between the Australian Bill Lang and the American Negro Sam Langford. Such publicity ballyhoo heralded and surrounded the contest at Olympia, for which the papers were issuing special editions, that the fight itself had a lot to live up to. Hugh McIntosh knew it and was ready for it. The mere fact that Langford wore snow-white boxing gloves made the crowd conscious of a touch of sensationalism, but when the white gloves became more and more tinged with Bill Lang's blood, the atmosphere of a Roman circus pervaded the hall. After six rounds almost unparalleled in vehemence, Lang committed a foul. The fight went to Sam Langford at all events, but Bill Lang collapsed into the bargain and had to be carried out of the ring. The tumult in and around Olympia was fantastic.'

Eugene Corri was the referee in that contest and he later recalled a conversation he had with Langford after the fight: 'We talked about the relative values of brains and brawn in a fighting man, and I happened to remark that Bill Lang had the reputation of fighting with his head, carefully thinking out his plan of attack as he went along. Langford rolled his thick lips in a broad grin that revealed all the white teeth in his head, and said, "Mister Corri, he's pretty fast on his feet, but his brains ain't fast. While he was thinking, I was hitting him!"'

Sam's keen sense of humour was as legendary as his prodigious fighting skills. There was the time he was fighting Fireman Jim Flynn for Sam Berger in San Francisco, in December 1908. When Joe Woodman told Sam he was to get only $700 for the bout, while Flynn was getting $2,500, Sam was not too happy. He was even less happy when the promoter came into the dressing room before the fight and asked, 'Make it just a nice fight, won't you, Sam?' Langford looked at him before saying, 'He's getting $2,500. I'm getting $700. Mister Berger, this is going to be the shortest fight you ever did see!' It was. As Flynn came out of his corner, Langford exploded a right on his chin, then turned and climbed out of the ring. He knew without looking that the Fireman would be out for some time. Next day, one of the local papers reported, 'Fireman Flynn got hit on the chin. Amen!'

In the veteran stage of his career, his sight failing, Langford was matched with Tiger Flowers, who would beat Harry Greb for the middleweight title a few years later. 'Can you fight southpaws?' asked the guy who was handling Sam then. Langford grinned and said, 'Old Sam can fight fighters which does things right, an' southpaws does everything wrong. Of course old Sam can fight southpaws.' In the first round, Langford literally felt out the Tiger. He had to. He couldn't see him, had to locate him by feel. He came back to the corner and notified his handlers, 'This boy makin' mistakes. He makes 'em again, an' we go home.' Flowers made the mistake and Langford knocked him out in the second round.

In London for one of his fights at the National Sporting Club, Sam was asked if he had any problem as to the appointment of the referee. Without a smile, Sam answered, 'Ah carries mah own referee.' When the shocked official pointed out that the Club always appointed the referee and in no circumstances would Mr Langford be allowed to bring along his own arbiter, Sam repeated, 'Ah brings mah own referee, an' here he is.' With that, Sam held up his mighty right fist. Later that night, Sam's 'referee' gave the right decision – a knockout.

Sam always reckoned that his biggest purse was the $10,000 he received for his fight with Iron Hague at the NSC in London, while Hugh McIntosh paid him $7,500 when he boxed in Australia. 'The top money I ever got at home was $3,000 for fighting Gunboat Smith in Boston. Very often I got no more than $150 to $200 for my fights. I once fought Joe Jeannette on percentage in a house where the gate was only a few hundred dollars. Once I boxed for a Negro promoter in New Orleans. The bout only drew $75, and I got one fourth of that.'

Joe Woodman ended his association with Langford in 1917. 'Sam got badly busted up around the eyes in a fight with Fred Fulton in Boston,' he said, 'and I was afraid he'd go blind if he kept fighting. I told Sam he'd better quit, but he was stubborn. He insisted he'd keep going. I argued and pleaded, but it did no good. So we parted. I was right. Sam did keep fighting, and eventually became blind. It was too bad. He was a great fighter and one of the finest chaps, personally, I've ever had anything to do with.'

Early in 1944, sportswriter Al Laney, researching an article for the New York *Herald Tribune*, went looking for Sam Langford in Harlem. Laney would write, 'We found him at last in a dingy hall bedroom on 139th Street. He was just sitting there on the edge of his bed listening to the radio. That is all there is for Sam to do now, for he is old and blind and penniless.'

The story Al Laney wrote inspired a campaign that established a $10,000 trust fund that kept Sam Langford comfortable until the day he died, in January 1956. A few years later, a ninety-year-old Joe Woodman told *Ring Magazine*, 'I keep looking for another Sam Langford. I know I'll never find one, fighters like Sam come along only once in a lifetime. But I can dream, can't I?'

# The Mighty Atom 4

Dempsey? Louis? Marciano? Ali? Boxing fans will argue long into the night as to who was the greatest heavyweight champion of all time. It's a different story at the other end of the weight scale, however. Jimmy Wilde is still universally acclaimed the greatest flyweight fighter of them all, some eighty years after he was in his prime. Yet when this wonderful little Welshman was at the top of his game, he wasn't even a flyweight.

James Butler, doyen of boxing writers, penned this in 1954: 'The most extraordinary pugilist ounce for ounce I ever set my eyes on was Jimmy Wilde. The phenomenal little Welshman, who was not a flyweight and scarcely a paperweight, was aptly dubbed the Tylorstown Terror and the Mighty Atom. But Pedlar Palmer, the old "Box of Tricks", coined a *nom de guerre* that described Wilde even more accurately: The Ghost with a Hammer in his Hand. Wilde was indeed a fistic ghost who never in his prime exceeded 7st 4lb. A phantom who, when stripped, was the nearest living thing to a skeleton, yet when he went into action he became a ring slayer . . . His starchy complexion, drumstick arms and pipe-stem legs caused National Sporting Club members to retire to the bar when Wilde made his first appearance at the Club in a trial bout with tough Joe Wilson of Stepney . . . I can see him now, looking undernourished and sickly, crouching in the ring with both gloves resting on his thighs. That was Jimmy Wilde, who, despite his freakish physical appearance, was a born champion and a natural hitter, because nature had bestowed on him the gift every athlete covets, the art of perfect timing. Wilde at seven stone punched harder than most featherweights. With patience a novice can learn to box, but no man can be taught how to punch. Either he can or he can't.'

'No fighter was able to do more with less than the fabulous Mighty Atom,' wrote Mike Silver in *Ring Magazine*. 'The stats alone tell the story, standing 5ft 2½in and tipping the beam at a paltry 108 pounds or less, this freakish fighter knocked out 101 men . . . The poor bloke looked like he was suffering from malnutrition and when he first came to America as world flyweight champion, promoters thought he was ill. This impression lasted only until Wilde began fighting. He was a holy terror in the ring. He moved aggressively into range, his hands held low to draw leads. He had the knack of weaving under punches, making his opponents miss by inches, and then countering with vicious, well-timed blows to the head and body . . . At first glance, Wilde looked like a scrawny runt. But upon closer inspection, one could see that his shoulders were muscular and large, at least in relation to the rest of his body. And his arms, though thin, were as strong as steel cables.'

This amazing little man reckoned he'd fought some 864 ring battles from the canvas booths of South Wales to the vast Polo Grounds in New York City, and only four official defeats were registered against him in a twenty-three-year professional career. For seven of those years, Jimmy Wilde was flyweight champion of the world.

A contemporary British newspaperman, R B Cozzens, wrote, 'If you are one of these sawed-off little guys, five feet nothing, with arms and legs like broomsticks, don't get that inferiority complex, don't get scared and envious of your lusty brethren, the men with brawn and muscle. Just listen to the story about a little chap who conquered the world, Jimmy Wilde.'

It was quite a story, and it began in a humble miner's cottage in Station Road, Quaker's Yard, Tylorstown, in the South Wales coalfield, on 12 May 1892. From an early age this tiny boy loved to watch the mountain fighters, bare fists and bare chests, fighting to a standstill. 'I would spend my precious pennies and get as close to the ring as I could,' Wilde wrote in his autobiography, 'goggling at the clumsy fighting, inspired by the spell of the ring. How I loved its tawdry magnificence.'

There was nothing magnificent in the lifestyle already mapped out for young Wilde and hundreds of boys like him: at thirteen, finish school one day and be down the pit the next. The one bright light that shone for the boy in that dark, dank environment, was a working friendship with a rock of a man called Dai Davies, one of the greatest of the mountain fighters. Young Jimmy became his lad, and as they worked together at the coal seam a thousand feet below the ground, the dream of a boy who wanted to be a boxer began to take shape.

'Occasionally,' Jimmy would remember, 'Dai would break off, lay down his pick and, crouching in the gloom, with his face covered with coal dust and his hands and body black, demonstrate this punch or that.' Warmed by the lad's enthusiasm, the old fighter would take him home so that they could practise more. Dai's wife relegated them to a tiny bedroom where the few sticks of furniture had to be shoved aside to give them space to spar. 'But as Dai pointed out,' recalled

Jimmy, 'the less space to move in, the more important was quick footwork and bodywork. That showed me how a move of an inch or even less could make the difference to the power of a blow given or received.'

A champion was in the making. There was a street fight with Tommy Davies, a bigger, older, heavier lad who had fought in the touring boxing booths that were a part of every travelling fair. Angry at being made to miss by this pale-faced, skinny youth, Davies rushed in only to be met with a right hand driven straight to his chin, and down he went. There was the famous booth run by John Scarrott, a man who laughed when young Wilde asked for a job. The boy persisted, so Scarrott told him to watch the rear of the big tent and stop other lads crawling under the canvas. When Scarrott saw the way he handled the interlopers, he put Jimmy in a pair of outsize trunks and shoved him on to the platform at the front of the booth. 'Stay three rounds with one of my lads and earn a pound,' was his cry.

'His appearance ensured that he would never be short of challengers,' wrote the late Harry Mullan in his book *Heroes and Hard Men*. 'He looked almost tubercular, with a pasty complexion, matchstick-thin arms, and a chest measurement of only 31½in. But the men who fancied their chances of earning a pound for lasting three rounds learned the hard way that the scrawny frame concealed utterly disproportionate hitting power. Wilde was a natural puncher, with the rare gift of perfect timing and coordination. Punch power has little to do with physique, and that simple fact was never more dramatically illustrated than by Wilde.'

'One day at Aberdare,' remembered Jimmy, 'I fought no fewer than sixteen fights. In fifteen of them I knocked out my opponent within the three rounds, but the sixteenth, who stood 5ft 10in and weighed 9½st, managed to go the three rounds and earned the pound. My reward for that day's work was thirty shillings.'

On his visits to the home of Dai Davies, Jimmy had fallen in love with Dai's daughter Elizabeth, who was always called 'Lisbeth. But like her mother, she hated boxing and when Jimmy suggested they get married, 'Lisbeth laid down one condition: no more fighting. Jimmy thought long and hard before finally agreeing, and they were wed, he seventeen, she just sixteen, living on a miner's wage of £3 10s a fortnight. But Jimmy was soon back on Scarrott's booth. ''Lisbeth hated the fighting, I know,' he said, 'but there it was. Boxing was stronger than anything else in me.'

Becoming more ambitious, Jimmy went along to the Millfield Athletic Club in Pontypridd where a silvery-haired old fellow named Teddy Lewis was making the fights. Jimmy weighed only six stone soaking wet and Lewis shook his head, saying, 'Put a little weight on, grow a few inches, and come back again.' But the lad wouldn't take no for an answer and Lewis matched him with a local middleweight over four rounds. Jimmy promptly knocked the fellow out and when he went to Lewis for his five shillings purse, Teddy asked, 'How do you manage to punch like that?'

'I don't know,' said Jimmy, 'I just do it.'

'Well, just keep on doing it,' replied the promoter.

The five-shilling fights at the Millfield Club became regular, sometimes three on a Saturday afternoon, and always a box of chocolate almonds for 'Lisbeth, her favourite. As Jimmy progressed, Lewis started booking him around the country. On New Year's Eve 1912, he fought Billy Padden at the Victoria Athletic Club, Glasgow, £25 for the seven stone championship of England. A hostile crowd laughed at the skinny lad from Wales but after eight rounds they were cheering him as he left the ring. His well-timed punches had knocked all the fight out of Padden, whose second threw the towel in. That fight convinced Jimmy he had to leave the pit so that he could train properly for his matches. So he became a full-time fighter.

'Jimmy, you've a champion's punch,' said Lewis, 'and a champion's ringcraft, and you've nothing to back it up. You've got to put on weight.' He tried. He ate meat three times a day and eggs by the dozen, but the scales refused to budge over 6st 10lb. His weight, or lack of it, thwarted a planned campaign in the United States. 'There's nothing to fight,' said agent Charley Harvey on the phone from New York. 'We couldn't get you a match. If you had an extra stone, you'd be all right.' Les Williams of Tonypandy and Dai Bowen of Treherbert were chosen to go instead of him and sailed for New York – on the ill-starred *Titanic*. 'I sometimes shudder when I realize how desperately hard I tried to make Harvey change his mind,' recalled Jimmy years later.

'I first heard of Jimmy Wilde in 1910,' wrote James Butler, 'from the self-appointed Professor Joe Smith, a boxing promoter in London's East End. "I was in Wales last week," said the Professor, "and in Jack Scarrott's booth I saw the most amazing kid in my life. His name is Wilde. He's just five stone, but he's knocking out flyweights, bantams and feathers." I didn't pay undue heed, for although Joe Smith was a splendid judge of talent, I believed at this time that he was overenthusiastic . . . A year later, Wilde had his first fight in London and knocked out Matt Wells's Nipper in one round!'

In her autobiography, Bella Burge, adopted younger sister of the famous Marie Lloyd of music hall fame, recalled the great boxing days at the Ring in Blackfriars Road, which she helped her husband Dick run and in fact carried on after his death in World War I. 'Dick was persuaded against his will to give this so unlikely specimen of a fighting man a match. However, as at the time Matt Wells had a paperweight youngster whose skilful boxing the then lightweight champion was forever dinning into Dick's ears, my husband gave them a six-round contest. Said Dick to me, "Bella, old china, you must come to the Ring tonight and give a little Welsh miner the once over."

So along I went, taking Rosie Lloyd with me as she wasn't working at the time. How we laughed when we saw this scarecrowish-looking kid crawl through the ropes and shuffle across the ring to his corner. His frame was just a collection of bones with a skin drawn so tightly that any moment one expected it to burst and a bone pop out . . . A wag in the gallery started to chant, "Any old bones?" and when Matt's Nipper climbed perkily through the ropes and tripped smartly to his corner, there came cries of, "Nipper, don't swallow the Leek in one mouthful!" It was the other way about! After swaying away from Nipper's punches with an ease which ought to have warned onlookers, Wilde shot his right glove across to the London boy's chin and brought down the curtain with a tremendous rattle. The look of astonished dismay on the face of champion Matt was comical.

'"Indeed to goodness, didn't I tell you Mr Burge what a hitter my boy is," said delighted Teddy Lewis, bustling into the office to draw the meagre wages of a six-rounder. "Who will you put him on with next?" I felt sorry for Lewis when Dick told him that Jimmy Wilde was much too little and that therefore he couldn't entertain another match. Lewis went off to see Peggy Bettinson at the National Sporting Club, but the manager turned them down. So back they went to Wales, chockful of disappointment, but at the same time determined to carry on . . . This remarkable little fighter had to win half-a-hundred contests, mostly by the knockout route, before he earned recognition . . . Teddy Lewis brought his still scraggy-looking fighting machine to London . . . ultimately persuading Peggy Bettinson to match him in an exhibition at the Club with Joe Wilson, who some years before had given Sid Smith a stiff fight for the first Lonsdale Belt Championship at eight stone. Like Alexander, Jimmy Wilde came, saw and conquered. Members who were prepared to scoff, and did when this bag of bones took his corner, remained to cheer and applaud with all their might. For Joe Wilson was never in the hunt, and was handled by the little miner almost as easily as if he and a championship fight had never had the slightest connection. Dick, who saw the bout, declared that he wouldn't have believed it had he not seen it himself. "He's the cleverest thing I've ever seen with a pair of boxing gloves, Bella," he told me.'

From then on, Jimmy Wilde became the darling of the National Sporting Club. In *The Home of Boxing*, a 1923 history of the Club, A F 'Peggy' Bettinson wrote, 'When we come to discuss the flyweights, we must begin and stop with Jimmy Wilde. He is incomparable. Jimmy Wilde stands alone. Before he went to America, he could give stones away and win in a canter. Of this wonderful, strange, uncanny Welshman, it is impossible to employ words to express our admiration. We can only say that his name will endure for all time.'

Jimmy made that name with fights against men like Sid Smith, Young Joe Symonds, Tancy Lee, Johnny Rosner, Young Zulu Kid, Joe Conn, Joe Lynch, Pal Moore, Pete Herman and Pancho Villa. His first fight with Symonds came in November 1914, with Bettinson recording, 'Already the fashion had been set to speak of Wilde as a phenomenon, for such indeed he was, but it may be doubted whether, up to this period, he had met such a strong, stubborn, accomplished, relentless fighter as Symonds. Yet the belief that Wilde would win was unshakeable . . . Fully dressed, he did not scale more than 6st 12lb. Symonds was sixteen pounds heavier and looked the picture of health. It was a rare contest, and it may be doubted whether Wilde has shown skill more wonderful than on this night. Symonds never fought harder, and twice very early on in the bout he was severely admonished for hitting low . . . Wilde only once had a really anxious moment, when, off his guard, he was set rocking by a particularly hard right to the jaw. But at the end of fifteen rounds he was ever so many points in front.'

Wilde's fight with Sid Smith at Liverpool Stadium, where he had become a big favourite, was to select a challenger for the British flyweight championship. Both men sparred cautiously in the opening rounds and when the crowd shouted for more action, Smith opened out and jolted Jimmy with a right to the jaw. After taking another right, Wilde knew that Sid didn't have the punch to hurt him. But he could hurt Sid. In the ninth round Jimmy crashed a right to the jaw and Smith went down on one knee. He was badly shaken and after the Welshman dropped him three more times, the referee called it off. So in January 1915, Jimmy was matched with the tough little Scot Tancy Lee at the National Sporting Club, for the championship of Britain and Europe, the Lonsdale Belt, and a £500 purse. Wilde trained at Porthcawl under George Baillieu, but a few days before the fight he was in bed with a heavy dose of influenza. When 'Lisbeth visited him and saw his condition, she wanted the fight called off. But Jimmy wouldn't hear of it. So she went home and told Teddy Lewis to hedge their bets, saving them £500.

In his book *Life's a Knockout*, veteran boxing manager and journalist Charlie Rose wrote, 'Lee, a pawky Scot, had begun his boxing life at an age when most of the fraternity are thinking of packing it in. He had only eight professional contests before meeting Wilde, but as he had stopped clever, seasoned fighters of the calibre of Percy Jones, Bill Ladbury, Alex Lafferty, Johnny Hughes and Tommy Harrison, you must admit his greatness. All the same, his luck was in on that January night in 1915 when he met the Ghost with a Hammer in his Hand. For early in the morning a newspaper colleague rang me up from Cardiff with the startling information that Jimmy had been in bed for four days suffering from fish poisoning, and had risen from it only the previous day. The fact was kept secret and not a soul suspected anything at the weigh-in, because Jimmy invariably looked pale as a sheet at any time, and odds of four-to-one on him were laid. Tancy's backer, John McGuire, helped himself liberally. Early in the contest Lee burst Jimmy's left ear, which began to swell, and continued swelling till it was flapping at the side of his head like a boat's sail against the mast when being hauled down.'

'It was as though a steam hammer had hit me,' Wilde would recall later. 'My head rang. I went on in a daze. And the ear started to swell.'

'It will be remembered,' said Teddy Lewis many years later, 'that in Wilde's first contest with Tancy Lee, the towel was thrown into the ring during the seventeenth round as an acknowledgement of defeat. This was done upon my instructions. Some little while after, Wilde took me to task for so acting and expressed his annoyance that such a course was adopted without at least consulting him. My attempt to justify myself was cut short with the following instruction: "No matter in what contest I am engaged hereafter, please understand that however bad a time I may be passing through, under no circumstances is the towel to be thrown into the ring. If the other fellow can put me down and out, then let him have the full credit for it. Please don't forget this."'

In his book *Heroes and Hard Men*, Harry Mullan related a nice anecdote on the new champion. 'The porter who carried Lee's bag on his arrival back at Glasgow railway station saw the Lonsdale Belt in it, and asked Lee what he'd won it for. "Swimmin' the Channel," Lee replied. The porter, who was no boxing fan, was impressed, and assured Tancy, "It's no more than you deserve for doing it in January."'

Two months later Wilde was fighting fit and back in action with a vengeance. This diminutive dynamo started a run of twenty-nine fights over the next four years, with only one opponent surviving those hammering fists to the final bell. 'The deadliness of his hitting,' wrote Charlie Rose, 'the lightning speed with which he hit his victims, and the cleverness of his boxing rapidly made him one of the great favourites of the day.'

While Jimmy was fighting his way back to the top, Tancy Lee had lost the British and European titles to Joe Symonds, and Bettinson booked Wilde to fight his former victim for the title and the Lonsdale Belt. Once again the little Welshman was giving a chunk of weight to his opponent, Joe bouncing the scales at 8st with Jimmy at 6st 10lb. Like their first fight, this was another tough battle. Wilde would recall that in the fifth round, Symonds hit him so hard in the stomach that 'I thought the end of the world had come. My eyes went round and round, and for a moment there was only a red and grey mist in front of me.' But when the mist cleared, Jimmy took command. In the eighth, as Symonds stepped back and tilted his chin to avoid a punch, the blow caught him full on the Adam's apple, knocking all the fight out of him. He could not breathe properly and it was only heart and courage that kept him in there until the twelfth round. Before the controlled fury of Wilde's attack, Joe dropped to one knee and raised a gloved hand in surrender. Jimmy Wilde was British and European flyweight champion. He was on his way back to Wales with a black eye and a Lonsdale Belt.

In April 1916 Wilde was matched with the American Johnny Rosner at Liverpool Stadium, in a fight billed for the world title as recognized in Britain and by the International Boxing Union. Rosner had received a scalp wound in sparring and it was soon opened by Wilde's punches, as were cuts over both eyes. Jimmy recalled it was one of the goriest fights he had taken part in, adding, 'Perhaps the most remarkable thing about Rosner during that fight was that he never once retreated.' The fight was stopped in the eleventh round with Wilde a good winner, but world recognition was still not his.

One man Jimmy wanted to fight more than any other in that summer of 1916 was Tancy Lee, and he was happy when the National Sporting Club put up a purse of £500 and a sidestake of £250. 'Different as chalk from cheese was the Wilde who met Lee in the return contest,' wrote Charlie Rose, 'for after feeling Tancy out for two rounds, he got well on top and knocked out the Scot in the eleventh round. John McGuire, who came down from Edinburgh to back Lee again, must have lost a packet, as the odds went down to six-to-four and he stepped in to scoop the cream off the market. But McGuire was a real sportsman, for when I went to Tancy's dressing-room to console him, I found his backer was before me, trying to cheer the tearful ex-champion with champagne. "I couldn't find him at all tonight, Guv'nor," complained plucky little Lee, sipping his wine.'

Bettinson arranged an open-air show at Kensal Rise with Jimmy opposed to Johnny Hughes of Bermondsey, a strong fighter with a powerful right swing. Jimmy handled him well and, after hammering Hughes all over in the ninth round, knocked him out in the tenth with a right to the jaw. ''Lisbeth told me afterwards,' said Jimmy, 'that a man leaned over and called her husband a miracle, a mite of a boy with a punch like that of a sledgehammer. The gentleman in question, an officer in a Scottish regiment, turned out to be Paddy Slavin, who had been one of the heroes of the legendary battle at the National Sporting Club twenty-four years before when he fought Peter Jackson.'

In the autumn of 1916, London fight promoter Jack Callaghan received a letter from a Mr Giuseppe di Melfi, an Italian boxer living in Brooklyn, New York. Fighting as Young Zulu Kid, di Melfi was the American flyweight champion and he suggested a match with Jimmy Wilde to clear up the world title situation. The fight appealed to Callaghan and he replied to the American, offering him forty per cent of a £500 purse. A few weeks later, Callaghan was running a show at Hoxton Baths when into his office walked the American champion, along with his manager Joe Sarno. The big fight was on.

Now Callaghan had a problem: where to stage the fight? There was a war on, and the established large arenas had been taken over by the government during the national emergency. Then the promoter remembered the old Central Hall in Holborn. It had been used as a stable and warehouse by Carter Paterson, the well-known delivery firm, but was now derelict. Jack almost had second thoughts when he visited the place. The concrete floor was strewn with rubbish and broken glass, the gallery piled high with filthy straw. But financier Clarence Hatry, an avid boxing fan, agreed to back the venture and obtained permission for the work to go ahead by offering the place to the YMCA as a hostel for servicemen. The gallery became a dormitory with beds that could be folded away to make room for spectators, a kitchen was added, and the main hall became a club and dining room. Jack Callaghan had his fight arena, to be known as Holborn Stadium, and he announced that Wilde and the Zulu Kid would meet for the world flyweight championship on 18 December.

As usual, Jimmy Wilde trained at home, while the American set up camp at the Royal York Hotel in Brighton, where licensee Harry Preston had an excellent gymnasium. Zulu Kid had taken his ring name from the golliwog mascot given to him by a friend when he started boxing, and whenever he fought, the mascot was tied to the ring post in his corner. Watching this ritual, Jimmy murmured to Teddy Lewis, 'I should have asked the missus for a leek to tie around our post.'

'You've got the best mascot in the world for winning fights,' said Lewis gruffly. 'It's in your right hand, and don't forget to give it to the Kid at the first opportunity.'

A crowd of some 4,000 had jammed the new stadium, and they were surprised when the men came together to see that Wilde, for a change, was actually 4½in taller than the muscular Italian-American. The Kid wasted no time, charging across the ring with both gloves firing, and Wilde was surprised, taking a few blows around the head. The American was a difficult target as he bobbed and weaved and the

67

Welshman was missing with his punches. But in the second round, a hard left hook landed on Jimmy's ear and he was stung into action. As the Kid pressed forward, a sizzling uppercut flashed through his guard and sent him reeling into the ropes. Then a right to the chin had him stumbling into his own corner. The crowd was in uproar as Jimmy followed up with a left hook and three rights to the jaw that sent the Kid crashing to the floor for the first time in his career.

With no chance of beating the count, the American was saved by the bell and as his seconds hauled him back to his corner it was seen that his golliwog mascot was hanging upside down by one leg. But Young Zulu Kid was far from finished. He roared out for round three as fresh as paint, and Wilde was forced to give ground under the fury of his attack. 'Keep cool,' counselled Lewis as Jimmy returned to his stool. 'You've got twenty rounds to go, he'll tire long before that.' But the Kid was still fighting strongly in the ninth round and Jimmy was forced to defend. In the tenth, however, Jimmy made every punch tell and the American started to come apart. The end came in round eleven. As the Kid came out swinging, Wilde smashed home a terrific left that almost took his head off and another knocked him back into his own corner. Jimmy moved in fast and a tremendous right knocked the Kid spark out, still standing up, and it took three more rights to bring him crashing to the floor. Manager Joe Sarno threw the towel into the ring and Jimmy Wilde was the undisputed champion of the world.

'There was a sequel,' remembered Jimmy. 'The Kid had smashed some heavy punches to the body and I went into a nursing home under the care of that fine medical man, Sir Herbert Barker. His treatment was little short of miraculous.'

By the summer of 1918, Jimmy Wilde had convinced the Army that he could be of some use, despite his size, and he was rapidly promoted to Sergeant Instructor in the Physical Training Corps –

which gave the promoter a problem when Jimmy was matched with Joe Conn at Stamford Bridge Stadium. Gilbert Odd told the story in his book *The Woman In The Corner*. 'A scientific instrument maker engaged on government work, Conn was free to accept a professional contest, but Wilde was a soldier. He could get leave to train for and take part in a public boxing match, but would not be allowed to accept any monetary payment. Jimmy would have been quite happy to box for nothing, but he had the future to think about and defeat by Conn, five years younger and 21lb heavier, might ruin his reputation. He turned down the proposal, but the promoters were so keen to have his services that they offered to make him a present of any commodity he might choose in lieu of cash. He advised them to approach his wife and without hesitation she plumped for diamonds, saying she had always wanted some. How many she expected I do not know, but the purse was £3,000 and she was delighted to receive a bagful after her talented husband had demolished his bigger opponent in the twelfth of their scheduled twenty-rounds bout.'

In December 1918, a month after the Armistice, the Inter-Allied Boxing Tournament was held at the Royal Albert Hall in London, all contests of three rounds' duration. 'There was only a medallion to be won,' recalled the famed referee Eugene Corri, 'and yet for two whole days, with the world looking on, they fought with all the hardness that was in them. The King's Trophy was won by the British Army, with the American Forces runners-up. First I should treat with the defeat of Jimmy Wilde by the American Pal Moore. Wilde had previously disposed of Joe Lynch, whom he afterwards met at the National Sporting Club, and Digger Evans, a hard-hitting, rugged little fellow from Australia. To my amazement, Wilde, who in my judgement won each of the three rounds, was declared to have lost. Most people were dumbfounded, and there was long and loud disapproval. I cannot explain how it came about that the judges decided that Moore won.'

Seven months later came the fight Jimmy wanted, a return with Moore. Theatrical producer CB Cochran staged the contest at Olympia for a £5,000 purse with a £1,000 sidestake, Eugene Corri third man in the ring. CB had more success finding lovely young ladies for his stage shows than he had with his boxing promotions. 'Do you know, Jimmy,' he said, 'you and Georges Carpentier are the only two men who have ever earned me money in boxing.'

'Jimmy Wilde was in a class by himself,' Cochran would later write. 'When he fought, he was nearly always giving weight away. Even when he boxed Pal Moore for me at Olympia he was about 7st 4lb to Moore's 8st 4lb . . . One of the greatest moments of Jimmy Wilde's career must have been that last round when he scored with left and right, and in the last couple of seconds came near knocking Moore out . . . If his body had been in proportion to the size of his heart, we should have had and held for several years the heavyweight boxing championship of the world.'

'Something almost unique in my contests happened at the end of the ninth round,' recalled Jimmy of the Moore fight. 'I had punched his ears sharply just before the gong went, Moore's head was ringing, and he did not hear the gong. As I dropped my arms, he came at me like a tiger and I took more punishment than I wanted.' The crowd booed referee Corri for not warning Moore, but the official whispered to Jimmy as they passed in the ring, 'I can't caution him, Jimmy – General Pershing is here, it would look so bad.' The American general was indeed sitting ringside, along with Mr Cochran and the Prince of Wales, an avid supporter of boxing and a great fan of the little Welshman.

Wilde's defeat of Pal Moore following his victory over Joe Lynch sparked interest across the Atlantic, and Teddy Lewis accepted terms for a fight with Jack Sharkey, a New York bantamweight, in Milwaukee on 6 December 1919. With Lewis unable to make the journey, David

Hughes went along as manager and Benny Williams as trainer, along with 'Lisbeth, of course, by now a permanent fixture at the ringside of Jimmy's fights. When they sailed into New York harbour aboard the *Baltic*, police had to control the crowds that turned out to catch a glimpse of the fighter they were calling The Mighty Atom. Among them was promoter Tex Rickard, who laughed as he shook hands with Wilde. 'I can't make you out, Jimmy,' he said. 'You're just a bag of bones!'

Within six months, the 'bag of bones' had fought eleven times, winning six and boxing five no-decision bouts, and earning himself the magnificent sum for those days of £23,500. But by the time he came home to Wales, Jimmy Wilde was ready to retire. He was now happier playing golf or snooker and relaxing with 'Lisbeth and their two boys at the house at Radyr, near Cardiff, which he called 'Lonsdale'.

Then in January 1921, eight months after hanging up his gloves, Jimmy was tempted back to the ring with a purse of £8,000 for a fight with Pete Herman of the United States. When the fight was proposed Herman was bantamweight champion of the world, and he signed a contract to box Wilde at the championship weight of 8st 6lb over twenty rounds. But Sam Goldman, Herman's canny manager, took out a little insurance before leaving New York. Pete boxed just bad enough to drop his title to Joe Lynch and was an ex-champion when he arrived in London to fight Wilde. On returning home, Herman regained his crown from Lynch without too much trouble.

In every way this was a bad match for Jimmy Wilde. Teddy Lewis had signed on the understanding that Herman would weigh at ringside on the night of the fight, but the American's manager had a contract calling for a two o'clock weigh-in. Herman had weighed in at 8st 6lb and gone off to eat a hearty meal. When he arrived at ringside that night he was weighing about 8st 9lb and he absolutely refused to go on the scales again. With Jimmy scaling just over 7st, Lewis realized the handicap was too great and was for calling the fight off. But the crowd was already in an angry mood after the proposed fight between Bombardier Billy Wells and Battling Levinsky was cancelled, the American appearing in the ring with his arm in a sling. Aware that the Prince of Wales was at the ringside, Jimmy Wilde climbed into the ring to face almost certain defeat. Denzil Batchelor would write, '. . . rather than disappoint his Prince, he accepted an invitation to professional suicide.'

'Within a couple of rounds,' wrote Gilbert Odd, 'it was as plain as daylight that Jimmy was no longer the great fighting machine who had thrilled us in the past. He had gone back to almost an unbelievable extent. In fact, in all ring history there has never been such a falling-off in form so complete or so rapid.'

The game little Welsh terrier fought his heart out, but the bigger, heavier American, a fine fighter, punished him mercilessly until in the seventeenth round referee Jack Smith had seen enough. Stopping the fight, he carried Wilde to his corner, saying, 'I've got to pick you up, Jimmy, you don't know the way to stay down.'

There would be one more fight, one too many for the Welsh idol. Inactive for two-and-a-half years after the Herman fight, he was lured to New York to defend his world title against Pancho Villa for a purse of £13,000. Jimmy was no match for the fiery little Filipino and was hammered in seven rounds, the final blow leaving him senseless on the bloody canvas.

Nat Fleischer would write, 'Jimmy showed he could take it besides dish it out. His was an unconquerable spirit. That is why, when asked for a definition of the word "champion", I always reply, "Jimmy Wilde."'

# The Manassa Mauler 5

Recalling the sporting heroes of the Roaring Twenties, Joseph Durso wrote in the *New York Times*, 'The performer who captured the public's fancy in the most basic way was Jack Dempsey. He started to capture it on the Fourth of July 1919 when he destroyed Jess Willard and won the heavyweight title, while Johnny came marching home. Tough, hellbent, savage, the right man at the right place at the right time.'

In 1969 Nat Fleischer of *Ring Magazine* wrote, 'Who had the most destructive single punch KO? Whom would I pick to end a fight with power, dispatch and classic form? The answer is Jack Dempsey. In Dempsey, it was his speed of hand and feet, combined with a powerful attack, that made him the promoter's magnet. He was a killer! Dempsey represented the true fighting man . . . Teeth bared, he sprang into action bent on destruction . . . Jack possessed steel fists and an iron jaw. His blows were explosive. He could take it and dish it out. Dempsey might be likened to a combination of a polar bear and a panther. Strong as the first. Agile as the second.'

Veteran fight manager 'Dumb' Dan Morgan said, 'Dempsey was the most spectacular fighter ever to hold the heavyweight title. The Tiger Man was electric. He created excitement. For the first time, the public poured millions into the box office because they knew they would get their money's worth and more in spine tingles any time Jack defended the title he cherished and fought so savagely to keep . . . Dempsey's great magnetism drew to boxing, for the first time, the general public. Before Dempsey exerted his mass appeal, the ring was, for the most part, a magnet only for the roughneck, the race tout and the sporting character. In Dempsey's time, boxing finally achieved eminent respectability.'

The man who would become king of the ring was named after an American president when he was born on 24 June 1895 in Manassa, a potato town in the San Luis Valley of Colorado. The ninth child of Hyrum and Celia Dempsey, he was named after President William Harrison.

'My brother Bernie nicknamed me Jack,' he would recall. 'I am basically Irish, with Cherokee blood from my mother, plus a Jewish strain from my father's great-grandmother. A lot of people have said that the Indian showed more in me than it did in my eight older brothers and sisters or in the boy and girl who were born after me. I have the high cheekbones and jet-black hair of an Indian, and they say I still walk with the Indian's pigeon-toed glide.'

Celia Dempsey was a tough, wiry little woman, and Jack always said it was his mother who influenced his decision to become a fighter. 'Just before you were born,' she would tell him, 'a stranger came to the door selling magazines. I told him I had no money but he was welcome to a glass of milk. When he left, he wanted to pay for the milk, but I wouldn't hear of it. So he gave me a battered old book about John L Sullivan. I sure did enjoy it. When you were born, so big and strong, I said to everybody, "He's going to grow up to be the world's heavyweight champion, just like John L Sullivan."'

'My older, bigger brother Bernie had become a fighter,' recalled Jack many years later, 'and knowing of my ambition to be a fighter, he started teaching me a few professional tricks of the trade. Bernie was a good fighter, but he had a glass chin. He taught me to chew pine gum, straight from the tree, to strengthen my jaw. Then, after a spell, he would test me to see if I had done enough chewing by throwing a left hook to my jaw. Invariably I would be knocked down. After dusting myself off, I would chew some more of the bitter-tasting stuff.

'I bathed my face in beef brine to toughen the skin. Bernie called it pickling and said if I ever got cut, I wouldn't bleed. Once a day, I would trek to and from the butcher shop, carrying back pails of the stinking stuff. At first the brine burned like hell, but then I got used to it. Eventually my face got as tough as a saddle. Bernie was a good coach. He taught me a lot about rhythm, ducking and sidestepping. My instinct and his teaching combined to make speed my best defence. My best offence proved to be the punch I was born with.'

When Jack was sixteen, Bernie got him a job in a copper mine in Bingham County, Utah, and he worked the mines on and off for five years, digging for gold, silver, copper and coal. 'There have been a thousand and one things I enjoyed doing through my life,' he would say, 'but the two things I enjoyed most were fighting and digging coal. I know it's hard to believe it, but I actually enjoyed going into a mine to fight chunks of coal out of a wall. And whenever there was time, I would fight. I lived to fight, just as later I would fight to live.'

He started fighting as Kid Blackie. He fought in grubby saloons and old dancehalls and rough and tumble mining towns like Montrose and Durango, where his painted image still adorns old brick buildings. He would walk into a saloon and announce, 'I can't sing and I can't dance, but I can lick any man in the house!' He only weighed around 130 pounds and when the local bully heard Dempsey's high-pitched voice, he would step forward, fists raised. A few minutes later he would be flat on his back, and the bartender would pass the hat and split the few dollars with Dempsey.

Out on the road from his early teens, Dempsey discovered a class structure, as he later recalled: 'The hobo worked when he could and travelled wherever the wind blew him. The tramp, on the other hand, travelled all over but didn't work. Nevertheless, they had respect for each other. Bums were a completely different story. They didn't travel and they didn't work. In fact, they didn't do a damn thing!'

In 1914 Jack lost to Andy Malloy, who had beaten his brother, then knocked Malloy out a couple of weeks later. Malloy offered to teach Jack what he knew about the fight game and became his first manager. 'I learned many things from Malloy,' Jack would say when looking back on his early days. 'He was a good teacher.' Bernie, who fought as Jack Dempsey, signed for a fight in Cripple Creek, then had second thoughts and wired his brother to take his place. Harry, as the family called him, duly climbed through the ropes and was announced as 'Jack Dempsey'. It was a tough scrap and he stopped the guy inside seven rounds. But the promoter refused to pay, annoyed at the substitution. Not getting paid was something young Jack Dempsey would get used to. He slugged through ten rounds with big Johnny Sudenberg in Goldfield for $100, but when he woke up next morning he discovered the guy who had acted as his manager had blown the money in the local saloons and skipped town.

By the summer of 1916 Jack was ready to try his luck in the East. He hooked up with Jack Price and they headed for New York City. 'Nobody threw any ticker tape the day I got into New York, in June 1916,' he recalled. 'I was skinny, beetle-browed, needed a shave every four hours, had a broken nose, wore cheap clothes and was scared stiff. I talked with a Western accent, but it wasn't one of those manly drawls; I talked soprano and real fast. I must have set a new record for greenhorns!' They hung around Grupp's Gym on 116th Street and Price finally got Jack a fight with a 215-pound giant named Andre Anderson. To build up his strength, and his weight, Jack would buy a nickel beer in a saloon and gorge himself at the free-lunch counter, stuffing his pockets with as much food as he could for later. He gained ten pounds and weighed 167 for the fight with Anderson, a big blond fellow from Chicago, at the Fairmont Athletic Club run by Billy Gibson. When Gibson saw Dempsey, he yelled for Price. 'What the hell is the matter with you? I ought to put you in jail for allowing this kid to fight Anderson. Why, he'll get murdered!'

The big fellow bounced Jack off the canvas a couple of times in the early rounds, but by the fifth he grew tired from hitting Dempsey and the rawboned slugger from the West finished strong over the last half of the fight. Decisions weren't given in those days in New York, but Damon Runyon wrote in the *New York American* that Dempsey looked very promising and with the right training and management could get to the top. In the *New York World*, Ned Brown wrote, 'Dempsey is a great young fighter. There is one thing wrong with him, however. He looks like he needs a square meal!'

A black giant named John Lester Johnson ended Dempsey's first brief visit to New York. 'Johnson gave me a terrible beating,' he remembered. 'In the second round, he hit me with one of the hardest punches I ever took, and that includes anybody who ever hit me any time, anywhere and with anything. It busted three ribs like matchsticks. I was in agony. Every movement I made after that was torture. I was afraid he'd kill me.'

By this time, Jack Price had gone back home. Before leaving, however, he sold Jack to a guy named John the Barber for fifty bucks.

John Reisler, who got his name from a big barber shop he owned on Broadway, was a gambler of whom it was said he would have sold his mother's blood if the price was right. He was ready to throw Dempsey to the wolves, offering him fights with Sam Langford and Gunboat Smith. It was time for the kid to go back home. When he felt his ribs were back in place, he returned to New York, but there was nothing for him. He visited newspaper offices, showing sportswriters the wilted, well-fingered clippings that told of his many knockouts out West. They didn't even read them. Damon Runyon did. He remembered seeing Jack fight somewhere and told him not to give up. Next day, Jack Dempsey hopped on a freight train heading West.

'There is quite a difference between riding the rods and bumming it in freight trains,' he would explain. 'Most hobos aren't steady enough to ride the rods, the two narrow steel beams beneath a Pullman. There are only a few inches between you and the tracks, and death. If you fall asleep, you may roll off your narrow steel bed and die. Or if you're so cold you can't hold on any longer, you die. You have to be desperate to gamble like that, but if you weren't desperate, you wouldn't be on the rods in the first place.'

Dempsey arrived in Kansas City to learn that Frank Moran and Carl Morris were training to fight each other. Moran's people chased him when he applied for a job as sparring partner, but he was hired at the Morris camp for seventy-five cents a day. 'Boxing with him in the gym,' recalled Dempsey, 'I made a stunning discovery. I could beat him if I wanted to. I could beat Carl Morris, one of the top heavyweights in the world! I saw openings so clearly that it took all the strength I had not to do something about them. But I needed that seventy-five cents a day, plus the extra dime he was now paying me for rubbing him down after he had worked me over. Carl Morris stood six-feet-four and weighed around 235 pounds. There was an acre of him to rub for that dime!'

Dempsey was fired on the fifth day when the fight was called off after Moran hurt his hand. He hit the road again and ended up in Murray, Utah, where he was matched with Fireman Jim Flynn. Brother Bernie was in Jack's corner, and after Flynn had him going up and down like a yo-yo in the first round, Bernie threw the towel in, much to Jack's disgust. But his luck was about to change. Early in 1917, he received a letter from Jack Kearns asking if he still wanted to be a fighter. When Dempsey replied that he was ready to fight anybody, anywhere, any time, Kearns sent him a train ticket to Oakland, California, and five dollars eating money. 'Imagine a manager putting out money to a fighter who hadn't made him a nickel,' said Jack. 'This Kearns, as far as I was concerned, had class!'

Born in Michigan, raised in Washington State, John Leo McKernan was just fourteen when he ran away to join the Klondyke gold rush in Alaska. He did everything from selling Bibles door-to-door to weighing gold in a saloon; he was a fighter, a wrestler, a gambler. His biographer, the sportswriter Oscar Fraley, would write, 'Here was a combination of the swashbuckling D'Artagnan, the rollicking Robin Hood, the daring Jimmy Valentine, the wily Richelieu, and, withal, one possessing the charm, wit, impishness and *savoir faire* of a larcenous leprechaun. He was a poised rapier of a man with quick-silver tongue, puckish grin and powder-blue eyes that hinted alternatively of Arctic ice and Killarney mischief.' In 1917 he was called Jack Kearns and he had a new fighter, a kid called Dempsey. Kearns took him home to his mother and she fed him and gave him a room.

When Kearns figured his new boy was ready, he matched him with Willie Meehan, a fat ex-sailor who had faced such ring luminaries as Jew Goldberg, Racehorse Monroe and Bow Wow Flanagan. But Willie had also been in there with some real fighters, guys like Billy Miske, Gunboat Smith, Tom Gibbons and Bill Brennan, and he was as tough as an old boot. Dempsey found that out in their four-rounder that

79

night in San Francisco. He won the decision, but would recall, 'Willie kept coming into me, no matter how hard and often I hit him. There was no way to stop him. Fighting him gave me a feeling of complete frustration. I was disappointed and embarrassed I hadn't done better for Kearns. But he wasn't the least bit upset.'

In two further meetings with Willie, Dempsey came out with a draw before in September 1918 the little fat guy slapped his way to a hometown decision in 'Frisco. Dumb Dan Morgan said, 'Meehan was what we call a freak, but he was the biggest and best freak we ever had in boxing.' By the time of that loss to Willie Meehan, Dempsey was starting his climb to the world heavyweight championship and Kearns decided to test him against old Gunboat Smith in San Francisco. Smith had fought them all and he was a helluva puncher with his right hand, as Jack discovered in the second round. In his 1936 biography of Dempsey, Nat Fleischer wrote, 'The punch caught Dempsey squarely on the point of the jaw. It came down with a sort of sweeping motion and the force of impact was like that of a sledgehammer coming down on a plate of steel. The leverage was perfect. The timing was most accurate. The power behind the punch was with full force of the shoulders. Dempsey's knees sagged . . . Kearns, who had been standing on a stool at the ringside, became so excited that he fell off the chair . . . When he arose, there was Dempsey boring in, milling away with both hands as if nothing had happened. What a marvel Dempsey proved himself in that fight. He was out on his feet, yet didn't know it.'

'In that fight,' remembered Kearns, 'Dempsey showed me without question that we could go all the way to the top. Gunboat hit him with a shot in the second round, it almost tore Jack's head off. But the kid kept right on coming and won a unanimous decision. How hard Gunboat had hit him came to me on the ferry on our way back to Oakland when Jack suddenly looked at me and said, "Smith was too tough for me, that's all. What did he hit me with?"

"He hit you with a right hand, kid," I told him, "I thought it'd kill you. But instead you nearly killed him. Kid, you're gonna be the champion of the world, and I'm the guy who's gonna get it for you!"'

Carl Morris was next, at the Dreamland Pavilion in San Francisco, and the man they called the Sapulpa Engineer was glad of the California rules limiting bouts to four rounds. With Al Jolson, Wyatt Earp and Rube Goldberg among those cheering at ringside, Dempsey gave fifty-two pounds and a savage beating to the giant from Oklahoma. A couple of months later they went at it again, with Morris taking a worse beating. Dempsey battered him all over the ring and when Morris sent in a low punch in round six, the referee threw him out. Still not satisfied that Jack was his master, Morris faced him again, this time in New Orleans. A smashing left hook to the body put him down and out in the opening seconds of the first round. 'I knew the bum wouldn't get up,' growled Jack.

On their way to Chicago, Dempsey and his manager stopped over in Denver and bumped into the heavyweight champion of the world, Jess Willard. Kearns tried to make a fight for his tiger right there in the street, but the Kansas giant stated flatly that he wouldn't defend his title while the war was still on. But Kearns did get him to agree that Dempsey would get first crack, although Willard probably said so just to get away from Kearns. The secret agreement was soon leaked to a local newspaperman and the *Denver Post* brought out special editions with the news.

Arriving in Chicago, Kearns booked rooms at the swank Morrison Hotel. 'Don't ever check into a crummy joint, kid,' he told Dempsey. 'People'll think that's all you're used to. Remember, in a dump they'll always ask for their dough in advance, while a classy place waits till the end of the week, or month.'

In February 1918, after belting out Fireman Jim Flynn in one round to avenge his only stoppage defeat, Dempsey fought Bill Brennan at the Milwaukee Arena. He had sparred with Brennan at Billy Gibson's gym in New York, and Leo P Flynn, Brennan's manager, remembered him. 'Everyone's underestimating you, kid,' he said to Jack, 'but I've got a feeling you pack dynamite in those hands.'

Those dynamite hands had big Bill down four times in the second round, but he got up four times and was still coming at Dempsey in round six when a right to the jaw spun him completely around and when he fell, he broke his ankle. The fight was stopped and in the dressing-room afterwards the reporters crowded around Brennan's manager. 'Can Dempsey hit?' said Flynn, wide-eyed. 'Say, he hit my man so hard he broke his ankle. Did you ever hear of anything like that?'

In six months of 1918, Dempsey had knocked out ten of the dozen men he had faced and Kearns was clamouring for a shot at the title. In their way stood the towering figure of Fred Fulton, all 6ft 6in of him, the man already matched with Willard for the world championship on 4 July 1919. But there were so many protests at that fight being scheduled so soon after the war that the promoter promptly dropped the idea. So Mike Collins, who managed Fulton, came looking for Kearns and Dempsey, offering them a fight. Terms were quickly agreed for the bout to take place at the old Federal League Ball Park in Harrison, New Jersey, and Dempsey went into training at Long Branch. Kearns hired Jimmy DeForest to get his boy in shape for this most important fight and they hit it off from the beginning. DeForest was one of the top trainers in the fight business, always chewing an unlit cigar as he put Dempsey through his paces in the gym.

Because of his greater experience and physical advantages, Fulton was a hot seven-to-five on favourite to win, and even money to win by a knockout. A crowd of 10,000 paid to see the fight – what there was of it. It was all over in 18⅗ seconds! At the bell, Dempsey rocketed from his corner and waded into Fulton with a vicious barrage of lefts and rights to the body, then smashed over a right to the jaw and, as one reporter told it, 'The big fellow dropped like a safe from a ten-storey window!'

This is how sportswriter Dan Daniel recalled the affair many years later: 'It was a sunny Saturday afternoon and a fair house was there. Dempsey already intrigued the fans. Both men sat in a sun-drenched ring; Dempsey young and defiant, Fulton somewhat jaundiced, apparently scared stiff. Right behind me sat Joe Weber, the actor, part of the famous duo of Weber and Fields. Joe was a little guy and he tapped me on the back with the request that I shift my camp stool a bit so he could see beyond me. I turned to say something to the actor, adjusted my chair, and then saw Fulton sitting on the canvas, a picture of agony. I reported that fight from hearsay, because I never saw the one and only punch!'

It was a punch Dempsey called, 'the hardest I ever hit a man. It felt as though his jaw had shattered and my fist was going right on through his face.' Back in their hotel, Jack told Kearns the hand wasn't sore, but it was swollen. Kearns marched him into the little pharmacy in the lobby of the hotel and said to the guy behind the counter, 'I want something for this man's hand. About equal parts of iodine, wintergreen and sweet olive oil to take down this swelling.'

'All right, Doctor,' said the man. 'Is there anything else, Doctor?'

'No,' replied Kearns, 'just have that sent up to "Doctor" Jack Kearns's room when it's ready.' From then he was Jack 'Doc' Kearns to everyone in the fight game.

In February 1919, promoter Ted Rickard invited Kearns and Dempsey to New York to discuss terms for a title fight with Jess Willard. Tex had already signed the champion for $100,000 but he wouldn't agree when Kearns demanded $50,000 for his man. They settled for $27,500 for the fighter Damon Runyon had labelled the

Manassa Mauler. Every city where boxing was legal across America was sounded out as the battle site, with Rickard settling for Toledo, Ohio, after receiving the assurance of city and state officials of every co-operation.

Tex built a brand new arena on the shores of Maumee Bay. It took two months and 520 workers, and on fight day the blistering sun boiled the resin and pitch out of the plank seating so you either ruined your clothes, stood up or bought a cushion from the smiling vendors, who made a small fortune. But not many people remained seated once the fight started. In fact, big Jess Willard sat down more than anybody else in that first round, seven times in all. Seven times Dempsey's cruel, hammering fists smashed this giant hulk of a man to the canvas, and the last time he didn't get up and referee Ollie Pecord said to Dempsey, 'You're the winner.' But it wasn't over, not yet.

'I stumbled down the ring steps and started up the aisle,' recalled Dempsey in his autobiography. 'Then I heard Kearns screaming to me to come back. I climbed back through the ropes. "It's still on!" he yelled. "The bell saved him. Nobody heard it. The round ended at the count of eight." Suddenly, I felt terribly tired and punched out. I came out cautiously. He hit me a pretty good right-hand uppercut that shook me up. I boxed him through the second, but in the third I really gave it to him good. I don't know how he made it back to his corner. But he didn't make it out. They threw in the towel before the fourth could start.'

Grantland Rice, one of America's finest sportswriters, recalled, 'Looking at Dempsey and Willard in 1919, it was hard to give Dempsey a chance . . . Willard looked on Dempsey as a little boy. The night before the fight, Bob Edgren and I called on Jess. He thought the fight was a joke. "I'll outweigh him seventy pounds," Willard said. "He'll come tearing into me, I'll have my left out, and then I'll hit him with a right uppercut. That'll be the end." Next day when the first round opened, Dempsey circled Willard for some thirty seconds. He was a tiger circling an ox. Finally, Willard couldn't wait any longer. He jabbed at Dempsey with his left, and the roof fell in. Jack ducked under Willard's left and threw a right to the body. At the same time he nailed Willard on the right side of the head with a smashing left. "I knew it was over then," said Jack later. "I saw his cheekbone cave in."'

Doc Kearns said, 'Dempsey was so dumb at being heavyweight champion of the world that you could have hit him with a hammer and he wouldn't have blinked an eye.'

'That night was to remain vivid in my mind for a long time,' recalled Dempsey. 'I managed to peel off my clothes and flop into bed, where I dreamed the fight all over again. In my dream, Willard knocked me out! I woke up in a cold sweat, confused . . . Pulling on my pants and shirt, I rushed outside. A newsboy was hollering, "Extra! Extra! Read all about it!" Then he asked, "Ain't you Jack Dempsey?"

"Yeah, why?" I said. I grabbed a paper. There it was, my name in big, bold headlines. I was the Heavyweight Champion of the World! All of a sudden, standing barefoot on the street with a newsboy at my side, I felt the full impact of my victory.'

Before he started writing short stories of Broadway's guys and dolls, Damon Runyon covered the sports beat, and this is what he wrote of Dempsey's savage victory: 'The right side of Willard's face was a pulp. The right eye of the fallen champion was completely hidden behind that bloody smear. His left eye peered over a lump of flesh in grotesque fashion. The great body of the giant was splotched with red patches. They were the aftermath of Dempsey's gloves thumping there and giving back a hollow sound as they thumped. At the feet of the gargantuan pugilist was a dark spot which was slowly widening on the brown canvas as it was replenished by the drip, drip, drip from the man's wounds. He was flecked with blood from head to foot.'

'The first change I noticed in myself after beating Willard,' recalled Dempsey, 'was that I could talk to nice people. I hadn't met many along the line, but those I had met frightened me. They were always using words I couldn't understand. It was embarrassing to say something and see their faces go blank . . . But suddenly people understood me. They started laughing at my jokes . . . But I was still a bum with a knife and fork, and I dressed like a guy an honest cop would arrest at a carnival. I had been wearing suits for two years but I dressed as much like Kearns as I could, and he was strictly patent-leather shoes and diamond stickpin happy.'

In 1920, Dempsey defended his title twice. In September, at Benton Harbour, Michigan, he met Billy Miske, a fighter who had already given him a stubborn argument in two no-decision fights. But by the time he got his shot at the title, Miske was a sick man, suffering from Bright's Disease which would eventually cause his death in January 1924. Dempsey liked Billy and knew the $25,000 purse would help him, so he agreed to the fight. But after knocking Miske out inside three rounds with a crashing right to the jaw, he would say, 'It was the only time in my life I was ashamed of being a fighter.'

Three months later, the champ met Bill Brennan at Madison Square Garden in New York City, thrilling a packed crowd of 15,000 in a sensational battle that tested the champion several times before the end came in round twelve. 'It was a right hook delivered with great force to Brennan's body just beneath the heart that started Brennan on his way to defeat,' wrote Nat Fleischer. 'As he doubled over and winced with pain, Dempsey quickly stepped in and whipped a well-directed left hook, delivered with all the power of his massive shoulders into Brennan's right side. The challenger dropped to his hands and knees. As referee Haukop began to toll off the fatal ten seconds, Brennan writhed in agony and strove gamely to regain his feet, but it was beyond human possibility.'

Yet more than once during the previous eleven rounds, Dempsey's title hung in the balance as Brennan fought like a man possessed. In the second round a terrific right uppercut almost brought the champion crashing down, and it was round five before he got back into it. Brennan was in trouble when a sizzling right almost finished him in the eighth, and both were rocked in fierce exchanges. In the tenth round, Dempsey bloodied the challenger's mouth, only to have his left ear half torn off by Brennan's swinging right hand. Kearns was going crazy in the corner, screaming, 'You're gonna blow the title, Jack! You gotta knock this guy out!' And after one minute, fifty-seven seconds of round twelve, Bill Brennan was knocked out. Dempsey was still the champ.

As Jack was having his ear sewn back on, Brennan called in to his dressing-room. 'It took you twice as long to get me this time, you lucky stiff,' he grinned. 'Next time, out you go!' For the brave Brennan, however, there was no next time. The Chicago heavyweight quit the ring a few years later and opened a speakeasy. When gangsters called in one night and advised him to stop buying a rival mob's beer, he threw them out. A few nights later, one of them came back and shot Bill dead.

'What seemed to be the worst mismatch in the history of the heavyweight division was my fight with Georges Carpentier on 2 July 1921 in Jersey City,' recalled Dempsey. 'Yet it became the first bout ever to draw a million-dollar gate, and the first ever to pull in anywhere near 91,000 spectators. The gross was $1,626,580. We had signed for either $300,000 or fifty per cent of the gate. But a week before the fight, Kearns waived the fifty per cent. "Just give us the three hundred grand and we'll be happy," he told Tex Rickard, the promoter. Doc's decision cost us $150,000!'

In his prime, Jack Dempsey usually weighed in around 188 pounds, not even a heavyweight by today's standards, but that day in Jersey

City Carpentier was no more than a heavy middleweight, his announced weight of 172 pounds said to be padded. Tex Rickard had arranged for him to train in secret. 'He wasn't a heavyweight any more than I was King Tut,' said Dempsey. 'If boxing writers had seen him, fast and skilful as he was, they would have laughed the match out of existence.'

In his preview of the contest, Ring Lardner wrote, 'It is doubtful if Carpentier will last through the introductions.' Even Rickard was worried, visiting Dempsey in his dressing-room to say, 'Don't kill him, Jack. We got a million dollars in already, and they're still coming. If you kill him, you kill boxing. I just want you to knock him out, and not with one punch or in the first round. Give them a run for their money.'

Dempsey took the first round, but received a shock in round two. 'Carpentier, to my surprise, had a terrific right,' he recalled. 'It landed high on my left cheekbone in the second. He followed it up, like a real pro. He bounced five in a row off my head before I could hit him. But then I busted him a right in the mouth and I thought I had him licked. In the fourth I hit him with a left hook and he went down for nine. Another left sent him down again and while he was falling I nailed him with a right. Time, fifty-seven seconds of the fourth round.'

Nat Fleischer wrote, 'Gorgeous Georges Carpentier, gracefully formed as some statue of an ancient Greek, and brilliant in his ring performances, went down before a surly bulk that was fighting man incarnate. Jack Dempsey held his title through the exercise of brute force, which was his mission in the ring at the Jersey City arena.'

It would be two years before Dempsey put his title on the line again, against Tom Gibbons in a fight remembered more for the colossal financial fiasco it became. Doc Kearns agreed to have his tiger fight Gibbons in Shelby, Montana, on Independence Day 1923, for a $300,000 guarantee. Dempsey won the fight under a broiling sun, and he and Kearns left town on a special train taking all the money that wasn't nailed down. Doc had already received two payments of $100,000 and he rounded up a further $72,000 at the pine-built arena in this Montana cowtown before heading for New York. The well-meaning promoters were out of their depth and by the final bell, with Dempsey taking the decision over a defensive-minded Gibbons, every bank in town closed its doors. Their assets had been stripped in what became known as the 'Rape of Shelby'.

The bankers weren't the only ones left with a headache after that fight. Dan Morgan recalled, 'Gibbons, well versed in the clever stuff, found more than his match in the champion and was hard put to go the distance. For days after the fight, Gibbons could not put on his hat because of the bumps Dempsey's iron fists raised on his head.'

On a September night in 1923, a cosmopolitan crowd of some 82,000 people paid Tex Rickard $1,188,603 to see Dempsey defend his title against Luis Angel Firpo at the Polo Grounds in New York City. Among them was gangster Charlie 'Lucky' Luciano, who used his influence to round up a hundred pairs of ringside tickets. 'It cost me about twenty-five grand,' Luciano later recalled, 'and I never regretted it. My two hundred seats mixed up everybody from whores to politicians, from society to Delancey Street. I had made up my mind I was gonna make friends from everywhere.'

Firpo was a shaggy-haired, beetle-browed Argentinian who was slow, clumsy and awkward, but he was 6ft 2½in and weighed 216 pounds, strong and dangerous with a clubbing right hand. Damon Runyon called him the Wild Bull of the Pampas and in a sensational opening round he gored the champion clean out of the ring, and that after being smashed to the canvas seven times himself. The champion landed on top of a typewriter in the press row and was pushed back into the ring by a reporter who wanted to see the rest of the fight!

'He half-hit and half-shoved me with a right to the face,' Dempsey related in his 1959 autobiography. 'I went out of the ring backwards.

I don't remember getting back in. The first thing I recall clearly is sitting on my stool in the corner. "What round was I knocked out in?" I asked. "You just slipped," Kearns said. "You're coming out for the second." I went after Firpo again, but this time with respect. I wasn't going to get nailed again.'

Describing round two, Nat Fleischer wrote, 'A left to the jaw and Firpo went down for a count of two. That was the beginning of the end. Firpo was beginning to show the terrific effects of the body battering. He arose, but a series of lefts and rights to the body and a solid smash to the jaw sent him down again for a count of five. He got to his feet again only to be met with a left hook to the jaw followed by a right to the jaw as he was falling, and the most sensational bout in modern ring history was over.'

'The wildest, most tumultuous of all Dempsey's battles,' recalled Dan Morgan, 'was against Firpo at the Polo Grounds. The cyclonic action in the battle pit projected itself among the spectators like I had never seen. For example, Mickey Walker, then welterweight champion, found himself beating another man in front of him on the back and shrieking madly for Dempsey. Suddenly the fellow turned and smote Walker on the chest, knocking him four rows back. When some semblance of sanity was returning, the big man turned to Walker and apologised. Walker gasped, "Gee, no wonder you hit me so hard. Honest, I didn't know it was you," he added as he recognized Babe Ruth.'

Even the Corona Typewriter Company got in on the act. It was a Corona machine Dempsey landed on when he was knocked out of the ring, and it still worked. Within days the company had a new advertising slogan: 'Dempsey knocked out Firpo, but he couldn't knock out Corona!'

This was the last fight Dempsey would have with Doc Kearns as his manager. 'We never had a contract,' Jack would recall, 'but we split everything fifty-fifty. Kearns never gave me an accounting. Prior to the Firpo fight, the New York Commission insisted we file a boxer-manager document stipulating a one third-two thirds split. I never signed the Commission contract. Nevertheless, Kearns produced such a document. He had three lawsuits pending against me. I was afraid to shake hands with anybody, fearing it might be another process server. Eventually I won in court, but, as can be imagined, the suits did not contribute to my peace of mind.'

Dempsey's purse for the Firpo fight was just over $500,000, and he collected it himself from Rickard. When Kearns came to his hotel the following day, Dempsey said he 'counted out what was coming to Kearns and took out what he owed me. This time, I got more than he did, and it burned him. "What are you going to do with that money?" he yelled at me. I had to say it then. "Doc, I'm going to put that money where I know I'll have it when I'm old."'

For three years, Dempsey engaged only in exhibition bouts, which all lasted one or two rounds. There were vaudeville tours, marriage (his second) to a lovely film star, Estelle Taylor; he had his nose remodelled, did a play on Broadway. Meanwhile, Harry Wills, a black heavyweight, was looming as his next contender. 'The New York Commission demanded I fight Wills,' Jack told *Ring Magazine* in 1965. 'There was no reason I shouldn't, although the move was politically motivated. I was willing and signed with Floyd Fitzsimmons, who guaranteed me a million dollars. Wills got a downpayment of $50,000. The promoter never came up with my end and all I received was a $25,000 cheque that bounced. Tex Rickard talked vaguely about Washington being opposed to a title fight involving a Negro. Eventually, he offered Gene Tunney as a challenger and I accepted.'

When the New York Commission refused to sanction the Tunney fight, Rickard put it on in Philadelphia on 23 September 1926, and a huge crowd of 120,757 paid $1,895,733 to sit in the

Sesquicentennial Stadium as the drama unfolded before their unbelieving eyes. Grantland Rice, wrote in the *New York Tribune*, 'Gene Tunney, a superbly cool and efficient boxer, marched out of his corner at the opening bell and hit Dempsey, the fighter, with a high, hard right hand. That blow sealed Dempsey's doom. It started to rain in the fourth round and by the tenth and final round it was a deluge. At the end, Dempsey's face was a bloody, horribly beaten mask that Tunney had torn up like a ploughed field. Speed of foot, a sharp jab and a right cross that ripped Dempsey's face like a can opener were going for Tunney that night, against a man who, despite a rocky training period, had been installed a one-to-five favourite. Tunney, at twenty-nine, had arrived on his toes. Dempsey, at thirty-one, departed flat-footed.'

In his heyday as heavyweight champion of the world, Dempsey had suffered criticism for being a slacker during the war, even though he had registered with his draft board and been deferred from military service because he was the chief support of his parents and his first wife Maxine. In the fight with Carpentier, Jack had been booed while the Frenchman was cheered as a war hero. But on that rainy night in Philadelphia, as the bloody, battered ex-champion walked from the ring, America found its hero again. 'The people were cheering for me, clapping for me,' recalled Jack, 'calling out my name in a way I had never heard before.'

Nat Fleischer, sports editor of the *New York Telegram* at the time, wrote, 'Jack Dempsey was far greater in defeat than was Gene Tunney in victory.' Tex Rickard was well aware of that fact and he talked Jack out of retiring, matching him with Jack Sharkey, with the winner to fight Tunney for the title. Rickard lined up Leo P Flynn as Jack's new manager and the veteran had some words of advice when they started training. 'Sharkey's a better puncher than Tunney,' said Flynn. 'Get that in your head. But he's got one weakness. He can't take it around the body. You keep punching to the body until he drops his hands. When he drops them, let that right hand go, and then the left, and knock him out.'

Rickard had himself another million-dollar gate at Yankee Stadium when 75,000 turned out to cheer Dempsey in his comeback against the erratic Boston fighter. 'He gave me a terrible beating for the first five rounds,' remembered Dempsey. 'I thought he was going to knock me out . . . In the seventh, after I had hit him half a dozen times just above the belt, he stepped back, dropped his hands, turned his head to Jack O'Sullivan, the referee, and yelled, "Hey, he's hitting me low!" I hit him with one of the last good punches of my life. I couldn't miss. What was I going to do, write him a letter? He went down and it was all over. The crowd went crazy.'

Rickard was a happy man that night. The right man had won: Dempsey, the fighter who had drawn boxing's first five million-dollar gates, and was now set for number six. It was Tunney-Dempsey again, this time in Chicago, and when the first bell rang out there in Soldier Field, a vast throng of 104,943 had paid $2,658,660 to see a prize fight.

'I won't forget the seventh round,' Jack related in his auto-biography. 'It was my first good shot at Gene. I got to him with a pretty good right, and then I hit him with a real good left hook. He started to go. I hit him seven times while he was going down, hit him with all the punches I had been trying to land in the ring and in my sleep for a year.' Reverting to habit, Dempsey stood over the fallen champion, waiting for him to rise so he could slug him again. But referee Dave Barry was intent on seeing the rules obeyed, and he shepherded Jack to a neutral corner before returning to start counting over Tunney. But instead of picking up the count from the knockdown timekeeper, he began his count at one, and by the time he reached nine, the champion was on his feet and in full retreat as Dempsey tried to cash in his advantage. Tunney had rested on the canvas fourteen seconds before getting up to win what would become known as The Battle of the Long Count.

Describing Dempsey's last three rounds in a boxing ring, Paul Gallico wrote, 'His legs failed him altogether. He stopped. And over his swarthy, blue-jowled fighter's face there spread a look the memory of which will never leave me as long as I live. It was the expression of self-realization of one who knows that his race is run, that he is old and that he is finished . . . And from his second losing encounter with the ex-Marine, Dempsey emerged the greatest and most beloved popular sports hero the country has ever known, a title that, curiously, his greatest victories never won for him.'

It was a title he would hold until death took him in 1983, aged eighty-seven.

# The Rochdale Thunderbolt 6

Jock McAvoy was one of the hardest punchers in the history of British boxing. They called him the Rochdale Thunderbolt, a nickname that fitted him like an eight-ounce glove. In eighteen years as a professional fighter, he lost only fourteen of 147 fights and sent ninety-one of his victims off to an early shower. He was British middleweight and light-heavyweight champion, fought for the European light-heavyweight, world light-heavyweight, and British heavyweight titles – and he did it all with bad hands!

In August 1929, barely two years into his career as a money fighter, McAvoy fought Jack Jukes at the Winter Gardens in Morecambe. Jukes came from Tyldesley, near Leigh in Lancashire, and, as McAvoy recalled in his autobiography, 'was a bullet-headed fighter of the stubborn type, and he kept boring in, irrespective of the punishment I was giving. Eventually I dropped him with a strong right to the jaw, but when I tried to land another in order to finish him off, he ducked his head and my blow landed on his rock-like cranium. A pain shot up my arm and I realized that something had happened, so I tried swinging and hooking with the left. He was on the deck twice in the fifth, and twice more in the sixth, after which the referee called enough. I ought to tell you hereabouts that my hands were never bandaged for those early fights.

'My damaged hand caused me to rest up for a few weeks, but it was never given real attention, and because it stopped paining me, I imagined it had righted itself . . . Had I had the sense to have my hands properly looked after whenever they were damaged and waited patiently until they were well before using them again, I might have realized my ambition and won a world title. As it happens, I was bothered with my right hand for the rest of my career.'

As recorded by Denis Fleming in his book *The Manchester Fighters*, it was not until McAvoy joined Harry Fleming at his gym in Manchester's Collyhurst district that his hands received some proper care and attention. It was the summer of 1931 and Jock, having just won the Northern Area middleweight title from Joe Lowther, figured he was ready for the big time. He had already racked up sixty-one pro fights, winning all but five (one draw) and scoring thirty-nine victories inside the distance. But his own hands had taken a hammering as well as his unfortunate victims. 'Incorrect punching had already caused havoc to his hands,' wrote Fleming. 'The two middle knuckles of the right hand were almost shattered, with bits of bone and tissue permanently dislodged and driven back against the metacarpals between knuckle and wrist. Harry Fleming was appalled when he examined them . . . After some experimenting he finally designed a method of taping and bandaging Mac's hands which would prevent any further deterioration and moreover give their owner the confidence to punch with more force and conviction. In order to get his taped hands to fit more snugly into the gloves, Mac developed his most famous ring characteristic: biting, gnawing, and pulling at his gloved thumbs.'

When *Ring Magazine* put McAvoy on its cover after his sensational American debut in 1935, writer Eddie Borden asked Jock why he chewed his gloves. 'I hurt the knuckle of my right thumb some years ago,' explained the fighter, 'and often when the glove is extremely tight I feel a sensation which causes me a little uneasiness. To relieve the pressure, therefore, I simply take the glove thumb in my teeth and yank on it to loosen it up so that I can close my fist tighter.'

Dr JW Graham, with a practice on the outskirts of Manchester, was medical officer at Belle Vue for many years, becoming a steward of the British Boxing Board of Control and later its chief medical officer. 'McAvoy had a badly set broken thumb,' he would recall. 'No matter how carefully bandages were applied and the gloves put on, this irritated him during a contest and he could often be seen worrying away at the glove with his teeth. Incidentally, this worrying often happened before McAvoy produced what he described as a "husker".'

Boxing writer Reg Gutteridge put it nicely when he wrote, 'Jock McAvoy is the only fighter who bit the hands that fed him. When he chewed his gloved thumbs and snorted, opponents were usually doomed. With him it presaged the pay-off. It was a mannerism of man-eater McAvoy interpreted as bad temper, but truth was he was loosening the joints of thumbs broken working in Lancashire's cotton mills. This gave McAvoy a better grip to be the only British fighter I have seen who could lift an opponent off the floor with a single blow.'

In his book *England's Boxing Heroes*, Frank McGhee wrote of Jock's glove-chewing habit, 'Some thought it was a sign of rage and frustration. Some thought it was an attempt to tear the padding inside the gloves to enable his knuckles to do more damage. It was, in fact, McAvoy's way of loosening joints that were already afflicted by arthritis.'

Jack Doughty's excellent book *The Rochdale Thunderbolt* is the definitive biography of McAvoy. Doughty wrote, 'Mac would have trouble with both hands throughout his career, particularly the right. It has been claimed by several people who knew him that Mac did not have particularly strong hands to begin with. They have even been described as being smallish and delicate. If that was the case then another factor must be taken into account, his tremendous punching power. He would not have been the first fighter to suffer with his hands for this reason. McAvoy himself said that his thumbs were so short that he could never find a glove that fitted him comfortably, and that this was the reason he developed the habit of repeatedly tugging at the thumbs of his gloves with his teeth during a contest. If this was in fact so, then those who insist that his hands were on the small side might just be right.'

Whatever the reason, one thing is certain. When Jock McAvoy stopped chewing his gloves and threw them at an opponent, he was a very dangerous person. Tough Heywood scrapper Joe Rostron had beaten Mac in April 1930, and agreed to fight him again a few months later, this time over fifteen rounds at Manchester's Free Trade Hall. 'Rostron managed to keep out of serious trouble until late in the fourteenth round,' wrote Doughty, 'when, backed up against the ropes and covering up, with his right hand held high and left arm protecting his body as McAvoy came at him, he suddenly felt Mac lift his left elbow. The next moment, Joe thought his ribs had caved in as McAvoy banged a piledriver of a right hand into his body. Rostron had never been hit as hard in his life and was sure that his ribs must be broken. At that moment he was badly winded and in agony, but before Mac could follow up, the bell rang.'

Rostron somehow got through the fifteenth and final round as McAvoy took the decision. Many years later, Joe told Doughty, 'It was like being hit with a sledgehammer. When that punch landed, all the breath went out of my body. It was just like a football being punctured. I'll tell you straight, I couldn't bend down to tie my own shoe laces for a week! What power that man had. Strong as a bullock and almost unstoppable.'

They called him Joe Bamford when he was born in Burnley, and when he first fought for money on a Sunday afternoon in November 1927, they called him Jock McAvoy. Promoter Joe Tolley was running shows at the Royton Boxing Club, between Rochdale and Oldham, and when he agreed to give the nineteen-year-old Bamford a fight, he asked the lad's name. Not wanting his mother to find out he was fighting, he told Tolley to announce him as Jack McCoy. But that afternoon when he climbed in there to fight local lad Billy Longworth, Tolley announced him as Jock McAvoy. It was a name he would make famous throughout the boxing world. He won the fight, swinging like a gate until he connected in round two and Longworth went out like a light.

'I signed for ten shillings and was given seven shillings and sixpence,' he recalled years later. 'That's when I learned there was more to this game than taking punches.'

Just after McAvoy won the Northern Area middleweight title in 1931, his promoter/manager Joe Tolley closed his stadium down and filed for bankruptcy. It was about this time that manager Harry Fleming approached Jock and offered to take over his affairs if he could come to an agreement with Tolley. Joe still had a contract with the fighter he had brought from nothing to contender status, and he had his price. And, according to author Jack Doughty, the people who were prepared to meet Tolley's price were the members of the Belle Vue Syndicate.

'This so-called syndicate was apparently made up of Henry Illes, the licensed promoter; Jack Madden, matchmaker; Harry Fleming, official manager of, among others, Jackie Brown and Johnny King; and

Norman Hurst, one of the country's leading sports journalists . . . The real power behind the organization, however, was Hurst, a man whose involvement in boxing went back a good many years. He wrote for the *Daily Dispatch* and the *Empire News*, whose sports coverage was excellent . . . Though Hurst could obviously not afford to have his connection with the syndicate made public, it was well known in boxing circles that he was not only involved, but was in fact the main man, who provided the financial backing and made all the major decisions. In other words, a shadowy figure who remained discreetly in the background pulling the strings.'

Tolley and McAvoy met the syndicate, terms were agreed, a sum of money handed over, and Jock McAvoy was on the road to the championship. Fleming and his able trainer Jack Bates gave Jock an intensive course of coaching, stressing correct punching on the heavy bag and regular sparring with the stable's two welterweights, Jack Sloan and Billy Kelly. Jack Bates had been a pretty good fighter himself and he taught Mac many of the tricks of the toughest game of all.

Dr Graham recalled a humorous anecdote about Fleming and Bates. 'Fleming's gym was a room over a coalyard and, in spite of its insalubrious surroundings, was a great success . . . Harry Fleming was a real manager and trainer. He knew all the tricks and always kept one jump ahead of his boxers. In the vicinity of the gym was a dance hall and Fleming did not think that dancing and training went hand in hand. I went into the small massage room on one occasion to be met by an appalling smell. This came from an evil-looking concoction that Jack Bates was, with his usual poker face, massaging into the limbs of a recumbent boxer. An equally poker-faced Fleming assured me in a loud voice that it was a special Indian rubbing oil from America. When we got outside the room, I said, "Harry, what the hell is that stuff?" He told me it was chiefly rancid cod liver oil and that the boxer had been going to the dance hall. He said, "With that stuff on him, he will be lucky to get in, let alone find anyone to dance with!"'

McAvoy started his climb to the title with a fight against Jack Hyams, a Jewish lad from Stepney who started fighting as Kid Froggy. Hyams was in the gym one day when his manager Joe Morris said to him, 'There's a promising boy in Rochdale they want an opponent for at Leeds. He's called Jock McAvoy. He's been knocking a few over, but you can take care of him.' So on a Sunday afternoon the London boy was in the ring at the Brunswick Stadium in Leeds fighting McAvoy, over fifteen rounds or less.

'I was giving away a stone,' recalled Hyams, 'and I hadn't been in the ring for more than thirty seconds before I realized that I had bitten off more than I could chew. McAvoy was no novice. He could box a bit and his hitting was tremendous. When he slugged me to the body, it shook me up from top to bottom, and I quickly made up my mind not to get my chin in the way of any of his punches. The only thing I could do was grab hold of him when he came in with his body slams, and I did this so successfully that by the eighth round I was still on my feet, but found myself disqualified for persistent holding.'

McAvoy's hammering fists stopped seven of his next nine opponents, and in March 1932 he was fighting Len Harvey for the British middleweight championship in the Belle Vue ring, the packed arena cheering him to a man. 'This was a complete contrast in styles,' wrote Frank McGhee in *England's Boxing Heroes*, 'because Harvey was a man of infinite patience, ice-cool, allowing all McAvoy's aggression to be countered by his own defensive mastery, then, in the fifth round, unleashing a right that lifted McAvoy through the ropes into the ringside seats. McAvoy landed on his head but scrambled back, beat the count and started biting at the thumbs of his gloves . . . The thirteenth round, and a terrible mistake. When Harvey dropped his arms in apparent exhaustion, McAvoy jumped in, chin first, into another right so perfectly delivered that Harvey confessed afterwards he was astonished that it had not knocked McAvoy down and out. "I thought it was hard enough to kill a horse," said Len.'

Just over a year later, Harvey put his title on the line again in the Belle Vue ring and this time McAvoy was a better fighter. In eighteen fights, he had lost only to Jack Casey on a disqualification, and fourteen of his victims were out of there before the final bell, seven by clean knockouts. This time Len Harvey was a flawed fighter. He had suffered damage to his right hand on the cast-iron jaw of Jack Casey in a title defence at Newcastle, and further aggravated the injury in a light-heavyweight eliminator against Eddie Phillips which ended in a draw. Harvey was given a two-week postponement, much to Mac's annoyance. Fleming demanded Harvey be examined by a Board doctor, despite the fact that he was attending Guy's Hospital and had a certificate stating that he was not yet fit to box. Charlie Rose, managing Harvey at the time, urged him to show the paper to the Board doctor, but Len stubbornly refused, saying, 'I'll fight him even if my right hand is tied behind my back!'

'It might as well have been for all the use it was during the fight,' remembered Rose. 'Jeff Dickson, the promoter, who was sitting just in front of me, voiced his readiness to lay six to four on Harvey. Leaning forward, I whispered in his ear that he would be chucking money down the drain if he backed Len, as he had only one weapon to fight with. My fighter lost on points, and a narrow margin at that. Was he worried about losing his title? Not a bit. He was happy as Larry at supper afterwards. McAvoy must have got the shock of his young life when Len wandered into his dressing-room, and, congratulating him on winning the title, told him that, as champion, his troubles were about to begin.'

Troubled or not, Jock McAvoy reigned as British middleweight champion from that night in April 1933 until he hung up his gloves in

1945, winning the Lonsdale Belt outright and putting two notches on a second one. His first challenger was Archie Sexton, then having a good run with victories over Johnny Summers, Joe Lowther and Jack Casey. Sexton, the Bethnal Green man, had a fine record with an impressive eighty-four knockouts in 174 fights, and both were mindful of the other's punch when they met in the Belle Vue ring. Mac eventually set the pace but Sexton did not want to get involved and it was round ten before he caught the champion with a terrific shot to the jaw. Mac staggered, hurt, but for some reason Archie didn't follow up. Jock recovered and stormed into the attack, determined to bring his man down. With the capacity crowd roaring him on, he smashed the Londoner halfway through the ropes. As Archie tried to grab the champion, McAvoy ripped home a tremendous right uppercut that struck Sexton on the jaw, and he crumpled in a heap to be counted out.

Al Burke, born in Shepherd's Bush, London, went to Australia as a lad, won their welterweight title and returned home to try his luck in the Old Country. His luck ran out one night at the Royal Albert Hall when he clashed with Jock McAvoy in a charity show. There was no charity in Mac's fists, especially the right uppercut in the fifth round. 'The referee broke us,' recalled Mac, 'and from my toes I brought up the most perfect right uppercut I think I ever delivered. It took Burke full on the chin and travelled on to smash his nose. Al was lifted off his feet, and then collapsed like a wet sack on the canvas . . . If he got up from that one, I reckoned, he would be a game one. But he did get up . . . He backed into a corner and I led him into a trap . . . I feinted with the right and Burke stooped down and away from that hand, covering his face and jaw with both gloves. Bending even lower, I brought up another right uppercut that went clean under his gloves, tore through and landed solidly on the point of his chin. Al couldn't have known what hit him and he went down as if he had been poleaxed . . . Gamely he pulled himself to his knees, then conscious-ness failed him and he fell on to his forehead and slithered forwards flat on his face. There he remained while they counted him out.'

That knockout stayed with Al Burke for a long time. In June 1935 he boxed McAvoy again, this time for the British title, and on this occasion he was determined to stay out of trouble. It was a poor fight, with Ted Scales reporting in the weekly *Boxing*, 'One punch beat Al Burke at Belle Vue, Manchester, on Monday night. It was a right uppercut delivered by Jock McAvoy over a year ago at the Albert Hall. Burke did not feel the punch on Monday night. He remembered it . . . Burke was so obsessed with the necessity of keeping out of range of that right uppercut that he did hardly any effective work . . . Burke was regarded as the boxer and McAvoy the fighter, but in this fight McAvoy not only outfought Burke but also very clearly outboxed him.'

The Cuban boxer Kid Tunero had done well in European rings, even beating Marcel Thil over twelve rounds in Paris. Thil was then recognized as world middleweight champion by the National Boxing Association of America and the International Boxing Union, and he gave the Cuban a rematch for the title, winning the decision. When they brought Kid Tunero to Manchester to fight McAvoy in December 1934, Belle Vue was buzzing. In training locally the Cuban had impressed onlookers, and Norman Hurst wrote, 'Subtle as a Greek lawyer, fast as a featherweight, and as cunning as a fox in matters fistic, that is Tunero.'

The visitor even impressed Jock McAvoy, who recalled, 'I have met some fine specimens of manhood, but Tunero was tops in my reckoning. His body was black-bronze in colour, and his muscular development and proportionate figure were well-night perfect. His whole body seemed to be of shining metal as he stood under the arc lights, while he flashed me a smile to show a mouth of gleaming white teeth as the referee called us together for the customary lecture.'

At the bell, Tunero moved across the ring on ball bearings, muscles rippling under that dark, satiny skin. Mac came out crouching, looking for an opening to land those savage punches. A vicious right crashed against the Cuban's jaw and he was shaken. Referee Percy Moss, a steward of the Board, got between the fighters and spent precious seconds illustrating to Tunero that he must not hold. As he stepped back, the bell rang before Mac could do any more damage. In the second round a whistling uppercut nearly tore the Cuban's head from his shoulders and the Kid stopped going back to fight it out with McAvoy, much to the delight of the spectators. By the fifth there was a lump under Tunero's left eye. Round six was a sizzler. Mac landed a piledriver to the body that would have felled an ox, yet the Kid set himself to take it and when the smoke cleared he was still standing. With McAvoy standing there expecting his man to drop, the Kid stepped forward and banged a beauty on Mac's jaw that made him blink.

In the interval, Ted Broadribb was demonstrating to the Cuban how to cover his chin while in the other corner McAvoy just chewed away at his gloves. Coming out for the seventh, Tunero was still fast, stabbing in the left, then a right bang on the chin. But Mac slipped a punch and shot a terrific right uppercut, his favourite punch, screaming upwards at the Cuban's chin. It lifted him clear of the canvas and his body landed with a crash that could be heard all over the hall. 'Immediately, seven thousand people went wild,' wrote Norman Hurst. 'Here was what they wanted. A match-winning punch! A champion's punch served up by a champion! Shrieks and yells came from the Cuban's compatriots. At eight he managed to stagger up and he reeled round like a drunken man. Someone in his corner tried to toss in a towel, but it fell outside the ropes. Instinct made Tunero back away and cover up. McAvoy crowded in, smashing blows to the body to bring down Tunero's guard. Having done this, McAvoy made as if to drive a right to the jaw, up went Tunero's left to block the blow, and like a flash, McAvoy's dynamite-laden right shot under the arm and up to the defenceless jaw. Tunero was lifted from his feet and dropped in a heap to the canvas. Human flesh could take no more. The game Cuban was "out" for the first time in his life.'

'I was told McAvoy was just a puncher,' said Tunero in the dressing-room. 'Take it from me, he can box far better than anyone dreams of. I was never hit so hard before. He is a great fighter.'

Jeff Dickson, the American who was promoting in Paris, matched McAvoy with Thil at the Palais des Sports, but the cagey Frenchman insisted the fight be for his European light-heavyweight title rather than his middleweight crown. Dr Graham recalled, 'McAvoy came from the same stable as Jackie Brown, and like Brown a few years before, developed a troublesome boil during training. It was on the middle of his forearm. McAvoy, remembering Jackie Brown's trouble, told Jeff Dickson that Dr Graham was "the best boil doctor in the world" and to get me over to see him. Jeff Dickson told Norman Hurst, who phoned an SOS from Paris. Flattered by McAvoy's innocent faith and jumping at the chance to see an outstanding contest, I agreed to go. Unfortunately, they had left it a bit late and in spite of getting the first train from Manchester and aeroplane from London, I was unable to arrive in Paris before lunchtime on the day of the contest. I did what I could for McAvoy, which wasn't very much, but I am sure that this disability contributed in no small way to his defeat at the hands of a very tough opponent.'

Sportswriter Peter Wilson would write, 'Marcel Thil was a tough, dour Frenchman, most of whose hair seemed to have slipped off his head on to his massive chest. There was nothing very spectacular about his technique: there's nothing very spectacular about running smack-dab into a telegraph pole, and meeting Thil was very like that, except that he took the initiative when it came to sustained bouts of body punching which gradually slowed his opponents down until they were clinging on like fly-paper. In January 1935, when he beat McAvoy, the defeat was about the worst McAvoy ever suffered during his peak period. Against Thil, McAvoy was outstayed by an ever grimmer battler than himself, and he took a beating, including two long counts.'

Late in 1935, his contract with Harry Fleming running out, McAvoy was introduced to Dave Lumiansky by Norman Hurst. The suave American had brought Panama Al Brown to Britain and had recently taken over the affairs of Mac's stablemate Jackie Brown. He proposed a trip to America with a view to getting McAvoy a crack at the world title. The New York State Athletic Commission, which recognized Eddie 'Babe' Risko as champion, insisted on McAvoy proving himself against a top contender. They gave him Al McCoy, a French-Canadian light-heavyweight, over ten rounds at Madison Square Garden.

Mac's right hand was still giving him pain, so Lumiansky brought a doctor to the dressing-room shortly before Jock was due in the ring. Mac got the shock of his life when this fellow suddenly produced a hypodermic syringe and jabbed it into the back of his right hand. The fighter promptly passed out, and his handlers had to pick him up and walk him around the dressing-room until he came out of the fog. He was feeling better by the time they called him for the ring, and his right hand felt like a rock.

In the Garden ring that night, McAvoy hit McCoy with every punch in the book and dropped him in the third. McCoy got up and fought back but Mac was a good winner at the final bell. He was also a winner in the New York press the next day. 'Jock McAvoy is the best English fighter to drop in since the day smiling Jem Driscoll came to electrify us,' said the *New York Evening Journal*. The *New York Daily News* described Jock as 'a little middleweight from London with the amazing habit of gnawing at his own gloves between punches, who showed the fans over at Madison Square Garden last night just how British fighters do battle.'

In his prestigious *Ring Magazine*, Nat Fleischer wrote, 'England sends us a real fighter in Jock McAvoy . . . The British champion, in practically every movement, has American style stamped all over him. He has adopted the American "stand-up" and in addition he has mastered the weaving of Dempsey, the crouch of Jeffries, the sharp-shooting of Jack Johnson and the speed of Jim Driscoll. He can throw more punches per minute than any fighter I've seen since Jackie Kid Berg made his American debut five years ago.'

Mac had certainly impressed the New York fight crowd with his showing against McCoy, but three weeks later he would blow them out of their ringside seats. Matched with Eddie 'Babe' Risko in a non-title bout, the Rochdale Thunderbolt struck the Garden in the middle of a snowstorm and warmed the great arena like no other British fighter before or since. Jock once again had a pain-killing injection in his right hand just before going into the ring and he was anxious to get the fight over before the effects wore off. How well he succeeded was described by Nat Fleischer. 'It was a case of savage attack from the clang of the gong to the finish. Jock opened up with the drop of the mallet, with a left and a right to the chin. The blows took Risko by surprise. He hadn't expected such rapid-fire action. The second punch was the destroyer. That right contained TNT. It struck with such thunder that the fans were amazed at its power. It sent Risko to the mat with a crash. He bounced up but was dazed. Another right to the chin sent Risko staggering towards the ropes and he retreated with faltering steps as the Britisher followed him. Three more rights, each landing with a thud, sent the Babe to cover, but scarcely able to stand on his feet. McAvoy gave no quarter. He crashed another right to the chin and down went the US titleholder for a count of seven. He arose and started to retreat, but another right and down he went again. This time he was down for five and when he got up, another smashing right sent him flopping to the canvas for four. So powerful was that punch that McAvoy hurled himself to the canvas as he floored Risko . . . A series of punches brought on the fifth trip to the canvas, this time for eight. With only half a minute of the round to go, McAvoy rushed in with another right on the chin, and that ended the fight. Risko rolled up into a kneeling position, but though listening to the referee, Billy Cavanagh, he couldn't raise himself before the fatal ten was counted.'

In just two minutes, forty-eight seconds, Jock McAvoy had blasted himself right into the world title picture, but when they did give him his chance it was against John Henry Lewis, newly-crowned light-heavyweight champion. John Henry's manager got word of Mac's hand trouble and that he was going into the ring with his right hand shot full of novocaine, so he delayed the start as long as he could, with the result that halfway through the fight the effects were wearing off and Mac was unable to use his vaunted right hand when he needed it most. He fought gamely, and practically wore his left hand out, but Lewis was not the man to fight with only one hand. He was a very competent box-fighter and after fifteen rounds he was still champion of the world.

Dave Lumiansky was a brave manager. When Mac challenged Lewis in New York, he was already signed up to fight Jack Petersen in London for his British *heavyweight* title, just six weeks later. The fight was a box-office winner from the start and Earls Court was sold out long before the opening bell. It was a case of a good big 'un beating a good little 'un. Petersen towered over McAvoy and was at least a stone heavier. Mac's right was still bothering him and it hurt him more than it did Petersen when he did throw it. Realizing he was well behind, McAvoy made a big effort in the final round but was chastised by a solid right that dropped him to his knees for eight. He was glad when the bell ended it.

The Rochdale Thunderbolt was still a force to reckon with, as Eddie Phillips found out when he defended the British light-heavy title at

Wembley in April 1937. Recalling this fight, Peter Wilson wrote, 'McAvoy was a heavy enough puncher to give away pounds in weight and inches in reach to the academic Eddie Phillips, to whom he administered a most bloodthirsty thrashing at Wembley in fourteen rounds. I shall remember the end of the McAvoy-Phillips fight as long as I watch boxing. Phillips had gone through a roughish period. But at one moment he was a lithe, clear-skinned, quick-moving athlete, the next he was a death's head of flaccid skin and grating bones, with a gash under one eye that might have been made with a chisel. Not for him the merciful anaesthesia of the clean knockout. He had to be supported out of the ring, and though dazed, he was agonizingly conscious all the time. When McAvoy hit like that, no man in the world within ten pounds of his weight could stand up to him.

Six months after beating Phillips, Jock retained his middleweight title against old foe Jack Hyams in the Belle Vue ring. Hyams, recalling that fight many years later, wrote, 'By this time I had bought myself a taxi as a sideline. About a thousand of my supporters made the trip, among them so many cab drivers that they told me you couldn't get a taxi anywhere in the East End that night. After three rounds, some sharp lefts to the face made an opening for a good right hand shot to his chin. It shook him up, but that was all, and the effect was to bring him back on the attack with increased fury. He threatened sheer destruction, so I backed away and fenced him off as best I could. But when McAvoy was aroused he needed some stopping and before long I was against the ropes, using every bit of ringcraft I knew to prevent him from knocking me out of the ring . . . It was like trying to outbox a tank . . . I was severely cut under the left eye, my cheekbone seemed gashed wide open. Then a swelling began to grow under the same eye, I just couldn't see out of it. In the eleventh round he almost tore my head from my shoulders with a series of right uppercuts that I couldn't see coming. At the bell, they tell me I walked in a zig-zag way back to my corner. Joe Morris wouldn't let me go on.'

There would be two more fights with Jock's nemesis Len Harvey. The Plymouth puncher took Mac's light-heavyweight title on a decision in April 1938, and a year later they clashed at the White City in a fight recognized in Britain as for the world light-heavyweight title, John Henry Lewis having retired with eye trouble. Harvey again came out the winner, but as usual Mac gave him all the fight he could handle. He always did.

There weren't many great fights left in Jock McAvoy. Harry Fleming urged him to retire but when he wouldn't listen, Harry left him. Jock signed up with London manager Harry Levene in 1939, with Tom Hurst looking after his training. But he did little under Levene and when both were fined £200 by the Board of Control for breaking a fight contract, Jock refused to pay and retired, still British middle-weight champion.

Jock was a man who always liked the ladies, but Lady Luck was not one of his favourites. In 1947 he contracted polio and was more or less confined to a wheelchair for the rest of his life. He died on his sixty-fourth birthday, 20 November 1971, from an overdose of sleeping tablets. Peter Wilson's words made a suitable epitaph. 'Joseph Bamford was not always a model citizen, but by the Lord Harry he was a good fighter!'

# Boxing's Clown Prince 7

'Max Baer was by far the best of the ring buffoons,' wrote Frank Butler in 1954. 'I don't mean Max was the most successful clown, but that he was the most impressive heavyweight who ever chose to be a funny man. Baer, in fact, only missed by a wise-crack going into the list of the truly great heavyweights.

'As it is, he will still go down in my memory as the best of the big fellows outside of Joe Louis . . . He was the biggest puncher I ever saw, an opinion that Tommy Farr, who fought him twice, vouches for from personal experience, having fought twenty-seven rounds with Baer, and if Tommy couldn't find that out in eighty-one minutes of throwing and taking punches, nobody else ever will . . . Baer had the physique of a Greek god, the strength of Hercules and the occasional fury of a jungle beast. And he was born with a trip-hammer in his right fist.'

That big right fist saw Max finish work early in fifty-two of his seventy winning fights, was the direct cause of one opponent's death and was blamed for contributing to the death of another in a subsequent fight. Those who survived its impact remembered it for a long time afterwards. Lou Nova, who twice stopped Baer at the end of his career, recalled, 'Baer's shots hurt more than Louis's did. I can't possibly imagine a man throwing a harder punch than Max Baer. After the first fight I went to Palm Springs to recuperate, and for a month afterwards I couldn't move my head without feeling like there were loose marbles in there. It was a frightening experience. I attribute it to Baer's punching power. I have no doubt that he was the hardest puncher who ever lived. And I could take a punch better than anyone who ever lived.'

Jim Braddock caused one of boxing's biggest upsets when he took Baer's world title on a decision in 1935. He would say afterwards, 'I kept talking to Baer. "Max, you're way behind," I kept saying. I should have kept my mouth shut. Max hit me with a right in the ninth. It was so hard that if I had electric light bulbs on my toes they would have lit up! I can still feel the shock, here on my cheek. He was a harder one-punch hitter than Joe Louis.'

Jack Dempsey sparred with Baer as a promotion gimmick while Max was training for his fight with Max Schmeling. Dempsey was promoting the fight and had already sparred with Schmeling at his camp before getting in there with Baer. But Max wasn't feeling too good that day and was anxious to end the session. Raising one eyebrow at Dempsey, he said, 'Sorry, Jocko, but this Baer is going into hibernation. Bye!' Max punctuated his parting words with a right swing that hit Dempsey full in the stomach. Jack's face contorted in agony and he did a rubbery-legged stumble backwards to the ropes. They helped him back to the corner and as his breath came back to him, Dempsey said to the reporters crowding round him, 'Baer will knock Schmeling out. I've never been hit that hard by anybody.'

'Learn?' the young Baer would ask his handlers. 'What do I need to learn? I've got the hardest punch in the world. In any fight, I'm bound to hit a guy and that's all I need is one sock, and away they'll go!'

Yet as a boy growing up in the American west, as Max freely admitted, 'I was afraid to fight in those days, and actually it was my big sister Frances who was still fighting my battles for me. My mother loved boxing and wanted a heavyweight champion in the family, but it was my brother Buddy who was labelled as the future champ. Me, I was just going to be a cattle rancher like my father.'

Max's grandfather was a Jew from Alsace-Lorraine, his father Jacob was born in Michigan, and his mother Dora was of Scottish-Irish descent from Iowa. They were living in Omaha, Nebraska, when Max was born on 11 February 1909. Jacob Baer, a powerful man standing over six feet, was a boss butcher and cattle-killer in the Omaha slaughterhouse of the Swift meat-packing plant. He later took jobs in Colorado before settling in Livermore, California, where he operated his own plant. At sixteen, already a strapping youth, Max was an expert butcher and cattle-killer, spending ten to fourteen hours a day swinging a huge cleaver and the short meat axe that developed his right arm. 'I'd bite clean through muscle, sinew and bone,' he would recall, 'and this was the work that gave me my right-hand punch. The more gory the better. I loved it. I had the glorious feeling of sheer physical power.'

He got that feeling again one night at a local dance. By this time Max was twenty, stood six feet in his socks, and weighed 190 pounds. In an argument with a burly railroad engineer, Max found himself with nowhere to run and had to stand his ground when the other guy bounced a big punch off his chin. Amazed to find himself still on his feet, young Baer fired his own right hand and knocked the other fellow spark out. 'In that big-thrill moment,' wrote Nat Fleischer, 'a new Max Baer was born. For the first time he realized that he could punch hard enough to knock any man he landed on galley-west, and what is more, he enjoyed the sensation. The fighting instinct was awake, never to slumber again.'

Tiring of ranch life, Max headed for Oakland, where he got a job in the Lorimer plant which manufactured diesel engines. Encouraged by a local middleweight, he bought a punch bag and a set of gloves and started training in a quiet corner of the plant, where he was spotted by the owner's son, J Hamilton Lorimer. 'Max worked for me,' he would recall, 'and he was always talking fight. I listened, and when he began to train in an amateur sort of way, he asked me to hold the watch for him. He was big and powerful, but I thought him too good-looking to go in for fighting. I wanted to cure him of his nonsense, so I matched him with Chief Caribou, an Indian heavyweight in Stockton.'

Baer swung that mighty right hand and missed more than he connected, but when he did find the Chief's chin its owner hit the deck, three times in the first round and twice in round two for the knockout. In that first year as a professional fighter, 1929, Baer's sledgehammer blows flattened his first twelve opponents, with only one of them making it to round three. By August 1930 he had won twenty-three of twenty-six fights with nineteen knockouts, and San Francisco promoter Ancil Hoffman paid him $10,000 to fight Frankie Campbell before a 15,000 crowd in the old Recreation Park.

Campbell was on a winning streak and the papers were calling him the 'Italian Jack Dempsey'. But Max, already tagged as the 'Livermore Larruper', had distinct height and reach advantages and weighed in fifteen pounds heavier than the local favourite. At ringside were Dempsey, his old manager Doc Kearns and former heavyweight champ Jim Jeffries. At the bell, Frankie set up a body attack but was caught by that swinging right hand and crashed down on his face. He beat the count, but the blow had dazed him and he was lucky to get through to the bell. In the second round, Baer slipped to the canvas as Campbell threw a left hook. Frankie walked away but Max had jumped to his feet and went after Campbell, who caught a big right hand to the head before he could get his guard up again. Although shaken, he came out to win rounds three and four. Round five saw the finish of the fight, and of Frankie Campbell.

Baer trapped Frankie in a corner and landed a tremendous left hook to the head. Campbell sagged against the corner post but he didn't go down, and Baer continued to slug him with crashing punches, finally bringing him down with that right-hand hammer. The referee didn't bother counting, raising Max's glove as Campbell's handlers raced into the ring to the aid of their stricken fighter. An ambulance was called to take Frankie to Mission Emergency Hospital, where he died the next morning from a double cerebral haemorrhage. Baer was charged with manslaughter and the newspapers had a field day, banner headlines screaming, 'Murderer!' and 'Ban The Kill From The Ring!' Max was comforted by Campbell's pregnant widow, holding eight-months-old Frankie Jnr as she told him, 'It might have been you. It wasn't your fault.'

As Baer would later tell Nat Fleischer, 'It was a tremendous relief when the surgeons announced that Frankie had died of a brain concussion and the court ruled that it was an accident and cleared me of the manslaughter charge. But for the time being, I felt as if I never wanted to see a boxing glove or enter a ring again. My enthusiasm for the game had gone.'

'There is no doubt that Max, as kindly a chap as ever lived,' wrote Fleischer, 'suffered keenly from the consciousness that he had unwittingly caused the death of a fellow creature. Yet Campbell's regrettable demise certainly helped to ballyhoo Max's name on a big scale. Newspapers all over the country published full details of the fight and the commotion it subsequently created. It was the sort of advertising no decent fellow, least of all Max Baer, would desire, but in the end he was to profit by it.'

Ham Lorimer had sold his interest in Baer to Ancil Hoffman and, after Max had rested away from the fight game for a few months, his new manager lost no time taking him to New York, where he was quickly fixed up to fight Ernie Schaaf at Madison Square Garden. By this time, the playboy in Max Baer was getting him more publicity in the society pages than in the sports pages, and his name was linked with wealthy divorcee Dorothy Dunbar. New York City loved the big, handsome, extrovert Baer, and he loved it right back. He wasn't too happy when he had to swap the neon lights of Broadway for the arc lights of the Garden ring, and Ernie Schaaf jabbed him silly to come out with the decision. Hoffman gave him an ear-bashing next morning but the Garden people were impressed with Baer's box-office appeal and offered him veteran Tom Heeney. This time Max trained and was in top condition when he faced Heeney, hammering him all over the ring and in the third round knocking him clean through the ropes for the knockout.

When the Garden offered Hoffman Johnny Risko or Tommy Loughran, the canny manager opted for the former light-heavyweight champion Loughran, explaining to Max, 'I expect him to box your ears off. But you may learn something. If Loughran trims you around the mug, maybe you'll begin to figure that it's about time you were picking up some pointers on how to defend yourself, or in a couple of years you'll be lucky if you're half as good as you think you are now.'

Max just laughed, but in the Garden ring he quickly got the point of Ancil's logic. Loughran avoided his big swings, making him look foolish. 'In the fourth round Tommy began to run the show,' wrote Lester Bromberg. 'His left became a many-splendoured thing – he would fend off a piledriver with it and then bring in a hook to the body, he would rat-a-tat with three, four jabs and then hook to the face . . .

**Left:** Terrible Terry McGovern: world featherweight and bantamweight champion.

**Below:** 'Little Chocolate' George Dixon, who lost the featherweight title to McGovern.

**Left:** 'The Old Master' Joe Gans lost to McGovern in a suspicious contest.

**Above:** Stanley Ketchel (left) stopped Joe Thomas in 32 rounds.

**Left:** Ketchel, shot dead while middleweight champion.

**Right:** Sam Langford was the greatest fighter never to win a world title.

PHOTO BY
SPORT & GENERAL.

SAM LANGFORD.

156 T
BEAGLES' POSTCARDS.

**Far Left:** 'Mighty Atom' Jimmy Wilde, the Welsh wonder.

**Left:** Tough American Pete Herman outweighed and outpunched Wilde in London.

**Below:** Dempsey (left) retains his title against Tom Gibbons in the Shelby fiasco.

**Left:** Giant champ Jess Willard, seen here with Kid Williams.

**Below:** Gene Tunney beat Dempsey twice in championship upsets.

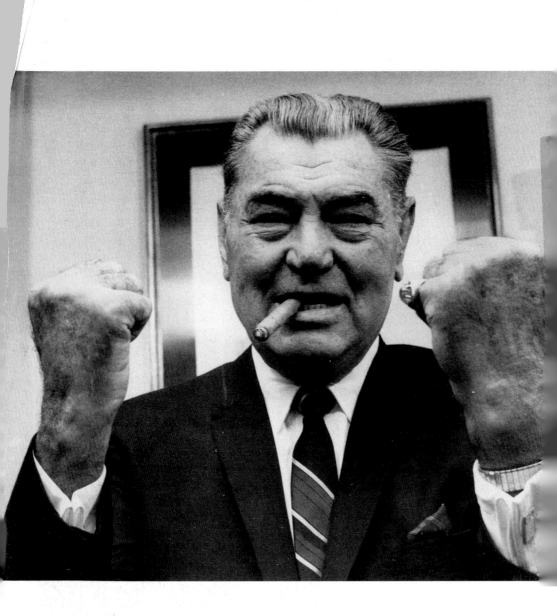

Dempsey shows massive fists during his 1967 London visit.

**Left:** Frenchman Marcel Thil beat Jock McAvoy in Paris, 1935.

**Below:** Brilliant Len Harvey beat McAvoy three times in four contests.

**Above:** Max Baer poses in training.

**Above:** Carnera, on one of his many trips to canvas, as Baer takes his title.

**Left:** Jimmy Braddock takes Baer's title.

**Above:** Featherweight champion Henry Armstrong (left) beats Enrico Venturi in New York, 1938.

**Left:** Armstrong (left) retains welterweight title as he beats Ernie Roderick in London.

**Right:** Donald 'Reds' Barry takes count against the young Joe Louis in 1935.

**Right:** Joe Louis (left) had to go fifteen rounds against Welsh hero Tommy Farr to keep his title.

**Below:** Louis (left) wins split decision over Joe Walcott in their first fight.

**Below:** Lew Jenkins, who had the kick of a Texas mule in his right hand.

**Above:** Tony Zale sends Rocky Graziano crashing for KO in the third fight of the titanic series.

**Right:** Sugar Ray Robinson: pound-for-pound the greatest fighter of all time.

Kid Gavilan (right) took punches like this one from Sugar Ray Robinson for 25 rounds in two fights.

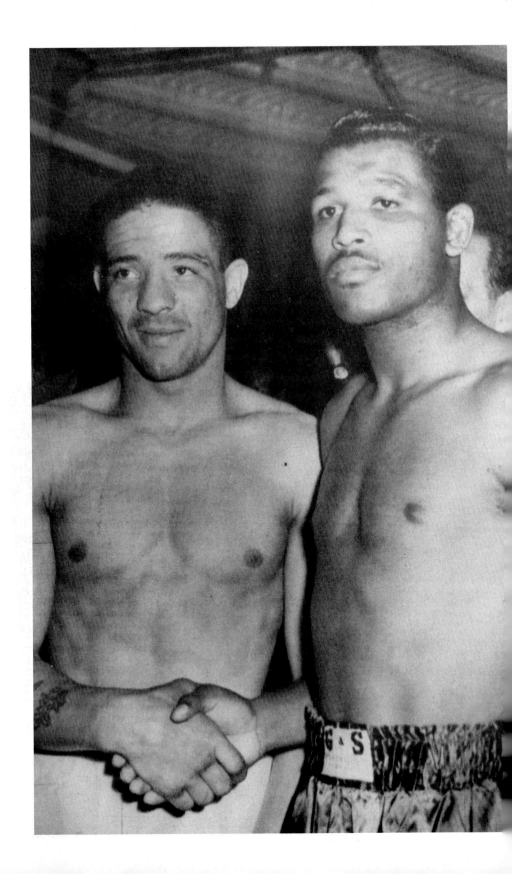

**Far left:** Randolph Turpin (left) at the weigh-in for his shock win over Sugar Ray in London 1951.

**left:** Sugar Ray, who became a night-club star when he retired in 1952, was soon back in the ring.

**Right:** Roland LaStarza heads for the canvas in his first fight with Rocky Marciano.

The computer made Marciano a winner over Ali in their 1969 'fight', which was filmed shortly before Rocky's untimely death.

Now the crowd had changed its attitude, it was noisily admiring the finesse with which Loughran conducted his laboratory demonstration of basic boxing . . . The jeering galled Baer into wilder attacking, and his sheer roughness was starting to tire Tommy. In the eighth he reached him with one overhander that shook up Loughran. In the ninth his tempo was faster and the old man more intent on protecting himself. In the tenth Baer was bombing . . . the crowd unashamedly rooting for Tommy to finish . . . As the final gong sounded, the building rang with applause even before the decision, unanimous for the veteran Loughran.'

That doyen of sportswriters, Grantland Rice, recalled, 'I was having breakfast with Jack Dempsey and Max Baer at the Warwick Hotel. The day before, Jack had refereed the Baer-Tommy Loughran fight at Madison Square Garden. Max had been decisioned in ten rounds. "I've been looking at left jabs all night," Max said. "Lefts, lefts, lefts, that's all I've seen."

'"The funny part," said Dempsey, "is that you could have stopped that 'lefty' in the first round."

'"How?" said Baer.

'"Take off your coat," replied Jack to big Maxie, six-feet-three and 220 pounds. Max shucked off his coat and faced Dempsey. "Now, lead with a left, just as Loughran did," said Jack. Max led, and there was an immediate yelp.

'"You broke my arm!" Max howled as he backed away, holding it. As Baer led with his left, Dempsey had dropped his huge right fist across the left biceps with paralysing force. The left arm became useless for thirty minutes.'

The old Manassa Mauler liked Baer and took an interest in him, teaching him things you wouldn't find in any boxing manual, and promoting some of Max's fights. The first, against Spaniard Paulino Uzcudun on a blistering hot Fourth of July in 1931, was over twenty rounds in Reno. Dempsey was third man in the ring that day and Baer was less than happy when Jack gave the decision to the Basque woodchopper. Paulino had trainer Whitey Bimstein in his corner, which was like having another fist.

'It was 110 degrees in the shade,' recalled Whitey, 'and right off I had a bathtub lugged down to our corner and stocked it with ice and water. I had eight one-gallon bottles of mineral water, and another bottle that was filled with brandy and unchilled water for drinking. I had a great stack of towels and kept soaking them in ice water for Paulino. I also covered the soles of his feet with adhesive tape and kept pouring ice water into his shoes, so the burning-hot ring canvas wouldn't bother him.'

Dempsey would later say, 'Baer was much the better fighter that day and in fine condition, but at the end of twenty rounds he was a mess and Paulino looked as if he could go another twenty, so I gave the decision to Paulino. But Paulino didn't win that fight himself. Whitey Bimstein won it for him.'

As consolation, Max wed Dorothy Dunbar in Reno a few days after the Uzcudun fight. When the minister said, 'Are you Max Baer?' he replied, 'I do.' When the clergyman went on, 'The name of your wife, please?' he said, 'Max Baer.' At the wedding breakfast, fifty strangers turned up. When the new spouse was presented with the bill, she handed it to Max. 'Go see my manager,' he said. The marriage didn't last.

Baer bounced back with victories over Johnny Risko, King Levinsky, twice, and Tom Heeney again. Then they signed for a rematch with Ernie Schaaf, on 31 August 1932. Schaaf, an ex-sailor, was handled by heavyweight contender Jack Sharkey and his manager Johnny Buckley, and was the number three contender after victories over Young Stribling, Jimmy Braddock and Jim Maloney. But a couple of months before going in with Baer, Ernie fought Tony Galento in

Newark's Dreamland Park, where 'Two-Ton' Tony's tremendous strength, lethal hook and a vicious right-hand chop behind Ernie's neck took their toll. Schaaf won the fight but couldn't leave his dressing-room for a couple of hours, and although he won three of his next four bouts, the spark was lacking.

That night in the Chicago Stadium, the big Baer wanted revenge over the guy who had ruined his New York debut. Schaaf held his own, however, and going into the eighth round Max needed a big finish. He produced it, a savage attack that culminated in a looping right swing in the tenth and final round with only eight seconds left on the clock. The punch caught Ernie flush on the jaw and he dropped with his arms and legs tangled in a fantastic contortion. Schaaf was carried from the ring and it was two months before he fought again. He won two of three fights and was matched with Primo Carnera, the winner to meet newly-crowned champion Sharkey, who was in Schaaf's corner. Madison Square Garden was jammed with 20,000 fans to see the clumsy Italian giant score a knockout in round thirteen with a punch that brought cries of 'Fake!' from the crowd. But Ernie Schaaf was carried from the Garden across the street to Polyclinic Hospital, where he died four days later. Once again the finger was pointed at Max Baer, Ernie's death being attributed to his last-minute knockout by Max rather than Carnera's punches.

Max Baer had only one fight in 1933, but it was hailed as the finest of his zany career. He was matched with former heavyweight champion Max Schmeling in New York's Yankee Stadium and a crowd of some 55,000 turned out on a blistering hot night to see Max v Max. Jack Dempsey promoted the fight and helped publicity by sparring with both men. In his autobiography, Schmeling recorded, 'I received a visit at my training camp from Jack Dempsey, who was one of the backers of the fight. Since he had announced that he would spar with me, several thousand spectators showed up. Dempsey greeted me cordially as in the old days, then he asked me if I would go easy on him in sparring and try not to hit him in the face. Dempsey had also entered the movie world and had recently gotten a nose job for an upcoming role. I jokingly promised that I would be careful.

'But my trainer Max Machon had barely left the ring when Dempsey stormed over to me and decked me with a barrage of punches. For a moment I had the wind literally knocked out of me, but I felt compelled to be a good sport about it. However, when Dempsey continued to attack and landed a hard right on my headgear, I forgot our deal. I countered with a hard right to his nose, whereupon he staggered backwards and, laughing, put up his hands in surrender as the crowd applauded. To the reporters, Dempsey said, "Max is in excellent shape and still has an outstanding right hand."'

On the big night, the ringside teemed with celebrities, among them Dempsey, his old rival Gene Tunney, champion Sharkey and con-tender Carnera. Al Jolson, a big Baer fan, was there with his movie star wife Ruby Keeler, whose new picture *Gold Diggers* was opening at The Strand. 'As Baer stepped into the ring,' ran one contemporary report, 'he arrogantly threw his head back, and slowly rolled the thick muscles in his neck, which bulged and glistened with sweat. As his head came to rest, his eyes seemed to be on fire as he stared at Schmeling. And when he curled his tongue around his upper lip, like a famished wolf about to devour a chicken, it seemed, in retrospect, to serve as a portent of things to come.'

In the first round, the German took a wild right from Baer and came back with a smashing right of his own that gave Max something to think about when he returned to his corner. The second round went to Baer as Schmeling weighed his man up, and in the third Baer clowned for a moment, but not for long. He took charge of the ring and belted Schmeling with savage punches, and he looked so good that after six rounds Al Jolson grabbed Baer's little trainer, Issy Kline, down by the corner and shouted, 'What happened to him? What did you shoot into his arm?' Issy just smiled and kept his eyes on the big Baer up there in the ring, hammering his way to the greatest night of his life.

In the eighth round, Max Baer was seen at his sensational best. He smashed punch after punch into Schmeling's weary frame; he rabbit-punched, back-handed and bullied the German around the ring. The fight nearly ended there and then, for just before the bell ended the session, Max Machon was about to toss the towel into the ring, but Schmeling's manager Joe Jacobs grabbed Machon's arm just as the bell rang. Jacobs was vindicated somewhat in the ninth when Schmeling went out and fought the best round of the fight. He boxed well, countered Baer's big punches and won the round on all three of the official scorecards. In the corner, Ancil Hoffman yelled at Baer, 'This guy could still win the fight with some more rounds like that one!'

Baer left his corner for round ten with those words ringing in his ears. His handsome face contorted in a snarl and he stormed across the ring to smash two left hooks into Schmeling's body before the German knew what was happening. As Schmeling tried to hold, Baer shoved him away and another crippling body shot almost broke him in half. Referee Arthur Donovan yelled at Baer to keep his punches up, and Schmeling stalled for time. As he hitched up his trunks, an old habit he would have done better to forget, Baer threw a mighty right swing to the jaw that lifted the German clear of the canvas. He crashed to the floor with a thud, his body as stiff as a board. As he lay there, only his head moved as he tried to look round the ring to see what was going on. Somehow, Schmeling hauled himself off the deck and Donovan wiped his gloves, giving him a few seconds' respite from the leather storm that was about to break over him.

Baer rushed in, throwing both gloves like he didn't want to see them again, and they crashed against Schmeling's head, rocking it one way then the other, as Baer was once again the savage fighter of the tragic fight with Frankie Campbell. But as the German bent almost double by the ropes, defenceless, Baer hesitated. Schmeling turned to grope his way along the ropes, and from the corner Issy Kline was screaming, 'Keep punching, Max! Don't let him get away now!' The big Californian stepped forward and that massive right fist struck Schmeling behind the ear, and as he sagged forward, Donovan moved in and grabbed him. It was over, and 55,000 people sent their cheers rocketing up into the night sky over Manhattan. Ringsiders cheered Baer as he came out of the ring, Al Jolson slapped him on the back and Ruby Keeler later said she didn't know what gave her the biggest thrill, Baer's victory or the opening of *Gold Diggers*.

'Despite the weeks of training, I decisively lost the fight against Max Baer,' Schmeling wrote in his autobiography. 'I can't say why. Maybe it was the brutal heat that day in New York. Even before the fight, sweat was pouring down my body. During the whole fight I felt paralysed. "Move, for God's sake, move!" yelled Max Machon between rounds. "Move away from him. Get him missing." But my legs were like lead and only rarely did I manage to avoid or neutralize Baer's punches. Standing still, I offered the Californian an easy target . . . In the dressing room, Max Machon said, "That wasn't a defeat, that was a disaster." Then the reporters swarmed in and asked how such a defeat was possible. I didn't have an answer . . . It was the worst defeat of my career . . . Max Baer had simply outclassed me as no one had before.'

Schmeling's manager Joe Jacobs recalled his fighter complaining about the terrible heat in the ring that night and the glare of the ring lights. 'But I knew it wasn't the heat,' said Joe. 'It was those murderous punches he had taken around the head.'

That sensational victory made Max Baer the leading contender for the world title, now in the clumsy hands of Primo Carnera, but Baer was in no hurry to fight the big Italian. He was having too much fun. Broadway was his playground and he had plenty of playmates. Ancil Hoffman seemed always to be settling some breach of promise suit brought by a leggy blonde showgirl, a night club hostess or a film starlet.

'He never trod a prosaic level of existence,' wrote Nat Fleischer. 'That simply couldn't be in the case of Max Baer. An ever-restless, dynamic, live-wire chap, always rarin' to go, surcharged with vitality, keenly responsive to the feminine beauty lure, a constant seeker for rose-tinted romance, a reckless looter in Lovers' Lane, his private life was one long, vibrant melodrama, shot through with scintillating streaks of comedy. Had he been born in the Middle Ages, Max Baer would probably have been a gay, irresponsible adventurer, a wandering man-at-arms, selling his sword and soldierly talents wherever fancy dictated, beloved by many fair damsels, breaking hearts and slaying opponents with equal zest.'

Baer was a natural for Hollywood and, in a bizarre situation, he found himself cast in a movie with Carnera, the world champion he would eventually meet for the title. The film was entitled *The Prizefighter And The Lady* and starred Myrna Loy, Otto Kruger and Walter Huston. Baer and Carnera were to fight ten rounds, with Jack Dempsey as the referee, with the script calling for Baer to win. The champ's backers wouldn't hear of that, so a compromise was eventually reached whereby the fight would end in a draw. Baer was in his element, but Primo was uneasy in this world of make-believe. Max took full advantage of the situation, but as well as enjoying himself hamming it up for the cameras, he was also making mental notes of just how he would handle Carnera when they fought for real rather than for reel. By the time the film was finished, Baer was convinced he could beat the giant Italian, because he was able to intimidate the champion in the movie ring and he discovered that Primo was a tremendous and slow-moving target.

So it proved on a June night in 1934 at the Madison Square Garden Bowl on Long Island when Baer challenged Carnera for the world championship. Max set up training camp at Ashbury Park in New Jersey and press agent Francis Albertanti would say to reporters, 'I still think this whole thing is a gag. Nothing about it is real. The ocean, the sky, the camp, the screwy characters. I can't get it into my head that this guy is training for a real fight. It's more like he is rehearsing for a musical comedy about the fight racket!'

Old-time physical conditioner Bill Brown, then a member of the New York State Athletic Commission, didn't spare Max when he watched him in camp one day. 'You're not in shape,' he growled at Baer, 'and what's more you are never going to be in shape. You are a big bum!' Brown even tried to get the Commission to stop the bout – to no avail, and a great crowd of 56,000 gathered to see the fight. Bill Brown had been right about Baer, he wasn't in shape. He just couldn't take Carnera seriously, not as he had Schmeling. It was decided by Baer's handlers, Hoffman, Dempsey and trainer Mike Cantwell, that Max fight in spurts, doing enough damage to allow him to rest before another attack.

And that is how Max Baer became heavyweight champion of the world. The big crowd went crazy as he battered the unfortunate Italian behemoth to the canvas eleven times in eleven rounds before it was stopped. Max would smash over that big right and when Carnera stumbled to the canvas, Baer would swagger around the ring, joking with ringsiders, gulping in air before exploding another fierce attack upon poor Primo. Max would hold up a glove, step round the champion and rub his boots in the resin in Primo's corner before resuming battle. In one round they both went to the canvas, and Max said loud enough for ringsiders to hear, 'Last one up is a cissy!'

Carnera didn't have an ounce of fight left in him as he stumbled out of his corner for the eleventh round. Baer closed in, smashed a terrific right to the head, and Primo fell against the ropes. As he lay there, upright but helpless, Baer slugged him with another overhand right that knocked him down for three. As he arose feebly, Baer, scenting the kill, hacked away at the huge carcass like he used to on a side of beef in his butchering days. An overhand right, flush on the chin, floored Primo again. He groped his way to his feet at the count of two and stumbled blindly forward, his eyes glassy and his legs caving in under him. As referee Donovan stepped between him and Baer, Primo mumbled in the referee's ear, 'Fini!'

The exultant Baer, strutting around the ring, mighty chest thrust out, the new heavyweight champion of the world, spotted Commissioner Brown at the ringside and yelled down at him, 'Well, Mr Brown, what do you think of me now?'

'You're still a bum,' growled Brown, 'and so is that big stiff in there with you!'

Champ or chump, in that summer of 1934 Max Baer was the hottest ticket in sports. *The Prizefighter And The Lady* had opened in New York to rave notices and he was also starring in his own radio serial, *Taxi*, in which he played 'Al Harper, a tough cab driver with a penchant for blondes'. The series was tied in with the radio broadcast of the Carnera fight, both being sponsored by the Goodrich Tyre Company. Max even entered the ring for the fight wearing a silk bathrobe emblazoned with the name *Steve Morgan*, the character he played in the movie, and left the ring wearing a robe with his radio name *Al Harper* across the back. Twelve months later, when he signed to defend his title against Jim Braddock, Baer was starring in another radio serial, *Lucky Smith*, a private detective with a punch. Garson Kanin, who would become a prominent playwright and director, was then an actor and played Baer's sidekick in both radio shows.

John V Grombach, a former Inter-collegiate heavyweight champion and member of the 1924 US Olympic team, was a programme director for a New York City radio company in the Thirties. In his book *The Saga of the Fist*, he wrote, 'For a year after winning the title, Baer did nothing but fight in exhibitions and appear in vaudeville, movies and on the radio. He could act quite effectively . . . he could sing and dance a little and was a natural showman. For a three-minute performance on a single radio programme in early 1935, he received $3,500 and all round-trip expenses from California to New York for three people. His coast-to-coast radio programme series, which did not even disturb his training schedules and was broadcast directly from his training camp at Ashbury Park, together with other radio and theatrical engagements, grossed him over $250,000. Baer and manager Ancil Hoffman took the Braddock fight because their share of proceeds from the sale of the radio series and the world fight broadcast rights (to Gillette) was far in excess of the forty per cent share of the gate the champion would receive for defending his title; and they furthermore knew that if Baer retained the championship, which was expected, the picture rights and renewed radio contracts would be worth a great deal more. If Baer defeated Braddock, these options would be worth half a million dollars. I should know, as I handled all of Baer's broadcasting and ancillary rights.'

It was money already in the bank as far as Max Baer was concerned. Braddock was just a recycled veteran who had been on relief before putting a few good wins together, and the bookies were offering ten, fifteen dollars for every one bet on Jim. Eddie Neil, then boxing editor of the Associated Press, took twenty-five to one and made a big haul on a $25 wager. Former champion Gene Tunney spoke for the majority when he said, 'It's ridiculous. Baer will win without trouble, he hits too hard. Braddock's too old anyway.' There was support, however, from old-time managers Billy McCarney and 'Dumb' Dan

Morgan. Billy told reporters, 'I know this Baer like a book. He won't even be in shape, he'll be lucky to walk fifteen rounds!' Morgan explained, 'Get the angle? Jim's great with a straight left, he can keep Baer off balance and win rounds without getting hurt.'

'When I beat Baer in 1935,' Braddock would recall, 'I was the most lop-sided underdog in history. But when it got to the fight, that's where being the underdog helped most. Baer believed I was a soft touch. He thought a big right swing would scare me into jumping out of the ring. Early in the bout I slipped one or two rights and he laughed. He must have figured missing me was an accident. I started sticking left jabs into his face. He laughed some more . . . It's an old story now that things didn't change very much over the entire fifteen rounds. I avoided getting trapped by his sucker punches and I scored enough points to get home free. I knew the way for me to win was to play it cool and I did. Had I tried to be a hero, Baer would have bounced me around like a rubber ball. He was a sensational puncher.'

'Max would have been champion longer,' said his big brother Buddy, 'but he injured his hands boxing an exhibition match with Eddie Simms in Cleveland prior to the Braddock fight. The promoters told Max he had to go through with the fight, and he could barely stand the pain in his hands every time he hit Braddock.'

Baer had enjoyed his year as heavyweight champion, and he wanted that title back. But there was a new kid in town, a black kid from Detroit named Joe Louis. He wanted the title, too. Mike Jacobs matched them for Yankee Stadium and boxing had its eighth million-dollar gate, a crowd of 88,150 paying $1,000,832. They didn't see much of a fight, Baer being counted out as he knelt on the canvas in round four.

Sportswriter Jimmy Cannon recorded, 'After the Baer fight, Louis's hands were bruised. Baer was sick with despair. Jack Dempsey, who worked his corner, said that Baer had been bragging in the dressing-room about what he would do to Louis. But when a man shouted it was time for the main event, Baer began to pant. "I can't go on," said Baer. "I can't breathe." "I conned him into the ring," Dempsey remembers. "And after the first round, Max came back to the corner and said he couldn't breathe. I told him I'd kill him with the water bottle if he didn't go back out there and get knocked out."'

Many at ringside that September night in 1935 slammed Baer for taking the easy way out. He didn't argue, saying, 'Sure I quit. He hit me eighteen times while I was going down the last time. I got a family to think about, and if anybody wants to see the execution of Max Baer, he's got to pay more than twenty-five bucks for a ringside seat!'

Baer had accepted a purse of $200,000 against thirty per cent of the gate, a decision that cost him $100,000. Trainer Issy Kline told me a funny story about the fight. 'Next morning, Hoffman and I walked into a bank near Central Park in New York, just in time to see four guards, with pistols drawn, escorting other guys carrying a big steel box. One of the bank officials, who knew us, said, "There's a sight for you guys. Fifty thousand dollars in that box!" Ancil and I just looked at each other. We had strolled over to the bank carrying $280,000 in our pockets! When we started pulling the dough out, the bank guy almost fainted.'

By this time, Max had settled down and married Mary Ellen Sullivan, a domestic, home-loving girl who was happy for her big Baer to retire to ranch life in California, and not long afterwards a son was born, named after his father. But Max was still only twenty-six, and in June 1936 he put the gloves on again for a barnstorming tour of the tank towns, knocking over such tigers as Buck Rodgers, Junior Munsell, Soldier Franks and Dutch Weimer. Eighteen fights, fourteen knock-outs. He was ready for the big time again. Hoffman had arranged for Max to fight Bob Pastor in New York, but when the Commission balked at giving him a licence, they set sail for England and Tommy Farr.

'When Baer arrived in London in the spring of 1937,' recalled Frank Butler, 'most of the boxing writers were talking of massacre. Farr had just won the British title but still had not won the affection of the British fight crowd. Baer had one of his off nights – he began scowling, grinning, and pulling faces, but such tactics were a waste of time against the dour Welshman, who wasn't afraid of anything on two legs. Tommy Bach, as confident as Tarzan in the jungle, just poked out a spitfire left hand, split open Baer's brow and walked away with the decision after twelve rounds, to the delight of thousands of his countrymen who stood and sang their national anthem with a fervour that only the Welsh can put to song.

'Yet it was quite a different Baer who crushed Ben Foord in nine rounds at Harringay six weeks later. I have a clear picture of the end as Baer let go with a terrible right which missed the South African's chin by inches. Like lightning, Max brought his right fist back and shattered Foord with the back of his fist and quickly followed up with a terrific left swing. This all happened so rapidly that not more than a few ringsiders could have seen it, although Baer risked disqualification with his speedy backhander. Foord looked in a bad way for a little while, and Maxie was concerned until Ben recovered and left the ring apparently none the worse for his shattering experience.'

Farr's great victory, followed by a three-round knockout of the big German Walter Neusel, won him a crack at Joe Louis, who by the summer of 1937 had knocked out Jim Braddock to become champion. Farr didn't beat Louis, in the Brown Bomber's first title defence, but he won over the crowd in Yankee Stadium by defying Joe's lethal fists to go the distance. Promoter Mike Jacobs was so delighted with the Welsh warrior that he signed him for a series of fights at Madison Square Garden. One of them was against Max Baer.

'From the date of his second marriage,' wrote Nat Fleischer, 'the playboy complex disappeared altogether from the make-up of Max

Baer. He was taking himself seriously for the first time in his hectic career, living only for Mary and the baby Max.' Against Farr in the Garden ring, Baer was a revelation to those who had written him off. He not only outfought Tommy, he outboxed him at times, and he did something Joe Louis couldn't do when he stuck Farr on the canvas in the sixth round. Tommy got up and fought back to close one of Max's eyes, but after fifteen rounds Baer received the decision and the Garden crowd nearly took the roof off. They turned out to see him take on the handsome new contender Lou Nova just over a year later, but this time he was out of luck. Baer fought well enough, countering Nova's jabs with heavy right-hand smashes to head and body, and in the fourth Lou suffered a cut eye. But in the fifth, a right from Nova cut Max's lip badly. The corner couldn't stem the blood from the inside wound which ran down his throat. 'Coming back to his corner at the end of the tenth round,' reported Fleischer, 'Max looked down at me in the press row and, opening his lacerated mouth, pointed down his throat. He was signalling me that he was choking. In the eleventh the referee refused to let the bout go any further and stopped it, declaring Nova the winner.'

There was one fighter Max Baer couldn't stomach: 'Two-Ton' Tony Galento, the fat beer-swilling bartender, a vicious left hooker with no regard for the Marquess of Queensberry and even less for Baer. At the weigh-in for their fight at Jersey City on a sweltering July evening in 1940, Tony called Baer a 'yellow bum' and promised to make him quit that night. In the days before the fight, Galento had already infuriated Max by mailing him a postcard showing two scraggly, unkempt bears pawing one another, across which he had written, 'Max and Buddy, and this goes for your whole family, you bums!' In the ring that night, Galento butted, heeled, bit and ripped at Max's face with the laces of his gloves. But Baer fought back with a savage fury not seen since the Schmeling fight and chopped the fat man to pieces. The fight ended with Galento, a bleeding, blubbering hulk, sitting in his corner and refusing to come out for the eighth round.

In April 1941, Max Baer was back in the Garden ring to fight Lou Nova again. For a few rounds he was the old swaggering Baer, clowning, laughing, pulling faces and belting Nova to the deck in the fourth round with that big right hand to the jaw. But Lou got up and he took charge in the fifth. The referee stopped it in round eight after Baer had been floored twice and had nothing left. A crowd of 22,114 jammed the Garden, and as Fleischer would write in his 1942 biography of Baer, 'From start to finish one couldn't but help see that it was Baer, not Nova, who was the thrill provider, and that it was Baer who drew that near-record gate. It was Max's socking powers when he did cut loose that caused the fans to get into a state of frenzy, so much so that one ardent enthusiast at the ringside toppled over as Max landed nine consecutive rights to Nova's head without a return, and died from a heart attack before aid could reach him . . . The Glamour Boy of the Ring had made his final exit as a pugilist, but his name will always be renowned in fistic annals as that of one of the most colourful figures in the long, royal list of Queensberry heavyweight monarchs.'

Final note. When America got into the war, Max badgered the services until they finally gave him a uniform. After all, as he explained, 'I started the whole damn thing, getting Hitler riled up by beating Schmeling and then making Mussolini mad by what I did to poor old Carnera!'

# Homicide Hank 8

Wirt Ross was a handsome giant of a man with snow-white hair, bright blue eyes and an accent that was pure Kentucky despite a lifetime spent roaming around places like Alaska, the Philippines, New York City and Panama. He was a fight manager who once slugged a referee and when he was hauled in front of the California State Athletic Commission, he turned the tables, placed the poor referee in the role of defendant and finished up defending him! They called him One-Shot Ross around the gyms and he had a weakness for heavyweights, but he could never find another Dempsey or Joe Louis. He did find Haystack Sloan, for whom he invented the 'Ice Tong Punch'. But Haystack couldn't fight, not even with real ice tongs in his mitt. The best fighter Ross ever had was a little black kid he picked up at the Main Street Gym in Los Angeles for two hundred and fifty dollars. The kid's name was Henry Armstrong.

They called him Henry Jackson when he was born in a sharecropper's cabin in the cotton fields around Columbus, Mississippi, a couple of weeks before Christmas 1912. There would be fourteen kids in the family, and when they were old enough they toiled in the fields alongside their father, Henry. When the boll-weevil pest hit the cotton, Henry took two of the older boys and went to St Louis to look for work. Soon the family was reunited in a big brick house on Papin Street in the south side of the city. They hadn't been there very long when their mother died, and Grandma Chatman did her best to fill the void. She made sure the kids got an education, and young Henry graduated from Vashon High School. But rheumatism was crippling his father and as he lost more work days, so the youngster shouldered the burden of looking after his brothers and sisters. Still a teenager, Henry Jackson was swinging a sledgehammer for the Missouri Pacific Railroad for twenty dollars a week. It was good money and good exercise for a kid who had taken wrestling lessons from a cousin and now fancied himself as a boxer. He was hitting the bag in the YMCA gym in Pine Street when he met Harry Armstrong, a big jovial fellow who was training some of the kids. Harry liked what he saw of young Jackson and started working with him.

Harry sparred a couple of rounds with Henry one day, then he laughed and said, 'Kid, you can fight, but you can't punch. Look, boy, when I jab with my left, you step to your right and cross my left with your right.' They tried it, Harry jabbed, Henry slipped the punch and crossed his right and Harry, all 170 pounds of him, hit the floor. Rubbing his chin, he laughed again. 'Henry,' he said, 'you can't box, but you sure can punch!'

The kid won some amateur bouts and Harry and another fighter named Eddie Foster took him to Pittsburgh, looking for money fights. They lived on cabbage and bread and slept where they could. Sometimes Henry would get a sparring job for a dollar a day. Then Harry got him a fight on a card at Apple Myer's Bowl headed by Teddy

Yarosz. The kid was calling himself Melody Jackson by this time, but he was out of tune against Al Iovino, a rugged southpaw, who hammered him with body punches and knocked him out in the third round.

'I had trouble getting bouts,' Al would recall, 'because I was a southpaw and I could hit. All I ever could do was punch. But I could punch! Melody was deceptive in build, he was all arms and shoulders. He came buzzing after me, boring in from the start, and I let him come, nailing him with lefts to the body and head. He was made to order for my southpaw counter-punching. He went down twice in the second round from punches to the stomach. The end came in the third round from another good one.'

'We were broke and living from day to day on a dime's worth of buns and water,' Henry would remember many years later. 'The night I fought Iovino, I went into the ring on an empty stomach and he caved me in with his hard left swings to the body.'

The thirty-five dollar purse soothed his pain and he was back a week later, beating Sammy Burns. Then the boys jumped into Eddie's old jalopy and headed back to St Louis. But young Jackson had the wanderlust now and he was convinced his destiny lay in the prize ring. He told Harry he was going to California, and next morning they hopped a Westbound freight train. A couple of weeks later, after living rough in hobo camps and eating whatever they could scrounge, the boys arrived in Los Angeles, dirty, dishevelled and flat broke. An old fighter gave them a handout and told them of a local Mission where they could stay. And during the day, they haunted the gyms around town, the Main Street, the Manhattan and the Ringside. They found Tom Cox, who ran a stable of amateur fighters, and after taking a look at Henry in the sparring ring he agreed to handle him. Harry said to Henry, 'Melody Jackson is dead, forget the two fights in Pittsburgh. From now on, we're brothers. You're Henry Armstrong.'

In a little over twelve months, Henry Armstrong had eighty-five amateur bouts and won sixty-six by knockouts. They paid him three bucks a fight while Cox took a dollar, and after Henry was beaten in the 1932 Olympic tryouts, Cox sold him to Wirt Ross for $250 and he became a professional fighter again. This time there was no going back. Ross kept him busy and in the summer of 1936 Henry was matched with Alberto Baby Arizmendi. The tough Mexican was recognized as featherweight champion in Mexico and California, and Armstrong had already given him a belting in two fights in Mexico City, but you were only a winner there if they let you live! This time the fight would be in Los Angeles, outdoors at Wrigley Field, and the Babe's titles would be on the line.

The big Mexican and Negro population in the city was all steamed up over the fight and the Main Street Gym was jammed every day to watch the boys go through their paces. Fight night was a cool, clear evening and a good crowd of 12,000 showed up at the ball park, the ringside studded with Hollywood celebrities.

Herbert G Goldman's fine book, *Jolson; The Legend Comes To Life*, is the definitive biography of the man they called the world's greatest entertainer. Goldman wrote, 'In that summer of 1936, Al and Ruby went to Wrigley Field in Los Angeles to see the ten-rounds fight between Henry Armstrong and Alberto Baby Arizmendi. Eddie Mead, a friend of Ruby's who had managed world bantamweight champion Joe Lynch in the Twenties, sat in back of the Jolsons. As the fight progressed, Ruby turned to Mead and said, "That's the kind of fighter *you* ought to manage, Eddie, that boy Armstrong."

'"There's just five thousand reasons why I ain't managing him," replied Mead. "I can buy him for five g's, and all I need is $4,995 more to make the deal." When the fight was over with Armstrong the winner, Al gave Mead a card and told him to call the next day.

'Al agreed to finance Mead's purchase of the Armstrong contract from Wirt Ross, Armstrong's manager since 1932. Mead, anxious for publicity, got Jolie's okay to tell Jack Singer of the *Los Angeles Times* that the sale price was ten instead of five thousand dollars. It proved to be a bad move – Ross raised the price to ten thousand dollars as soon as he saw Singer's story. Al was furious, and absolutely refused to give Mead the additional five thousand. George Raft soon came in with the necessary money and became Al's silent partner.

'Jolson, who never saw a quarter of the money he had lent Mead, finally washed his hands of the whole deal after an argument with Raft in Los Angeles' Roosevelt Hotel in February 1938. The experience, however, did not dampen Al's enthusiasm for boxing. Armstrong had been a winner, a sharp contrast to the nags that made up Jolson's racing stable. Miquelon, the stable's star horse, won only one race in his entire life.'

After that fight with Arizmendi, the papers were calling Armstrong 'Hurricane Henry' and 'Homicide Hank'. The boys threw punches non-stop for the entire ten rounds and when it was all over, Henry Armstrong had at last beaten Baby Arizmendi. Referee George Blake made it official when he held up Hank's glove. He had never thrown so much leather in any one fight. Arizmendi was a bull-necked power plug of a fighter who could take punches all night long, and against Henry Armstrong that was mandatory.

Eddie Mead had the right connections in the fight game and he arranged a match with Mike Belloise at the Los Angeles Olympic in October 1936. Belloise was recognized by the New York Commission as featherweight champion, a title he had lost to Arizmendi some time before, but when the Mexican failed to defend the title in the time frame set by the New York Commission, they conferred it once again on the New York boy. And they still recognized Mike after Armstrong gave him a beating in the Olympic ring because the fight had been over ten rounds, rather than the championship distance of fifteen.

Henry was delighted a few months later when Eddie told him he was going into Madison Square Garden – the big time, New York City. He was matched with Aldo Spoldi, a tough Italian lightweight, but a couple of days before the fight Spoldi cried off sick and Mike Belloise came in as replacement. As he walked down that long aisle to the most famous boxing ring in the world, Henry was nervous, ill at ease. Then a guy stepped forward from his ringside seat, took his hand and said, 'Hank, old boy, we've got to win for California tonight.' It was George Raft. Henry felt better. 'We'll win,' he smiled back at the movie tough guy.

For two rounds Armstrong bobbed and weaved as Belloise used the ring, getting behind his sharp left jab. In round three Henry stepped up a gear and the fans roared as he swarmed all over the New Yorker. He kept the pace up in the fourth, then slammed a left hook to the jaw. Belloise stopped in his tracks, then pitched forward on to his face. He never looked like beating the count, but the bell rang at seven and they dragged him back to his corner. Mike slid to the floor again and when they got him back on his stool it was obvious that he was all through for the night, Arthur Donovan stopped the fight, and boxing had a new star.

A week later, Henry made history by becoming the first fighter to headline at the Garden in successive weeks, taking on Spoldi, who was fit again but didn't feel too good after ten rounds with Homicide Hank. That fight was the only time in 1937 that Armstrong was taken the distance, in twenty-seven fights. One of his victims was Petey Sarron. Feisty promoter Mike Jacobs had just staged his Carnival of Champions at the Polo Grounds, an artistic success with four world championships but a financial flop that saw Jacobs lose a small fortune. But it did prove that Mike was the leading promoter, and he and the Garden people became partners – his dream had come true, he was sitting in Tex Rickard's chair at last.

Mike set his first card in the Garden for 29 October 1937 and looked around for a championship fight. This kid Armstrong was coming up like Halley's Comet, he came to fight and he didn't worry who was in the other corner. So Jacobs got Petey Sarron, who was recognized as featherweight champion by the National Boxing Association.

The champion was thousands of miles away at the time, in South Africa, and it cost Jacobs fifteen grand to bring him and his title back to New York. A boxer rather than a fighter, the little Syrian-American from Birmingham, Alabama, had beaten Freddie Miller for the title and defended it against Baby Manuel and Miller again, and now he readily agreed to come home and fight this new fellow Armstrong in the Garden. Fifteen grand was big money for little guys in those days.

For his first show in the House that Tex Built, Mike Jacobs counted $34,708 paid in by 11,847 fans – could have been better, but it was a start. For two rounds Petey Sarron boxed like a champion and Armstrong couldn't hit him with a handful of rice. Henry lost the third when the referee penalized him for a low blow, yet Eddie Mead told him to concentrate on the body coming out for the fourth. 'Cut the distance,' he told Henry. 'Stay inside his arms, work the body.' Sarron was now being bullied around the ring as Armstrong chugged forward, bobbing, weaving, punching, always punching – and the punches were beginning to hurt.

The end came in round six. Henry caught the champion with a shattering right to the jaw, dropping him to his hands and knees, on the canvas for the first time in over 100 fights over twelve years. He listened to Arthur Donovan counting, 'One, two, three . . .' Then the referee walked over to knockdown timekeeper Pete Hartley, and when he picked up the official count again, returned to the fallen champion. The next thing Sarron knew, Donovan was saying, 'Ten, and out!' The referee was criticized for leaving Sarron's side during the count, but

Petey wasn't bitter. 'Don't underestimate this Armstrong,' he told the reporters in the dressing-room. 'He's the kind of guy who never lets up, he'll beat a lot of fighters, lightweights, welterweights, anybody. This isn't the only title he's going to win.' Prophetic words.

Henry Armstrong was the new featherweight champion of the world, but three weeks later he walked into Mead's office asking why he wasn't fighting. 'You're a champion now,' growled Eddie as he studied a Racing Form. 'You can't fight every week, it'll cheapen the title. Why don't you go over to the gym and bang your head on the big bag a couple of times. You'll feel better!' So Henry went over to Stillman's Gym and boxed ten rounds with a lightweight and three welterweights, just for the hell of it.

Armstrong was an incredible fighter, and that night against Petey Sarron he started a ten-month campaign that was to establish him as a super fighter, one of boxing's greatest ever champions. Seven months after winning the featherweight title, he moved up two divisions and hammered welterweight champion Barney Ross into retirement. Then he dropped down to the lightweight division and relieved Lou Ambers of his title in a bitter battle, to become the only fighter to hold three major world titles at the same time. This amazing character didn't stop there. He would go against Ceferino Garcia, who held the middleweight title as recognized by the New York State Athletic Commission, and come out with a draw when most considered he had beaten the teak-tough Filipino.

As featherweight champion, the logical first move up would have been for Henry to challenge Ambers for the lightweight title. But Mike Jacobs had a score to settle with Al Weill, the manager of Ambers, who had demanded $82,000 for Ambers to defend his title against Pedro Montanez in one of the four title bouts on the loss-making Carnival of Champions. So Mike announced that Armstrong would instead challenge Barney Ross for his welterweight crown at the

Madison Square Garden Bowl on a May evening in 1938. At his training camp at Grossinger's in New York State, Ross told newsmen, 'I will never take but one bad beating. I will know then that I am going back and I won't stick around. When the day comes that I crack up, that will be my last fight.'

'Ross was twenty-eight,' recorded boxing writer Barney Nagler, 'long past his prime, and speed had fled from his limbs. Although he could not move fast, neither could he punch. Time had programmed him for defeat. At twenty-five, Armstrong was at his physical and combative peak. He molested Ross all the way, forcing the old pro back with machine precision. We remember averting Ross's pitiful gaze when, at one point in the mid-rounds, he spun helplessly into the ropes and caught our line of vision. Ross's legs were unwilling servants of a master's courage.'

In a fine career, Barney Ross had beaten such men as Jimmy McLarnin, Tony Canzoneri, Billy Petrolle and Ceferino Garcia, but that cold night on Long Island he couldn't beat Henry Armstrong. Not even with a huge weight advantage. The Commission stated that Armstrong must weigh in at least a pound over the lightweight limit, to protect Ambers's title, so Eddie Mead had Henry drinking beer till it was coming out his ears. The day of the fight, he saw his own doctor, who weighed him: still too light! Drink water, he was told. He drunk enough water to float a battleship, and when he stepped on the official scales he was bang on 138 pounds. He had done it, and he got a break when rain postponed the bout a further five days, allowing him to come in at his natural poundage after Mead talked the Commission out of a second weigh-in. Henry went in against Ross at 133½ pounds while the Chicago Jew hit 142.

'By his one-sided victory over Ross,' wrote Nat Fleischer, 'Armstrong gained a niche in the Fistic Hall of Fame as one of the greatest fighters of all time. Until that feat was accomplished, there

143

was considerable doubt about his true status, but Henry answered that by giving Barney the worst beating a champion had received in many moons . . . Ross lingered through those fifteen rounds to the amazement of even his staunchest supporters. He went out of the ring with the distinction of having stood up for forty-five minutes against an assault such as few other fighters, middleweights included, would have survived in a tilt with Hurricane Henry. Armstrong never stopped.'

For the first five rounds, Barney Ross held his own as the human buzzsaw they called Henry Armstrong climbed all over him, gloves, arms, shoulders, everything going in. Then it hit Ross, as it had so many ring veterans over the years. In his autobiography, Barney wrote, 'Sixth round. He came at me too fast and I danced away neatly . . . then suddenly, unbelievably, something happened to my legs. I couldn't seem to move on them, they were like Mack trucks. Armstrong sensed there was something wrong with me. He came at me with a rain of punches, I lifted my gloves to block them and another strange thing happened, my arms felt as if they had lead weights on them. It was all I could do to get them up to protect my face, let alone fight back.

'The eighth and ninth were the same. He rained left hooks on my mouth and blood gushed out. He hit me in the eye and closed it tight. Another punch cut my lip open. Another crashed into my nose, nearly breaking it and starting another flow of blood. Blood was all over me now, it was dribbling into my good eye so I was practically blind. And I was taking such a beating in the stomach I wanted to throw up, right in the middle of the ring. Ring that bell, I thought. Ring it! Ring it, dammit! It rang. The punches stopped. I had to get back to my corner – my corner, where the hell was my corner? I couldn't see. There was a man at my arm now guiding me. It was Arthur Donovan. What in God's name has happened to Barney Ross, I thought, that a referee has to take him back to his corner?'

Manager Art Winch told him what had happened to Barney Ross this night under the stars in the big wooden arena on Long Island. 'It's only old age,' said Art. 'It just caught up to you tonight. This is your last fight.'

It was. His corner wanted to stop the fight, the referee wanted to stop the fight, and Henry Armstrong, the one man who could stop the fight, didn't. 'I respected Barney,' Henry would recall, 'so I carried him the last few rounds, won the decision and my second title, from the man I consider the cleverest and finest all-around fighter I ever fought.' Ross was a pitiful sight in the dressing-room afterwards, Sam Pian and Art Winch almost in tears as they tended his wounds. Barney's face was swollen, his lips torn and bloody, his right eye shuttered tight, but he still had time for the boxing writers, telling them, 'Armstrong is a great little fighter. He was surprisingly strong and a good game fellow. I gave him everything I had and couldn't halt him. There is no doubt in my mind that Henry will stay up there a long time. He has the class . . . He never left me alone.'

Ed Van Every of the *New York Sun* said of Armstrong afterwards, 'With twenty more pounds he'd lick Joe Louis!'

Of this fighting phenomenon, Barney Nagler wrote, 'He had thrilled them, bounding down the aisle, dancing and snorting, with his body squirming inside his robe, working his arms and moving in a seeming glide. When the bell rang he would lean forward, punching to the body, his skinny legs spread wide and his neck taut, forcing his rival before him, fighting with a calculated fury, racing the clock, unmindful of pain; a champion!'

Now Mike Jacobs was ready to talk to Al Weill. For a purse of $32,000, Lou Ambers would defend his lightweight title against Mike's double champ, who would have to be happy with $25,000. Jacobs set the fight for Yankee Stadium but it rained and the boys finally got together in the Garden the night of 17 August 1938, and for once Henry was fighting a guy his own size. 'A rugged citizen, that Ambers,' wrote Lester Bromberg. 'He couldn't punch and he certainly didn't have a classic boxing style. But he had the heart of a lion and he never tired. His proper name was Luigi D'Ambrosio, and he had come from the bootleg amateur circuit in upper New York State near his hometown of Herkimer. Lou's durability was a legend.'

Armstrong was a seventeen-to-five favourite with the bookies, but Ambers was the overwhelming favourite with the crowd that jammed into the Garden that night. They cheered every punch he threw and every time Armstrong hit him below the chin they yelled foul. The opening round was pretty even, with Armstrong edging rounds two and three. Edward Brennan of the *New York Journal American* reported the fourth round, 'With a new purpose glowing in his eyes, Ambers strode out to meet the bouncing Armstrong. This time he followed Weill's advice. As Henry dashed in as usual, Lou suddenly lashed out with a right to the jaw. Henry staggered, he was hurt. The 20,000 crowd leaped to their feet, and the roar that erupted from their throats shook window panes across Eighth Avenue. Ambers chased his dazed foe around the ring, but Armstrong didn't go down, with masterful reflexes and ring generalship he fought off his tormentor to survive the round . . . Round five came with something like an explosion. The durable Armstrong rose like the mythical Phoenix . . . he rushed forward, swarmed all over the startled Ambers and, to the horror of the lightweight champion's backers, slammed stunning punches against his body and head . . . Then, as the round drew to a close, Henry hurled a left hook and right cross to the head. Ambers was thrown back as though shot by a .45 slug, then he fell flat on his face.

'Had referee Billy Cavanagh been able to finish counting, he would easily have reached ten . . . But Cavanagh reached the count of one and the bell rang. Weill leaped from the corner. With Whitey

Bimstein, he dragged Lou to his stool and administered feverishly to the stricken fighter. Somehow, they managed to get him ready for round six. Again the solid left-hook, right-cross combination dropped Lou in his own corner. This, the crowd agreed, was the end . . . But no, eight seconds later, the brave champion was on his feet. They cheered him again, and they kept on cheering.'

Armstrong had suffered a cut on his lower lip in a sparring session with Chalky Wright and Lou's hammering fists had the blood flowing as the wound opened again. By the tenth round, the referee, alarmed at the loss of blood, warned Armstrong he might have to stop the fight. Henry simply fought on without his mouthpiece so that he could swallow the blood. He wanted to win this one. Yet round thirteen was almost unlucky for him, as Brennan reported. 'A wicked right to the jaw sent Henry spinning against the ropes. So stunned was he that he tried to climb out of the ring through the ropes, but Cavanagh pulled him back in. By this time, everybody in the Garden was berserk with excitement. Coats and hats flew through the air, men and women jumped up and down and slapped one another on the back . . . As the round ended, people were running up and down the aisles, with the cops right after them.'

'But that thirteenth round effort took a lot out of Ambers,' wrote James P Dawson in the *New York Times*. 'He was practically out on his feet in the fourteenth and fifteenth when he again essayed rallies, only to be brought up short by the California Negro, who would not be denied . . . The writer gave Armstrong ten of the fifteen rounds . . . This margin in Armstrong's favour reflects the flow of battle. He was a perfect little demon, a human cyclone, a frenzied destroyer who did not encompass destruction as it is known in the ring only because he tired when the crucial moment came. Homicidal Henry or Hammering Henry, whichever you will, because he is a combination of both, won a two-to-one verdict from the bout officials. He left the ring with the derisive shouts of noisy protests ringing in his ears, victim of a sad demonstration after a glorious bout.'

'In his dressing-room,' wrote Barney Nagler, 'Armstrong lay on his rubbing table. "I'm sick," he said. "I'm almost out of my head with pain. He's a tough man. It was my hardest fight." We trailed Armstrong to the office of Dr Schiff, a few blocks up from the Garden. Dr Schiff used twelve stitches to close the laceration inside Armstrong's mouth.'

Boxing had its first triple champion. Armstrong was featherweight, lightweight and welterweight champion of the world, and he had done it in ten months and seventeen fights. No fighter before or since had equalled his astonishing feat. It was 1938 and Henry Armstrong and Joe Louis were kings of the ring, sitting on top of the boxing world.

'I fought hard and I lived just as hard,' recalled Henry many years later. 'I drank like a demon and I gambled, and if I didn't chase women it's because I didn't have to. They chased me. Those were the high old days and I made the most of them. I was a celebrity, owned by celebrities. Jolson was my friend, a big spender who passed out $100 bills, threw great parties and entertained from dawn to dusk. George Raft was my friend, a real sport. Mae West was my friend, too, and not at all like she seemed on the stage. That woman had a heart of gold.'

Of manager Eddie Mead, Barney Nagler would write, 'By the time we got to know Mead, Armstrong's purses had put him in the chips. He was hanging out in good saloons, away from his old haunts on the West Side, and had more than one suit of clothes to his name. He was a blubbery *bon vivant* with a round, soft face that had the mild look of a kid surprised with his hand in the cookie jar. He went to his pocket easily and lived at a pace only hustlers can set and only millionaires can afford.'

After beating Ambers, Armstrong surrendered the featherweight title and a few months later defended his welterweight title against Ceferino Garcia in Madison Square Garden. 'Garcia was the hardest puncher I ever fought,' Henry would remember. 'He had that bolo punch, a sort of wild-sweeping hook or uppercut. His bolo was a very heavy punch, it hurt you all over. He hit me with the hardest shot I ever took. I had a special mouthpiece made to protect that old lip scar. But my seconds were nervous and they forgot to shove it in before the eleventh round started. They called to me and when I turned my head to see what they were yelling about, Garcia hit me with a right-hand bolo to the chin that lifted me three feet off the canvas. To this day, I say I was unconscious when I fell. But I landed on my hands, causing my neck to snap, partially reviving me. I looked up and saw *four* Garcias. I jumped right up and in so doing, my head slammed against his chin. That shook him up. I grabbed him, twisted him, punched him hard and kept him busy until I recovered. Had Ceferino known how badly I was hurt, he could have knocked me out easily.'

In May 1939, Mead brought Henry to London to defend the welterweight title against British champion Ernie Roderick at Harringay Arena. The Liverpool man was a veteran of some ninety-odd ring battles, a good boxer with a knockout punch, and Johnny Best figured he would give Armstrong a run for his money. Best had just taken over as matchmaker at Harringay, but he ran into problems when he booked the American. Someone from the Madison Square Garden Corporation called to inform Best that unless Roderick, on the chance that he beat Armstrong, agreed to defend against an American of their choice, there would be no fight.

Johnny called in the lawyers but they didn't have the answer. Johnny had it all along! When he learned of Eddie Mead's passion for beef stew, the matchmaker took Eddie along to Stone's Chop House in Panton Street and sat him down to the finest beef stew in the city.

That did the trick. So far as Eddie Mead was concerned, Johnny Best was his kind of man and Armstrong would fight Roderick, no strings attached. They did haggle over the referee, but Eddie finally accepted the Board's appointment of Wilfred Smith. He did win one point, asking for a few feet longer bandages for Henry's hands, Roderick to have the same. Everything was set for a memorable evening, yet for some reason the fans stayed away in droves. That Thursday night, only about 5,000 were in the big arena.

British hopes were high as Ernie took the first round, boxing nicely behind the jab and landing a couple of solid rights. But round two saw Hurricane Henry blow across the ring and take Roderick with him. A leather storm engulfed the Liverpool man for three minutes and when the bell rang, the crowd cheered Ernie just for still being there. In the fourth Roderick bounced some heavy rights off Henry's chin, but in round five a cut appeared on his right eye. Round seven was probably the best round of the fight, as the British champion came off the ropes fighting for his very life, and the crowd raised the roof as he battled the American across that canvas battlefield. But try as he may, Ernie Roderick could not stop this phenomenal little fighter. Armstrong couldn't stop him either, and at the final bell the sparse crowd rose to two grand warriors, Roderick for his superb exhibition of sheer fighting guts, courage, fortitude – whatever you call it, Ernie had it that night. And Armstrong the champion, with that great heart driving him on all the time no matter what his opponent threw at him, fists hammering away three minutes of every round, taking punches like an anvil takes the hammer.

Famed British referee Moss Deyong said after watching the fight, 'Without doubt Henry Armstrong is the greatest of them all. He is the most sensational two-fisted fighter I've ever seen, and I've seen them all. But what I admired about him more than anything else was when he spoke to the crowd after he had travelled those fifteen whirlwind rounds. There wasn't a breath out of place as he spoke. Armstrong's stamina confirmed everything they said he was. Yes, you can say I told you that he's the world's greatest fighter!'

Armstrong had won his last forty-six fights, thirty-nine inside the distance. He would lose his next one. They matched him with Lou Ambers in Yankee Stadium, with Ambers going for his old lightweight title, and this time the officials voted Ambers the winner. The outcome was determined early when Lou's punches ripped open the skin around Armstrong's eyes. Blinded, Henry slugged away at Ambers's body. Some of his punches strayed too low and five rounds were taken from him, costing him the decision and his lightweight championship. Bitter accusations and arguments over the low blows and the decision led to the suspension of the respective managers, Eddie Mead and Al Weill, by the New York Commission.

'I never deliberately fouled anyone,' insisted Henry, 'but I was a body puncher who stayed on top of my opponents, so it may have seemed that way. If I punched low in the Ambers fight, it was because I was bleeding so bad I couldn't see. I know I gave him a body beating such as I gave no one else. I must say, though, that Ambers was a tough little guy and, outside of Barney Ross, the cleverest I ever met.'

Now the triple champ was down to just one title, the welterweight, so Mead kept him busy with that one, and just six months after dropping the lightweight title to Ambers, Henry was fighting for the *middleweight* championship! His old rival Ceferino Garcia had won New York State recognition as a champion, but the weight difference between him and Henry was more than New York would allow, so the boys fought in Los Angeles. One day in the Main Street Gym, Henry was approached by three mob guys who threw $15,000 in bills on the table, saying, 'That money is yours if you let Garcia put you down in three rounds.' The little champ told them to get lost.

'It was a wild-swinging fight for ten rounds,' wrote Henry in his autobiography, referring to himself in the third person, 'but neither man went down. Henry was sure he would get the decision; he was dumbfounded when the referee left the ring without casting a vote. The referee said it was too close, so did the judges. They called it a draw. The referee took two rounds from Henry, on what he said were fouls. Nobody else thought so. The press booed the decision, and so did the fans. But Henry did not get the title. He still thinks he was robbed, and so do a lot of others.'

Armstrong defended the welterweight title twenty times. He won nineteen of them. In October 1940, he climbed into the Garden ring to give Fritzie Zivic a shot. One of five fighting brothers, Fritzie was a flat-nosed Croatian-American, and sportswriters called him the dirtiest fighter to come out of Pittsburgh since Harry Greb. For the first six rounds Armstrong fought his usual fight, bulling his way in, everything going, and his fans were happy. Zivic wasn't happy. He did something about it.

As Fritzie told it to Red Smith some years later, 'You remember the Cadillac? Ever since I was a kid, that's what I always wanted. Figured then I'd be a success. So the day I'm fighting Armstrong for the title in New York, I go and look at the biggest Cadillac I can find. That night, Henry's givin' it to me pretty good and I can see that Cadillac rollin' farther and farther away from me. Henry's givin' me the elbows and the shoulders and the top of his head, and I can give that stuff back pretty good, but I don't dare to or maybe they'll throw me out of the ring. Well, in the seventh round I give him the head a couple of times and choke him a couple times and use the elbow some, and the referee says, "If you guys want to fight that way, it's okay with me." "Hot damn!" I told Luke Carney in my corner, "watch me go now." And from there out I saw that Cadillac turn around and come rollin' back!'

Fritzie Zivic got his Cadillac and he got Armstrong's title. In the fifteenth and final round, Armstrong, the great little champ, was stumbling blindly around the ring, nothing left but that great fighting heart driving him on. With the last punch of the fight, Zivic tossed a vicious right to the jaw and Henry fell on his face, the bell saving him from a knockout. 'Zivic was just nasty,' he recalled later. 'Bad! He couldn't punch and he ran, but he could box and he could fight dirty. I was running out of gas when I met him and I wasn't able to rough it up with him, which was the only way to fight a guy like that. My close friend, Dr Alexander Schiff, operated on me to get rid of the scar tissue around my eyes. He, and others, didn't want me to fight anymore, but it was hard for me to quit.'

Henry rested and he trained, and he went back with Zivic in January 1941 as a record crowd of 23,190 packed Madison Square Garden. It was an Armstrong crowd there to see an Armstrong victory, but they were disappointed. Their great little champion had nothing left and Zivic chopped him to pieces. They had to stop it in the twelfth round to save Henry from himself. And when he went to see Eddie Mead for his money, he found there was nothing left there either, nothing left of well over half a million dollars.

'I should have watched over my own money,' he said, 'but I didn't. That was my mistake. Still, I can't really complain. I didn't know how to take care of money any more than Mead did. He ran through a couple of fortunes of his own before he went through mine. Eddie felt bad, he didn't want to cheat me. Only thing was, Mike Jacobs gave Mead advances whenever Eddie asked, and Eddie was always asking. So I had to keep fighting so Eddie could pay back. It wasn't Mike's fault Mead and me blew all the dough.'

Armstrong didn't fight for over a year, and when he decided to make a comeback, he called Dr Schiff, Mead's closest friend. 'Too late, Henry,' Dr Schiff said. 'Eddie just died. He scored a big bet on a horse and it was too much for his heart.'

The old champ found somebody else to book him some fights – there's always someone out there willing to trade on a good name in the flesh market – but the magic was gone and he quit in 1945. He hit rock bottom, but overcame alcoholism to become a Baptist minister. He died on 24 October 1988, aged seventy-five.

# The Brown Bomber 9

Literary legend Ernest Hemingway loved a prizefight as much as he loved a bullfight. Speaking of another American legend, Hemingway said, 'Joe Louis was the most beautiful fighting machine I have ever seen.'

Sportswriter Bob Considine recalled, 'Heavyweight champ Joe Louis was a big, lean copper spring, tightened and retightened through weeks of training, until he was one pregnant package of coiled venom!'

Louis became world heavyweight champion in June 1937 when he knocked out Jimmy Braddock in the eighth round of their fight at Comiskey Park in Chicago. Remembering Joe's punch, Braddock would say, 'It's like someone jammed an electric bulb in your face and busted it. I thought half my head was blowed off. I figure he caved it in. He drove the tooth through the mouthpiece and right on through the lip. You see what power that guy had. When he knocked me down, I could have stayed there for three weeks.'

Sports Editor of the *New York Daily Mirror*, big Dan Parker, didn't mince his words when writing of the fight racket, but he used purple prose to sum up the Bomber's brilliant career in 1962, writing, 'Joe Louis fought all comers, knocked out most of them, defended his title more often than most of the others combined, and conducted himself with such dignity, decency and honesty that he made boxing a better sport, brought it a period of unprecedented prosperity, inspired his people by his example to make great strides, was a good soldier, made generous contributions to Army and Navy relief funds during World War II, and in short, was a champion in every sense of the word.'

Madison Square Garden's Harry Markson, who used to do publicity for promoter Mike Jacobs, once asked Louis if he had any super-stitions. 'Don't need superstitions,' replied Joe. 'I was born on the thirteenth, that's enough!' It wasn't Friday the thirteenth but on Wednesday, 13 May 1914, that Lily Reese Barrow gave birth to a boy in a pine shanty a few miles from the town of Lafayette, Alabama. 'I was a healthy boy,' recalled Joe in his autobiography, 'weighed about eleven pounds at birth. Momma was a big woman, my father was a big man. We come from big people, mostly blacks, some whites, and a few powerful Indians. Put that all together and I guess you get something.'

The boy was named Joseph Louis Barrow, the seventh child of Lily and Munrow, and a girl was born before they took Munrow away to the asylum. The few acres of red clay they rented often produced only heartbreak and hunger, and the years of struggle finally broke Munrow Barrow. Lily eventually heard that her husband had died, and she accepted a marriage proposal from widower Pat Brooks. Munrow actually lived long after Lily became Mrs Brooks and followed her new husband north to Detroit. It was 1926 and young Joe Barrow was twelve years old. 'One thing I knew,' he would say, 'Detroit looked awfully good to me!'

By the time he was seventeen, Joe was 6ft tall and weighed 170 pounds. He was going to the Bronson Vocational School, where he made wooden cabinets, tables, stuff like that. He was good with his hands, but Lily wanted something more for him and, renting a violin, sent him to a local music teacher. Joe didn't like that. Anyway, as he told me many years afterwards, 'My hands were too big. I couldn't hold the fiddle.'

What Joe did like was boxing. At the Bronson school he met Thurston McKinney, who had won the Detroit Golden Gloves light-weight championship. McKinney asked Joe to spar with him and took him over to the Brewster Recreation Centre Gym on the East Side. Young Joe Louis Barrow liked this place instantly and pretty soon he was spending all his spare time there, using the fifty cents his mother gave him for the violin lessons to rent a locker at the gym. In the ring one day with McKinney, Joe got tired of being knocked about and he belted Thurston with a cracking right to the jaw, almost knocking him out. McKinney rubbed his chin, grinned at Joe, and said, 'Man, throw that violin away!'

When his mother discovered that Joe was doing what he wanted more than anything, she gave her blessing, saying, 'Yes, son, you can be a boxer, but remember, you got to be a good one!' He was a good one. In fifty-four amateur bouts, he won fifty and knocked out forty-three of his opponents on his way to the Detroit Golden Gloves light-heavyweight title and the National Amateur Athletic Union championship at St Louis.

It was 1934 and the ring exploits of young Joe Louis Barrow had come to the attention of John Roxborough, a Detroit businessman who lived well and dressed well thanks to a thriving betting operation. Joe went to see Roxborough, who had helped him get a job at the Ford plant for $25 a week, and said he wanted to be a pro fighter. Roxborough knew if he turned Joe down now he might lose him, so he agreed to handle the young amateur sensation, taking him to Chicago where an old friend in the numbers racket, Julian Black, was running a stable of fighters out of Trafton's Gym. Roxborough and Black drew up a contract, with Joe getting fifty per cent and the other fifty going to the two managers, who would pay all expenses. They brought Joe Blackburn in as trainer on thirty-five dollars a week, with a promise of ten per cent if Joe got into the big money. Jack Blackburn had been a good fighter in his younger days before he ran foul of the law and did five years in prison for murder. 'He was rough-talking,' Joe would recall. 'When I first met him, he said to me, "You have to really be something to get anywhere. And you got to listen to everything I tell you. You got to jump when I say jump, sleep when I say sleep. Other than that, you're wasting my time." I told him that I'd promise him and myself there would be no time wasted. With a little tight funny smile, he said, "OK, Chappie." I smiled and said back to him, "OK, Chappie," and from that time on that's what we called each other.'

Blackburn found Joe a willing pupil in the gym. For a week all he did was punch the bag, learn how to set his feet before punching, balance, getting into position to throw a punch. Six miles roadwork every morning, skipping, sparring and, two weeks later, the fight. The Bacon Casino was at Forty-Seventh Street on Chicago's South Side. On 4 July 1934, the main event was Joe Louis v Jack Kracken. 'Chappie could see I was nervous,' Joe would recall. 'He kept talking. "Remember everything I taught you. You get in there and knock that guy out as fast as you can. One clean punch is better than a hundred punches." When the bell rang, I did just what Chappie told me. I went straight to the body. When Kracken dropped his guard, I gave him a left to the chin, and in less than two minutes I knocked him out. The fight was over. I won.' Roxborough gave Joe his entire purse of fifty-nine dollars and told him to send it to his mother.

Joe knocked out Willie Davis, Larry Udell went out in two rounds, and the fans came back to see Jack Kranz take Joe the full six rounds. Buck Everett fell in round two, then Joe went home to Detroit to fight Alex Borchuk at the Naval Academy. 'I knocked him out in the fourth round,' said Joe, 'but the crowd didn't know how tough that one was. This Borchuk hit me harder than any fighter hit me before or since. He fetched one to my left jaw that broke one of my back teeth.'

Joe remembered his fight with Art Sykes from New York. They fought at Arcadia Gardens in Chicago and for seven rounds Louis hammered Art all over the ring, finally knocking him out in round eight. 'I was glad it was over,' he said, 'but when I left the club, the doctors were still with him in the dressing-room. I called the hospital all night to see how he was doing. He was a boy Damon Runyon liked. Mr Runyon told me later, "You almost killed my boy." This Art Sykes never fought again.'

They brought Lee Ramage in from California to fight Louis at the Chicago Stadium. Joe always said Ramage was one of the cleverest boxers he ever met, and he had trouble nailing him with a decent punch. But by the eighth round Ramage was tired, Joe knocked him down three times and his corner threw the towel in. Two months later, Joe went out to Los Angeles and flattened Ramage inside two rounds, right in his own backyard. 'My picture and my name got in all the papers after I beat Ramage the second time,' he recalled. 'They called me Brown Bomber and it got out that the writers thought that up, but they didn't. Mr Roxborough was talking about me one night in Detroit to Scotty Monteith, who was a fighter then a manager. When Mr Monteith went home that night, he got the idea. He called Mr Roxborough on the telephone. He said, "I got a good name for your boy. You call him The Brown Bomber." That's how it was.'

Within nine months of becoming a professional fighter, the young Detroit heavyweight had won sixteen fights, thirteen by knockouts, and people were taking notice. People like Mike Jacobs, a New York hustler and ticket broker who was now promoting fights. He was calling himself the Twentieth Century Sporting Club and he was ambitious, he wanted to be in Madison Square Garden. Joe Louis could get him there. Jacobs worked out a deal with Joe's managers, and he told the young fighter, 'Joe, you can fight on the level when you fight for me. If you win, you win. You don't have to drop for anybody. I'll make a lot of money for you.'

Louis was matched with Natie Brown in Detroit and Jacobs hired a special train to bring the New York sportswriters out to see the fight. Among them was Nat Fleischer, editor and publisher of *The Ring* magazine. 'What impressed me most in the fight with Brown,' wrote Fleischer, 'was Joe's coolness, both prior to his entrance into the ring and under fire; his great left hook, a devastating punch; his powerful right hand sock and the manner in which he hit, stepped away and then stepped in again with his follow-up blow. That is the style that brought success to Jack Johnson and Kid McCoy, and was the style employed by every great fighter of the past.'

'He is cold as ice,' wrote Caswell Adams in the *New York Herald Tribune*, 'and when he moves, he does so as would a tiger or a lion.'

Joe knocked Brown down in the first round but Natie was there to stay the limit and he did so. 'It was Joe's severest test since he started his professional career,' wrote Fleischer, 'and the scribes voted that he had come through with flying colours, though they hadn't seen his devastating punch in action.'

'People think I felt the best the night I won the world's heavyweight championship from Jim Braddock,' recalled Joe. 'I felt good when I got to be champ, but the biggest night was 25 June 1935 when I beat Primo Carnera in Yankee Stadium, and the biggest days were the days before the Carnera fight. I was a kid then. When I came into New York, the people liked to have swept me away. There were so many newsreel and newspaper cameras the lights got me blind. I was never asked so many questions, not in all my life put together. I got to see Mayor LaGuardia down in City Hall and I met Jack Dempsey on Times Square.'

Primo Carnera was a former heavyweight champion, and he stood 6ft 5¾in in his ring boots and bounced the scales at 260 pounds. But he couldn't fight very well and he couldn't punch very hard. Nobody cared, New York City was fight crazy – got to see this new guy Louis, the Brown Bomber. Mike Jacobs was on a winner, with a huge crowd of 62,000 paying their way into Yankee Stadium. They got what they came to see. 'When I climbed in the ring and looked around, I saw the most people I ever saw in one place at one time,' Joe would recall. 'This was my first fight in New York and this was the night I remembered the best in all my fighting. If you was ever a raggedy kid and you come to something like that night, you'd know. I don't thrill to things like other people, I only feel good. I felt the best that night.

'Chappie said for me to work on Carnera's body until I had him weak there, with his guard down, before I try for his head. I got some hard ones in before the end of the first round. Carnera tried to scare me with his weight. In the fourth round we come into a clinch and he tries some of that weightlifting on me. I got him first. I lifted him clear and swung him around. I see his jaw come open and a funny look on his face. Before he got his jaw closed I hit him on the head and his eyes went glass. I got in more body punches in the next round. I heard his breath stick in his throat. In the sixth I got the nod from Chappie. I went after Carnera's head. I got him on the jaw again and he went down. He came up slow and wobbly and I got him with a left hook and a right cross to the head, and he went down again. He tried to pull himself up by the ropes but I could see by the way his mouth worked he wasn't coming up again. When they count my end that night it was

$60,000. Mr Roxborough told me that was the biggest money ever made by a fighter who was pro less than a year.'

'The first time I saw Louis fight,' recalled sportswriter Jimmy Cannon, 'he humiliated Primo Carnera. The knockout didn't impress me as much as the first left hook that tore Carnera's slack mouth. It ripped Carnera's high-curved upper lip and his mouth seemed to be crawling up the sides of his face in an agonized grin. The eyes in the big head rolled in terrible wonder, marvelling at the force of the blow. Ask me the way Louis punched and I'll tell you about Carnera's mouth breaking into that idiot's smile.'

Recalling the Carnera fight in a *Fight Magazine* article in 1953, Ed Linn wrote, 'Primo was sitting unattended on his rubbing table after the fight, his face still bloody, his forehead lumpy, his mouth battered out of shape, when H Allen Smith, then doing colour for the *New York World Telegram*, interviewed him. "Did he hit you hard?" Smith asked.

'Primo stared at him through narrow slits for a long minute, then lowered his lopsided head into his gloves. "Jesus God, does he hit!" he said.

'"Do you want to fight him again?" asked Smith.

'"Oh, Jesus God, no!"'

Next on Joe's hit list was King Levinsky at Chicago Stadium. Boxing writer Ted Carroll remembered 'Levinsky's abject terror just before going into the ring with Louis. So panic-stricken was the Kingfish that Mike Jacobs, fearing the Chicagoan might pass out, rushed the bout into the ring before schedule "due to weather conditions" although the night was clear as a bell.' The fight ended in the first round with Levinsky sitting on the middle rope begging the referee, 'Don't let him hit me again!'

The next big one for Louis was in September 1935 against Max Baer, who had blown his title to Jimmy Braddock three months previously in a lacklustre performance. Baer was still only twenty-six and needed to get back up there, but Maxie wasn't sure fighting Joe Louis was the right way to go. Memories of the terrible beating Louis had given Carnera still haunted Baer. Meanwhile, young Joe Louis had other things on his mind. He was in love with beautiful Marva Trotter. A few hours before his fight with Baer, Joe wed Marva at a friend's apartment in Harlem, and that night, when he climbed into the ring to fight the former champion, Marva sat in a ringside seat, surrounded by a crowd of 88,150 who had paid just over a million dollars for their seats in Yankee Stadium.

They didn't see much of a fight. Baer fought like he would rather have been somewhere else that night, and in the fourth round, Louis belted him with a left hook and a quick right to the head and Baer went down. By the time the referee counted six, Maxie was on one knee. 'Baer's on one knee, seven, eight, nine,' shouted Clem McCarthy over the NBC network, the radio rights having been bought for $27,500 by the makers of Joe's favourite car, Buick Motor Company. 'Baer is not up, and Baer is on his knees at the count of ten. Your fight is all over, your fight is all over. The boys are coming into the ring with the speed of a Buick. Of a new Buick.' Referee Arthur Donovan would later tell columnist Red Smith, 'Joe Louis had the most vicious jab I ever saw on a fighter. If Max Baer was alive, you could ask him, "Max, what did Joe's jab feel like?" He'd say, "What did it feel like? Like a bomb bursting in your face!"'

Joe and Marva didn't have much of a honeymoon. He had to start training for his fight with Paulino Uzcudun at Madison Square Garden. The veteran Spaniard was known as the Basque Woodchopper and he'd been in with the best. It was his proud boast that nobody had ever put him on the canvas, at least not until that December night in 1935. It happened in the fourth round and this was how Jimmy Cannon remembered it. 'Paulino looked up and his head came out of the cage of his arms. One punch did it. It was a right hand and Paulino was down. Gold teeth sprinkled on the dirty canvas, the way tiny charms might fall off a woman's broken bracelet. Paulino began to push himself up. His back was to Louis. But he was in another country, lost and hurt through. The boxing journalists forgot they were reporters. They stood up and shouted to referee Arthur Donovan, "Stop it!" And Donovan stopped it.'

In June 1936, America went into shock. Superman had been beaten by a mere mortal! At Yankee Stadium, Mike Jacobs had offered up another ex-champion for Louis in Max Schmeling, then in the throes of a comeback. Joe trained at Lakewood, New Jersey, but he was no longer the hungry kid fighting his way to the top. In his autobiography, Joe wrote, 'I know I'm going to win anything I want. My record speaks for itself. I married a fabulous woman, I bought a beautiful home for my mother, I'm sending my sister Vunice to Howard University, women are running me crazy. Big, important people are my friends. Shit! I can't go wrong. I got the money, I got the power.'

Ray Arcel watched Joe in training one day and was shocked at what he saw. 'Chappie,' he said to Blackburn. 'What's wrong with your fighter?'

'Ray,' answered Joe's trainer, 'he's here on his honeymoon, and she's here with him.'

Even when they sent Marva back to New York, Joe found female company impossible to resist. There was also the golf. He had got hooked on the game and would cut training short to head for the course, and Jack Blackburn was not a happy man. 'Chappie,' he warned Joe, 'that ain't good for you. The timing's different. And them muscles you use in golf, they ain't the same ones you use hitting a man. Besides, being out in the sun don't do you no good. You'll be dried out.'

Meanwhile, Max Schmeling was training hard at the Napanoch Country Club in the Catskills, his mind on one thing: beating Joe Louis. Sportswriter Harry Grayson watched him work out one day, accompanied by veteran New York promoter Tom O'Rourke, who had managed George Dixon and the original Joe Walcott. 'You should lick Louis,' the old-timer said to Max. 'All he can do is hit. Bend to your right, keep your head down and shuffle backward. Louis is the big guy. He has to come to you. He'll lean forward with a left jab. Let him lean until you get him leaning far enough and then throw your right hand like you never threw it before. Hit him anywhere on the head. He's got a glass noggin.'

On fight night, Grayson took O'Rourke to Schmeling's dressing-room before the fight and the old man repeated his advice, telling Max, 'Now remember, bend to your right and keep your head down.'

'Those were the last words Tom O'Rourke ever uttered,' Grayson would recall. 'He gasped for breath and started to crumble. Schmeling, Joe Jacobs and the trainer Max Machon helped the old gent to a rubdown table. Jacobs tried to lead Schmeling away, but Max wouldn't budge. "He's just fainted," said Jacobs. "No, Joe, he's dead," said Schmeling. It was with this knowledge that Max Schmeling went down the runway, on to the field and into the ring to face the supposed executioner, Joe Louis. He was reminded of old Dr O'Rourke's prescription from the opening bell, as Jacobs kept shouting from the corner, "Bend to your right and keep your head down."

'The puzzled Louis groped, just as old Dr O'Rourke had predicted, and after two minutes was leaning too invitingly forward with a lowered left jab for even the unimaginative Schmeling not to do something about it. A booming overhand right came like lightning from the crouch and landed smack on Louis's chin. The Detroit Tiger cat's knees buckled. He was badly hurt. Schmeling had Louis practically out on his feet ten times before Joe fell from terminal shellshock and complete exhaustion and was counted out after two minutes, twenty-nine seconds of the twelfth round. Louis, the Brown Embalmer, who, it was reckoned, would annihilate his foe, was himself embalmed in a manner that left the entire fight world gasping in amazement.'

Joe was out of the ring for two months before Jacobs brought him back via another former heavyweight champ in Jack Sharkey, on the way out and needing the money. Louis had learned his lesson, he was as sharp as a tack, and Sharkey was destroyed inside three rounds. The old Boston Gob liked to tell how he was the only man to fight both Dempsey and Louis. 'Who hit you the hardest?' Jack would be asked. He always answered, 'Well, Dempsey hit me $211,000 worth, Louis only $36,000. Those are the purses I got for those fights.'

A few weeks later Joe went in against Al Ettore in Philadelphia, which was Al's home town. But Al didn't give his fans much to cheer about as Louis cut him down in five rounds. Jorge Brescia was a highly promising Argentine heavyweight and he belted Louis clear across the ring with a sizzling right-hand shot when they met at the New York Hippodrome, but Joe blasted him out in three rounds and he was never the same again. Eddie Simms was next. Louis opened with four left jabs to Eddie's face, and when Simms moved within range Joe ripped a left hook to the chin and Eddie dropped like a stone. Up at eight, Simms asked the referee to take him up to the roof for a look at the stars! Although he was able to walk, Eddie was still unconscious. The time was just twenty-three seconds of round one.

In January 1937, New Yorker Bob Pastor gave Joe a run for his money, quite literally. Backpedalling, ducking, dodging, Bob ran like a thief for ten rounds and was still there at the final bell, well beaten, but he had snapped Joe's KO streak at nine since the Schmeling setback. Cagey veteran Natie Brown, who had defied Joe for ten rounds in their first fight, was knocked out in four when they clashed again in Kansas City. Back in New York, the news was good. Mike Jacobs had been after Schmeling to fight Joe again but the German wanted his old title back, he wanted Jim Braddock, and the New York Commission was backing him. They ordered Braddock to defend against Max in June and Schmeling went into training. But Mike Jacobs made Braddock's manager an offer he couldn't refuse and it was announced that Braddock would give Louis first crack at the title in Chicago on 22 June. Lawyers for Madison Square Garden filed a suit against Jacobs to block his fight but the court threw it out and Joe Louis went into training for the fight of his life, for the heavyweight championship of the world. Poor Max Schmeling got no further than weighing in for the fight that wasn't going to happen.

The real fight happened in Comiskey Park, Chicago, where Joe Louis climbed off the deck in the first round and knocked Jim Braddock out in eight rounds to become champ. Bill Heinz wrote a fine story on Braddock for *True Magazine* in 1958. '"Why did you try to punch with Louis?" I said. "I intended to box him," Jim said, "but in that first round I seen him get set to throw the right hand. I stepped back and naturally he come in, and I stepped in and let the right go. I didn't hit him on the chin, but he went down and I said to myself, if I hit him a good punch he'll stay down. I went after him and spent a lot of energy, and after the fourth round he started layin' it into me . . . In the sixth round, he hit me a terrific left hook in the stomach. I thought my stomach was in my mouth." At the end of the seventh, Gould wanted to stop it. He told Jim he was going to throw in the towel. "If you do," Jim said, "I'll never speak to you again as long as I live. If I'm gonna lose it, I'll lose it on the deck." He walked out and carried the fight to Louis and Joe finished him in one minute, ten seconds of that next round. When the last right hand went in, Jim pitched forward on his face and as the referee counted over him, he lay there in a growing pool of his own blood.'

At twenty-three, Joe Louis, the Detroit Brown Bomber, had become the youngest heavyweight champion of the world since John L Sullivan used gloves instead of his bare fists to fight Jim Corbett. Louis would be champion as long as he wanted to be, which was eleven years and eight months, longer than any other champion. He would defend his title twenty-five times, more than any other champion. Only three of those challengers made it to the final bell, and two of them were knocked out in return bouts. Jacobs didn't let Joe go rusty. In the past seven years there had been only seven heavyweight title fights. At one stage in his career, Louis fought off seven challengers in seven months.

Two months after beating Braddock, Joe gave a title shot to the tough Welshman Tommy Farr. Farr had won the British championship and beaten Max Baer and Walter Neusel in London, and when moves were made to put him in with Schmeling, Jacobs grabbed Tommy and offered him Joe Louis. Farr was dismissed by the American press, one writer suggesting he had as much chance against Louis as Shirley Temple! Tommy made them change their tune, battling the Bomber for fifteen rounds to a decision.

Tommy took the best Joe threw at him. He remembered some of them in what was almost an unlucky thirteenth round. There was a tremendous right uppercut – Tommy said he had never been hit harder, before or since, adding with his quaint humour, 'If I had been rubber, I would have starved to death bouncing!' Then a right to the jaw that had 'everything in that punch, short of murder. It sent red hot needles into my throat and I feared I would suffocate.' Another thudding right to the forehead shook Tommy, who would recall, 'I feared my spine was broken.'

Joe knocked out Nathan Mann and Harry Thomas, but there was one fight he wanted more than any other. He reckoned he wasn't the real champion until he had avenged the Schmeling defeat. It was June

1938 and Hitler sent Max Schmeling to New York as a prime example of Aryan supremacy . . . his mission, to whip the black man and bring the world championship home to Germany. It proved to be Mission Impossible. Before a baying crowd of 70,000 in that New York ball park, Joe Louis annihilated Schmeling in two minutes, four seconds.

'The first punches Louis reached him with were jabs,' wrote Jimmy Cannon. 'They made Schmeling's neck jerk as though he had run into an invisible wire. Louis never paused after that. Schmeling screamed and turned his back to Joe, holding on to the ropes. Louis had a fury which is seldom seen in the ring. It was a calculated rage and one controlled by intelligence. If ever a fighter made a perfect fight Joe did that night.' Bill Corum wrote that Louis had 'reduced a proud and perfectly trained athlete into a quivering, quaking, beaten old man.'

Now Joe Louis felt like the champion of the world, and now he lived like it. As well as being a perfect physical specimen, Joe was a prodigious sexual athlete. In his book *Joe Louis, The Great Black Hope*, author Richard Bak wrote, 'Joe was an equal-opportunity lover, bedding down waitresses, actresses, models, cigarette girls, singers, secretaries, showgirls and society mavens of every race, shape and creed . . . Joe's handlers cared about his sexual exploits only to the degree that they worried he might become the victim of a blackmail plot. Mike Jacobs was always trying to get his fighter to choose a downtown hotel for his dalliances, but Joe preferred staying at all-black establishments like Harlem's Theresa or at one of his friends' apartments where he could cavort in relative anonymity.'

There would be affairs with Hollywood headliners such as Lena Horne, Sonja Henie and Lana Turner, but discretion had been drummed into Joe by Roxborough and Black and there were no headlines such as Jack Johnson stirred up during his time at the top. 'We respected an athlete's private life,' said Washington sportswriter Shirley Povich. 'Joe was a womaniser, a lot of us knew that or had heard the rumours, but we didn't write anything about it, just like we didn't write certain things about Babe Ruth and other sports figures. They were the mores of the time. The feeling was that it was none of the public's business.'

When Louis hung up his gloves, Nat Fleischer reckoned his total earnings had amounted to $4,626,721. But he spent freely, on himself and others. Lester Bromberg, boxing writer for the *New York World Telegram and Sun*, wrote in 1963, 'There is no doubt Joe Louis still holds the record for the variety and voraciousness of camp-following chisellers. When he was new to big money and carried big wads of bills around with him, he rarely bothered to note how much he started a day with. Or finished with. The heels would see him home, insist on staying with him. While he slept, they virtually cleaned out his pockets. His ample wardrobe would be a target, too. Shirts, suits, sweaters, shoes, for their own use or resale. Later the circle of bums widened but Joe was no more discerning. Fly-by-night producers of nightclub shows tapped him for $10,000 or $15,000 as a "loan". Golf had become his favourite pastime and though he developed considerable skill, he wasn't as good as he hoped to be. Professional golf hustlers hit him and there were days when he lost enough to have bought an interest in a country club.'

There was always another fight, and another payday. In June 1939 they matched Joe with a little fat guy named Tony Galento, a New Jersey saloonkeeper who was his own best customer. But 'Two-Ton' Tony could fight, and he had a left hook that could take your head off. Going in with the champion, Galento kept muttering, 'I'll moider da bum!' He opened with a left hook that knocked Louis against the ropes, but in the second Joe thrashed him and dumped him with a right-left combination. Round three was sensational. Tony rushed Louis to the ropes, the referee separated them, and as Joe looked to throw the right, Galento's wild left hook smashed against his temple and knocked him down. 'Dumb' Dan Morgan recalled, 'The crowd was screaming like madmen. This thing couldn't happen. This freakish fat man could not possibly lick Joe Louis. We'll never know. Joe Jacobs screamed for Tony to keep his head, but it was like trying to win an argument with your mother-in-law. Tony always thought Louis was a bum, now he knew it. He would knock the bum out. You know what happened. Louis got off the floor, tore into the over-anxious Galento and knocked him out in the following round.'

London sportswriter Peter Wilson was in New York for the fight and this is what he reported of the fourth round. 'The most terrifying moment came when a barrage of lefts and rights dislodged the two collodion packs protecting Galento's eyebrows. Women screamed as first one then the other was sent flying high against the arc lights by the mahogany mallets which Louis called his fists. For, in truth, it really looked, under the lamps, as though Tony's eyebrows had been cut away from his face. Although he was trying to fight back, you could see the energy draining out of Galento like sugar out of a split sack . . . When a left hook ripped his mouth even wider open, women screamed again, for it seemed certain that a blood vessel had been severed.'

Arturo Godoy was a tough South American from Chile who embarrassed Louis with a crouching, weaving style in Madison Square Garden and became one of only three men to last the fifteen rounds with the Brown Bomber. Jacobs put them together again a few months later, in Yankee Stadium, and Joe was taking no prisoners this night. Godoy boasted he had never been floored in sixty-five fights, and in a publicity stunt a burly lumberjack hit him in the stomach with an eight-pound sledge hammer and couldn't budge him. But Joe Louis's dynamic fists did the trick. By round seven the Chilean was a mess, one eye shut, bleeding from the mouth and the other eye, and the bell saved him from a knockout. They sent him out for the eighth but the Bomber was on target now and after two more knockdowns it was stopped.

The message was clear: never fight Joe Louis twice. 'Louis did funny things to people he fought,' recalled trainer Ray Arcel. 'They never forgot it the second time around. He left something with you.' Willie Davis, Lee Ramage, Natie Brown, Max Schmeling, Bob Pastor, Arturo Godoy, Abe Simon, Buddy Baer, Billy Conn, Jersey Joe Walcott – they would all regret having a second helping of what Louis dished out.'

In December 1940, war was raging in Europe and Mike Jacobs figured it wouldn't be too long before America entered the conflict. He lined up what one of the sportswriters called the Bum of the Month Club, with Louis putting the title on the line against seven challengers in seven months: Al McCoy in Boston, KO six rounds; Red Burman in New York, KO five rounds; Gus Dorazio in Philadelphia, KO two rounds; Abe Simon in Detroit, KO thirteen rounds; Tony Musto in St Louis, KO nine rounds; Buddy Baer in Washington, DC, disqualified for not answering the bell for round seven after claiming Louis had hit him after the bell ending the sixth. Buddy, Maxie's bigger, younger brother, had popped Joe through the ropes in the first with a left hook, but paid for it over the next few rounds.

Challenger number seven was Billy Conn, in New York. He was no bum. The handsome Pittsburgh Irishman had given up the light-heavyweight title to campaign as a heavyweight and had beaten Lee Savold and Bob Pastor to earn his shot at the big title, although he was never more than a light-heavyweight. His weight that June night in 1941 when he faced Louis at the Polo Grounds was announced as 174 pounds, and it helped him give Joe a tough time for twelve rounds, outjabbing Louis to level the scoring going into the fateful thirteenth round. Some even had Billy out in front – if he could keep moving for another three rounds he could be the new champ. But

Conn wanted to knock Joe out. Mistake! Louis tagged him with a barrage of punches and it was all over.

'Do you know who had the best chance to lick Louis of anybody I worked with?' trainer Ray Arcel asked writer Bill Heinz. 'Lou Nova. When Nova was matched with Louis, we went up to the Maine woods for a month. When we came back we went into the Pioneer Gym to work out for the newspapermen, and when they got a look at him I think the same thought must have crossed their minds that crossed mine. How was even Louis going to lick a man like this? We pitched camp in Pompton Lakes and there was a man in camp by the name of Walston Crocker Brown who used to talk to Nova about something called the Cosmic Theory and the Dynamic Stance. When the fight was drawing close, I could see something was happening to Nova, it was like the day of execution was drawing near, and he was like a guy doomed to die in the electric chair . . . Louis came out in a crouch, and Nova was up too straight and too stiff, and it was the worst fight you ever saw in your life. Nova was so tense that once he got his feet crossed, and Louis had to smile. Near the end of the sixth, Louis hit him with a right and he went down. When Nova got up, Arthur Donovan had counted him out.'

In December 1941, Japanese aircraft attacked Pearl Harbour and America was at war. A month later Joe Louis defended his title in the Garden, knocking out Buddy Baer in one round, and donated his purse to the Navy Relief Fund. The next day, Joe Louis, the million-dollar champ, became a $21-a-month private in the US Army. In March 1942 he hammered big Abe Simon inside six rounds and gave his purse to the Army Relief Fund. Then he put the title on ice. By the time he got out of uniform, Joe had travelled some 70,000 miles, from Alaska to Italy, France, North Africa and Britain, giving exhibitions and talks to some five million servicemen. They gave him the Legion of Merit Medal.

It was 1946 and Joe Louis was still heavyweight champion of the world. The contract he had with Roxborough and Black had expired, and in any case the former was in prison. Old Chappie Blackburn was dead, and when Uncle Mike took over from Uncle Sam, Mannie Seamon stepped in as Joe's trainer. There was a fight to get ready for. Billy Conn wanted a second chance at the title, but even he couldn't buck that return fight jinx. With ringside seats at $100, the gate at Yankee Stadium hit $1,925,564, eclipsed only by the second Tunney-Dempsey fight in 1927. But it wasn't a very good fight and this time Louis caught up with Billy in round eight.

Next came Tami Mauriello, a tough guy from the Bronx who was Frank Sinatra's favourite fighter. Arthur Donovan, who refereed twelve of Joe's twenty-five title defences, would say to columnist Red Smith, 'Remember the night Tami Mauriello hit Louis the first punch and if it hadn't of been for the ropes Louis would have gone down? That Italian boy could hit. They said I got in the way, but what was I supposed to do? Take him by the arm and say, "Hit him again"? He was so shocked himself he didn't know what to do and just stood off five or six feet. Finally Joe came off the ropes punching, and that was that.'

In December 1947, in Madison Square Garden, a washed-up old guy named Jersey Joe Walcott knocked Louis down in the first and fourth rounds and came out with referee Ruby Goldstein's vote, seven rounds to six with two even. But Christmas hadn't come early for Walcott, as the other two judges voted for Joe, winner and still champion. And when they fought again in June 1948, Louis knocked Jersey Joe out in round eleven and announced his retirement from boxing.

But like so many old champions, he came back. Ezzard Charles, a fine fighter, had beaten Walcott and was recognized by the National Boxing Association as champion, but he was in the Bomber's shadow, as was Tunney all those years ago when he licked Dempsey. They talked Joe into a comeback and in September 1950 the thirty-six-year old former champion, balding and paunchy, was beaten up by Charles at Yankee Stadium.

Many years later, Joe told me he didn't regret his comeback. 'I thought I had a real good chance of being champ again. But I wanted four to five months to really get into condition for the Charles fight. They wanted the fight outdoors and there wasn't time. That's why Charles beat me. He wasn't a great fighter, just had better condition, that's all.'

The curtain came down when Louis was knocked out in eight rounds by Rocky Marciano. Recalling that night in Madison Square Garden, Red Smith wrote, 'This was an hour before midnight of 26 October 1951. It had been the evening of a day that dawned 4 July 1934 when Joe Louis became a professional fist fighter and knocked out Jack Kracken in Chicago for a $50 purse. The night was a long time on the way, but it had to come . . . A young man, Rocky Marciano, knocked the old man out . . . An old man's dream ended. A young man's vision of the future opened wide. Young men have visions, old men have dreams. But the place for old men to dream is beside the fire.'

When Joe Louis died on 12 April 1981, aged sixty-seven, Dave Anderson wrote in the New York Times, 'Shortly after Pearl Harbour, on 9 January 1942, the reigning world heavyweight boxing champion, Joe Louis, defended his title against Buddy Baer at Madison Square Garden. He knocked out Baer in the first round and, as he had promised, donated his $65,200 purse to the Naval Relief Fund. Not long after that, on 27 March, he again defended his title at the Garden for free. This time he knocked out Abe Simon in the sixth round and contributed $45,882 to the Army Relief Fund. "How does it feel," somebody asked him at the time, "to be fighting for nothing?"

'"I ain't fighting for nothing," he replied. "I'm fighting for my country."

'Put that on Joe Louis's tombstone in Arlington National Cemetery where he was buried Tuesday . . . When he entered the Army, he owed $98,000 to the Internal Revenue Service because of shoddy accounting advice. Within a decade, interest and penalties pushed his debt to more than $1 million, a debt that the IRS eventually forgave. But at the time of his original $98,000 debt, the IRS never took into account the $110,000 that Louis had contributed to the two service relief funds from his 1942 title bouts. If it had, the government would have owed Louis some money. Maybe that's what President Reagan remembered when he decreed that an old corporal could be buried in Arlington.'

# The Texas Mustang 10

'The one-punch knockout is to boxing what the home run is to baseball and the hole-in-one is to golf,' wrote Mike Pepper in a 1955 magazine article. 'A thing of beauty, more often the result of perfect timing and co-ordination than luck. No one who watched runtish Lew Jenkins, 135 pounds of skinny flesh and bones, go through his paces can ever forget the feverish anxiety he generated in a fight arena. When Sweetwater Lew stood in a prize ring, naked from the waist up and with a pair of red leather gloves wrapped over his protruding knuckles, the possibility of a perfect knockout was ever present.

'With the possible exception of Aurelio Herrera, there never was a more deadly-hitting lightweight than Lew Jenkins. Some will argue, insisting that Lew Tendler's ferocious left hook had greater power than Jenkins's right, or that Charley White's savage hook was a more destructive weapon than either, but I doubt if Tendler or White ever hit a man harder than Jenkins hit Lou Ambers in 1940. Ambers caught a right just under his mouth and actually bounced when he struck the canvas. Herkimer Lou was lightweight champion on the way down, but when Al Weill picked him up ten seconds later he was the ex-champ. I consider the punch that knocked Ambers out one of the ten deadliest of all time.'

Lew Jenkins knocked out Lou Ambers in three rounds to become world lightweight champion in May 1940, and six months later, when he turned back the challenge of Pete Lello inside two rounds, veteran Hype Igoe wrote in *The Ring* magazine, 'When Lew Jenkins popped Pete Lello on the button and knocked him out in the first defence of Lew's lightweight title, the old-timers about the ring rubbed their chins and asked themselves if this skinny, hollow-cheeked Texas cavalryman didn't belong among the quick finishers of all time. No question about the Jenkins punch. There is no doubt about his having earned the right to have his name enrolled among the best punchers in lightweight history. Once Jenkins tags a man, cleanly, the show is over. All that remains is to come in and pick up the victim.

'To look at Jenkins before he goes into the ring, one would have a feeling of pity for the fellow. Nature has made him scrawny. He has dicky-bird legs and there isn't a wasted ounce of flesh on his bones. In all my experience, I can't recall anyone like him in structure, unless it was "Spider" Welsh, the San Francisco "Pieman". The Spider looked enough like Jenkins to be his twin brother and, like Jenkins, the Pieman could punch.'

Boxing writer Ted Carroll said, 'Many smart boxing people insist that Lew Jenkins had everything it took to become a stand-out lightweight champion. It's a cinch that few men his weight could hit any harder.'

Welterweight champion Fritzie Zivic fought Lew Jenkins twice. 'Jenkins was one of the gamest guys in the world,' he said. 'He couldn't fight too much, but what a dynamite puncher! When he made a fist, never seen to this day knuckles, they stuck out this big. And when he put his gloves on, I found out later, he'd push the pads back so when you got hit with his punch, all he had was a little bit of leather in between there. He hit me in the forehead in the first fight, and I thought the building fell on me. If he'd hit me on the chin he'd have knocked me cold.'

'I could punch hard as a heavyweight, you know,' Lew would say. 'I loved to throw that right hand and watch those guys wilt. I never will forget, Chalky Wright watched me around the gym for several weeks. Then finally we started using him for a sparring partner. He said, "I been watching Lew throw that right hand. I watched you do that for months around here. I swore you couldn't hit me with it." And the first thing, I had him down! He couldn't believe it. And he was a good fighter.'

Lew Jenkins was a good fighter, too. He was born Elmer Verlin Jenkins in Milburn, Texas, on 4 December 1916, one of seven kids. 'We came from a poor family,' he told author Peter Heller for his book *In This Corner*. 'There was no money around. It was during the Depression. I grew up picking cotton. That was one of the most horrible jobs a man can do, pick cotton. A miserable job. Your hands chap and bleed from the burrs sticking into your fingers. Daylight till dark. I mean, humped over all day dragging fifty, sixty pounds behind you. Oh, man, a backbreaking job.'

Young Jenkins first became interested in boxing in 1926 in Brownwood, where his father was a blacksmith. His father took him downtown to listen to a radio broadcast of the first Gene Tunney-Jack Dempsey fight, and when they moved to Sweetwater the kid fought on street corners and they called him 'Dempsey' because he hit so hard with his right hand. After his father drank himself to death in 1932, Lew started boxing with the TJ Tidwell carnival which wintered in Sweetwater. Always hungry and dirty through the Depression years, he finally enlisted in the US Cavalry at Fort Bliss after getting out of jail for beating up some guy.

'When I was in the Army making twenty-one dollars a month and ten of that going home,' he told Heller, 'I had to do something when I went on furlough, so I took boxing up as a profession then. I went out on a sixty-day furlough, went to Dallas. I had six straight knockouts on my leave. I went back, got out and ran it up to nine straight KOs.'

Fighting around Dallas, Lew met and fell in love with Katie Jenkins, whose name he didn't have to change when he married her shortly afterwards. Theirs was a stormy relationship. She caught him out one night in a bar with another woman and threw a heavy water glass at him, cutting his left cheek. When he came back from the hospital, Katie refused to open the door to their hotel room. Still drunk, Lew took a run at it, crashing through, leaving his outline behind him on the door. Katie promptly smacked him with an ashtray, knocking loose his fresh stitches. But she loved the guy and she knew he could fight, and in the summer of 1939 Katie pawned her watch for sixty dollars, Lew bought an old beat-up Model A Ford and they drove all the way to New York City. They hit the Big Town in June with eight dollars between them and found an apartment on the West Side. They lived on Bologna sandwiches and Lew walked the fifty blocks to Stillman's Gym on Eighth Avenue every day to work out. Willie Ketchum, who would become Lew's trainer, told writer Bill Heinz, 'When he first came into Stillman's, he didn't look like anything.'

In the *New York World Telegram*, Joe Williams wrote, 'Jenkins looks about as much like a fighter as a Bohemian free-verse writer. A starved cannibal wouldn't take a second look at him. He has a hatchet face, a head of wild, stringy hair, and deep sunken eyes that seem to be continuously startled.'

The new kid in town did have something going for him, however, besides a right-hand punch that was like a kick from one of his Daddy's old mules. Katie Jenkins had been racing stock cars in the Texas carnivals when she met Lew, and she worked in his corner when he was fighting his way around the West and Middle West. In New York, the Boxing Commission wouldn't let her go in Lew's corner, but she helped with publicity. She looked like a movie star and the papers went for her in a big way.

Manager Frank Bachman, who had Maxie Rosenbloom, the light-heavyweight champion, had negotiated Lew's contract with Fred Browning, his Texas manager, and he booked Jenkins into the Queensboro Arena. The date was 18 July 1939 and this was how it was reported in *The Ring* magazine. 'Lew Jenkins, Texas lightweight, made his debut at the Queensboro Arena and while winning the official verdict over Baby Breese in their eight-round bout, he was hardly entitled to the award. Breese was rough in spots and fought without any regard for the rules, which may have militated against him. Jenkins was floored in the sixth round and he showed his gameness when the occasion demanded, but the decision did not belong to him.'

'You can hit all right,' said manager Bachman in the dressing-room afterwards, 'but you died in there.'

'I was hungry, man,' said Lew in his Texas drawl. Bachman saw to it that his new boy had a hotel room and started eating regularly. Two weeks later he whipped Brooklyn's Joey Fontana in eight rounds. Lew had Joey on the deck in the first round and again in the fourth, but couldn't keep him there. Then he got Baby Breese again and this time Lew gave him a beating. He knocked out Liverpool veteran Ginger Foran and Primo Flores, then took Flores again at the Bronx Coliseum. Flores, a rugged Puerto Rican, gave Lew a torrid time of it but in the fifth round, the Texan connected with a savage right and Primo was finished for the night. In the dressing-room, a reporter said to Lew, 'I thought you were going to get knocked out until you nailed him.' Jenkins opened his eyes wide, then gasped, 'You mean I knocked him out?'

Top sports photographer Sam Andre had been on the boxing beat ten years when Lew and Katie Jenkins hit New York, and after Lew had won six fights in a row, three by knockout, Sam saw the possibility of a good picture story. Lew was matched with Mike Belloise at the New York Coliseum and Sam was there with his cameras when the first bell rang. For seven rounds, Belloise gave Lew a stiff argument, with Katie yelling from her ringside seat accompanied by New York Giants fullback Nello Falaschi. One of Lew's Texas specials fractured Mike's ribs in the seventh round and the New Yorker almost collapsed when he tried to come out for round eight. The doctor refused to allow Mike to continue, Lew had his most important victory, and Sam had his picture story.

'Belloise wasn't too rough,' Lew told Heller. 'He was a good little boxer, but that's when I first realized, I quit smoking for two or three weeks, trained for that fight and I was in good shape for that fight. But I smoked all my life and that was the hardest thing on me, smoking. That was my reason for losing a lot of fights. They said there was no way in the world I could win the fight, the newspapers and everybody that knew me. I knew that I would. I knew it! I got drunk before the fight for a few days. But I knew, at that time, '39 and the first part of '40, nobody could beat me because I was just like a spring. Lightweights didn't have a chance with me.'

By this time Lew had a new manager, Hymie Caplan, who promised him a fight in Madison Square Garden. Hymie had managed four world champs in Ben Jeby, Al Singer, Lou Salica and Solly Krieger, but they were choirboys compared to this wild Texas Mustang. Lew had already signed himself into the Garden, against Billy Marquart. Telling the story in his marvellous book *Once They Heard the Cheers*, Bill

Heinz related, 'Jack Hurley had Marquart, who was another of those hands-down, walk-in left hookers like all of Jack's fighters, and he could hit. "Are you out of your mind?" Hymie screamed at Lew when he heard about it. "This guy is a murderous puncher. He'll kill you."

'"I'll kill *him*," Lew said. "This is gonna be a short trip. I'll knock this guy out so they'll have to give me a fight for the title."

'"You're crazy,' Hymie said, and tried to get out of the match. The contract had Lew's signature on it, though, and on the night of the fight, Marquart was a nine-to-five favourite. "Never mind," Hymie said to Lew in the dressing-room. "Don't worry if he knocks you out, because we'll start building you up again."

'"Ain't this awful," Lew said, and he looked around the room. "There ain't anybody here believes in me. I'm the lone man who believes." Eddie Joseph was the referee that night, and once he had to pull Lew off Marquart while Marquart was through the ropes and going down. It ended in the third with Joseph holding Lew off with one hand and counting Marquart out with the other.'

There was almost a full house at the Garden that night, 17,116 for a good card headed by popular slugger Al 'Bummy' Davis against Tippy Larkin. Reporting for *The Ring*, Eddie Borden wrote, 'Billy Marquart received a tough break in his affair with Lew Jenkins. He looked the better man but his opponent took advantage of "sneak" punches and was credited with a knockout in the third. Marquart had his opponent on the run all the way but ran into an unexpected right which put him on the floor for five. When he arose he was floored again and upon rising at the count of nine, as he thought, referee Eddie Joseph informed him that he was counted out. It did not look like Billy could have gone much longer anyway.'

That stunning victory put Lew Jenkins in the number nine spot in *The Ring* magazine's monthly ratings. With Christmas just ten days away, Lew and Katie headed home to Dallas in style; new clothes, new car. He was drunk most of the time, and a fight with old rival Chino Alvarez helped pay his bar bill. Alvarez had stopped Lew in 1938 but this time it took Lew just two punches to gain sweet revenge. Then they were back to New York. Hymie had a fight for him with Tippy Larkin in the Garden.

In his last fight in the Eighth Avenue arena, Larkin had boxed Bummy Davis silly for four rounds, but Davis got to him in the fifth with a savage hook and Tippy was finished for the night. Now they were bringing him back against Texas Lew Jenkins, and all this guy could do was punch! It was all over in two minutes, forty-one seconds of round one. Larkin was a smart boxer with a sharp punch but Lew told Willie he was going to knock him out.

'Hold the right hand,' counselled Ketchum. 'Go with your jab, he won't be expecting that. Then, when you got him confused, give him the right.' So Lew went out at the opening bell and he jabbed Tippy once, twice, three times, then he threw the right straight from the shoulder. As Larkin started to fall, Lew hit him with a hook, a right and another hook. Face down under the ropes, Larkin never moved. In the dressing-room, a jubilant Jenkins told the press, 'That man was the most convinced knocked-out man I ever knocked out!'

Mike Jacobs told Katie that her husband would be fighting Lou Ambers for the world title in two months' time. 'Get him here in shape,' rasped Mike, 'and you'll be married to a champion.' The Big Town was buzzing about this skinny sensation with the big punch, but the bookies couldn't see him beating Lou Ambers. The man they called the Herkimer Hurricane had licked guys like Canzoneri, Armstrong and Zivic, and had never been knocked out in one hundred pro fights; only Armstrong had decked him. He was three-to-one on to beat Jenkins in Madison Square Garden that night in May 1940.

'The first fight for the championship with Lou Ambers,' recalled Lew, 'I trained. I trained very good, but a week before, I broke all the rules. I did a lot of things. All the rules that you could break, I broke. Screwing, the whole goddamn thing. I couldn't go no further. I'd been on that training long enough.' The night before the fight, Willie Ketchum walked Lew around the block after dinner. They had done one circuit when Lew said to Willie, 'Go inside, you might catch cold. I'll go round once more and follow you up.' The next time Willie saw his fighter, dawn was breaking over the city and Lew was drunk. Willie got him to bed and let him sleep until the weigh-in. Lew scaled 132 pounds easily, while the champion barely made the 135-pound limit. But the smart money still figured Lou could take Lew.

The fight was about a minute old when Jenkins stunned Ambers with a left and a right to the chin, then another right high on the head, and the champion of the world was sitting on the canvas wondering what the hell hit him. Lou came up at five and he let Jenkins take him to the ropes, where he fiddled his way through to the bell.

Lester Bromberg of the *New York World Telegram and Sun* recorded, 'In the second Ambers started with a supercharge of speed. He went left, he went right. He was under, he was around. But beady-eyed Jenkins did not attempt to match his agility. He watched Ambers, in the words of Cas Adams, *Herald Tribune* fight writer, "like one of Frank Buck's famished leopards". Then, in a fast strike, Jenkins sent over a left hook. It clipped Ambers hard. He flopped to the floor. Again he got up at five. He was hurt but unruffled, and it was no shock that he was able to finish the round . . . Early in the third, Jenkins was scoring again, both hands drum-firing Ambers' head. Now he set his gauge again for a big single shot, one right hand to the jaw, then another. Lou was on the floor a third time. He was weaving erect at six. Again he was at the ropes but he was too far gone to weave or slip. A literal downpour of leather caught him. He fell to the floor. Up again, the punishment-generated stupor had him in its grip, and he could not have seen Jenkins winding up with another right to the head. When it crashed in on Lou, his limp body flew all the way across the ring and he landed against the ropes in his own corner. His legs were quavering and quivering. His hands were not where a fighter's ought to be for self-defence. Referee Billy Cavanagh stepped in without hesitation. The new champion had gotten his credentials at one minute, twenty-nine seconds in the round. Eleven months after Lew Jenkins had hit New York, broke, unknown and undernourished, he was the lightweight champion of the world. Hell, this was easy. A guy doesn't need to train, just show up on the night, hit them with the right hand, and pick up the cheque next morning!'

'If I'd had any type of an education at all,' Jenkins told author Pete Heller, 'I'd have stuck some money down in my socks. I went through all of it, a lot of money in those days. I used to make fifteen to twenty-five thousand dollars a fight. It's hard to explain, but you just spend it. I could go out and spend eight hundred, a thousand dollars a night. Whiskey was three dollars a bottle for Canadian Club in them days. I paid for everything. Always picked up all the bills. I was the champ. Cadillacs, I had about nine of them in 1940, four motorcycles, an airplane and two racehorses.'

Mike Jacobs now offered Lew a crack at Henry Armstrong, who was the welterweight champion; a non-title bout, but Lew liked the idea. He liked the $25,000 purse he would be getting for this fight, outdoors at the Polo Grounds, and they took him up to Grossingers to train. 'I wasn't training, no way,' he told Heller. 'Staying up all night, all them women. I couldn't even do no roadwork. I wasn't getting no sleep. I'd get up about nine o'clock in the morning, run a half mile or walk. I walked out, moved into town. I should have beat Armstrong. I must have got hurt very early. I was too small for them guys, really, and I couldn't get any bigger.'

A crowd of 23,306 turned out for the fight. Jenkins didn't do badly for three rounds, but he couldn't nail Henry's bobbing head with that right hand and by round four, Armstrong was in top gear and he rolled over the Texan. Lew was on the canvas in the fourth, twice in the fifth, three times in the sixth, and when he sat on his stool gasping at the end of the round, referee Donovan took one look at him and stopped the fight. 'How'm I doin'?' Lew kept asking Hymie in the dressing-room. 'What round did I get him in?' He couldn't believe Armstrong had beaten him.

They matched him with local boy Bob Montgomery in Philadelphia but near the fight, Lew had to go home to see his mother, who was dying. Then Hymie phoned to say if he didn't show up for the fight he would be suspended, so Lew set off in his new convertible with another fighter, Eddie Carroll. Eddie was driving when he fell asleep at the wheel and rolled the car off the road. Luckily it wedged against a tree and Lew was thrown clear. He had a couple of cuts and his hip didn't feel right, but he turned up in Philadelphia a few days before the fight.

'Hymie Caplan had come in from New York,' related Bill Heinz. 'He waited until Lew had gone into the bathroom. "Willie," he said, "what kind of shape is he in?"

'"What shape can he be in?" Willie said. "He's lucky if he can climb up the steps to the ring."

'In the third round, Lew was on the floor. He had just belted Montgomery with a right to the body and Montgomery had hit him with a long right on the chin, and he was face down on the canvas . . . He got up at nine, punching. He hurt Montgomery with a right hand and Montgomery went into a shell. While he was in the shell, he kept walking at Lew, and Willie said that if Montgomery had just walked away, Lew would have fallen on his face.

'"Lew," Willie said to him after the ninth, "it's the last round. That guy just about got to his corner."

'"I know," Lew said, gasping, "but I can't get off this stool." Willie lifted him off and pushed him out. Halfway through the round, Lew was bleeding from the nose and mouth, but he kept throwing punches, and they wrote on the sports pages later that this was the most savage fight in Philadelphia since Lew Tendler and Willie Jackson fifteen years before.

'"At the end," Willie was telling me, "the referee walks over and he lifts Lew's hand and he says, 'The winner, Lew Jenkins!' I just stood there and I said to myself, did I see this thing, can it be true with his hip and his knee and the way he's living?"'

In November 1940 Lew made the first defence of his lightweight championship against Pete Lello, who had stopped him in seven rounds in a Chicago fight eighteen months before. Hymie had Lew at Pompton Lakes in New Jersey, and Allie Stolz, himself a good lightweight, recalled those crazy days at camp. 'He'd disappear,' Allie said, 'and he'd be gone three or four days. He had three motorcycles then, one for straight speeding, one for hill climbing and one that, so help me, ran in curves and circles. One day, we heard a terrific clatter out on the road past the camp and there was Lew, riding at the head of about fifty guys on motorcycles and waving to us as they roared past.'

Hymie Caplan wasn't with Lew that night in the Garden. He had been arrested that afternoon and was being held in what the District Attorney called a $4 million marked-card swindle. Bill Heinz wrote that, 'Hymie went to Sing-Sing, but the word around New York was that he took the fall for somebody else.' Before he went into the ring that night, Lew managed to get a telephone call through to Caplan in the Brooklyn hotel where he was being held, saying, 'Listen, Hymie, when you hear the building shake, that's Lello hittin' the floor!'

'Lello hit the floor in the second round,' related Heinz. 'They were coming out of a clinch and Lew threw a hook and Lello started down. Lew was on top of him, and he came back with a right as Lello was going. Lello rolled over on the canvas and got up at nine. When he did, Arthur Donovan moved in to wipe Lello's gloves, and as he lifted them, Lew belted Lello with another right and he went down again. He was down three more times and was on his knees in Lew's corner, about to pitch forward on his face, when Donovan stopped it. "Did you miss Hymie?" one of the newspaper men asked Lew in the dressing-room.

'"I missed Hymie," Lew said, "but I didn't miss Lello."'

'Against Lello,' Dan Parker wrote in the *New York Daily Mirror*, 'Jenkins looked like a great champion. Certainly no lightweight within the memory of this present generation of fans could hit like this bag of bones.'

Lew set some kind of record when he fought three successive welterweight champions with none of them risking their titles. Henry Armstrong had stopped Lew, then lost his title to Fritzie Zivic. Uncle Mike put Lew in the Garden with the Pittsburgh hard man and they fought a savage draw over ten rounds, one official for Jenkins, one for Zivic, the third for a draw. Caswell Adams wrote in the *New York Herald Tribune*, 'Here were two youngsters in perfect condition and with the sole idea of knocking the other fellow out.' Mr Adams was obviously unaware of the fact that Lew Jenkins was in a Broadway saloon at three that morning boozing it up with some Texas pals.

Lew lost to Freddie 'Red' Cochrane, who had taken the title from Zivic, in another Garden fight that the Texan nearly didn't make. Red Smith wrote, 'When he was lightweight champion of the world, and Red Cochrane, the welterweight champion, knocked him down five times in a non-title fight in Madison Square Garden, the press declared that he was a disgrace to himself, to the title he held, and to the whole fight game . . . They didn't know that he had trained for the Cochrane fight in a New Jersey nightclub, drinking with the band. Not long before the fight date, he left the club about three in the morning and got on his motorcycle to find an all-night spot. Dead drunk, he crashed into a traffic island and woke up in hospital with his neck, back and arms taped. He had them carry him back to training camp at Pompton Lakes, where he stripped off the tape and tried to train, but he had three broken vertebrae in his neck.'

When Lou Ambers lost his lightweight title to Jenkins, he wasn't convinced Lew had his number. 'I begged Al Weill after the first Jenkins fight,' said Lou, 'to give me one more chance. I promised him that if I lost a second time, I'd quit fighting.' Ambers was Whitey Bimstein's favourite fighter. 'There was the best fighter a guy could train,' he said. 'You didn't have to drive him. I remember when he was going to fight Lew Jenkins the second time that Al Weill wasn't too sure he wanted Ambers to keep fighting. Weill said to me to watch Ambers close. I did, and told Al he didn't have much left. Weill went to Ambers and told him, "Lou, maybe you shouldn't fight Jenkins." Do you know what? Ambers cried and said he wanted to fight. He knew he could lick Jenkins, even if he got knocked out the first time. Cried like a baby, and Weill got soft and let him go. He got knocked out. It was too bad.'

Many years later, in 1980, Ambers and Jenkins met at an old-timers' convention. 'When my husband introduced me to Lew Jenkins,' recalled Margaret Ambers, 'I said, "Hey, Lew, do you still have that lucky punch?" Then his wife said, "He did it twice." So I almost got in a big argument with her. I told her that it really was a lucky punch, because he never actually knocked out Lou. The fights were stopped. Al Weill threw in the towel in the second fight.'

Lucky punch or not, Lew Jenkins certainly had a lucky charm. When he lost his title to Sammy Angott in December 1941, he had survived yet another motorcycle smash, in which he fractured his neck. On the day of the fight in the Garden, he removed the brace but every time he tried to throw the right hand, the pain surged through his entire body. Sammy Angott clinched so much the writers called him 'The Clutch', but with Lew's right-hand bomb defused, he won practically every round that night to take the title.

By that time, Katie had divorced Lew and the two homes he had in Texas and in Florida were gone. With his title also gone, Lew fought off and on for another nine years, and when he wasn't fighting in a ring somewhere, he was fighting in a war. He served on a US Coast Guard landing craft in World War II, putting troops ashore in Sicily, Normandy and Burma, and was in the Army for the Korean War. That was when he stopped drinking.

'I met my second wife Lupie when I was stationed at Camp Stoneman in 1947,' said Lew in a 1969 interview. 'That's the year we were married. In the Korean War, when I got cut off in the infantry, everybody else in the damn outfit got killed but me, and, brother, I straightened out. I lived a different life since then. I just prayed to God that I'd come through that thing and get back to my lines and see my wife and boy again sometime.'

Lew's prayers were answered; he did get back to his outfit and they gave him the Silver Star for bravery. And when he died on 30 October 1981, aged sixty-four, he was buried in a hero's grave in Arlington National Cemetery.

# The Old Mongoose  11

On a sunny afternoon in May 1958, a dark bay three-year-old colt named Tim Tam won the eighty-fourth running of the Kentucky Derby, earning $116,400 for his Calumet Farm owners. The night before the big race, at Freedom Hall on the State Fair Grounds in Louisville, a dark brown fighter of indeterminate age named Archie Moore won a split decision over Willi Besmanoff, a rugged German heavyweight, earning a purse of $10,000.

Archie, the light-heavyweight champion of the world, had come into town a couple of days before the fight and was delighted to find the place knee-deep in sportswriters. But they all seemed to have their minds on horses rather than fighters. So the day before the fight, Archie showed up in the stable area of Churchill Downs and chatted amiably with his friends among the journalists as they made their rounds of the Derby horses. 'I want to thank all of you gentlemen for coming to Louisville to see me fight,' he said, sounding genuinely pleased. Then, his eyes twinkling, he added, 'Oh, by the way, why don't you stay over and see the Kentucky Derby? I understand it's an excellent race.'

Against Besmanoff, Moore, forty-one going on forty-four, had to fight hard to come out with a split decision. The old champ was disappointed, even if the fans were happy. Had he racked up a knockout, Archie would have become boxing's all-time KO champ with a total of 127, beating the record held by Young Stribling, the Georgia heavyweight who fattened his record touring the tank towns knocking over guys who had hinges on their knees. 'I'll get that knockout record soon,' Archie told reporters after the fight. 'And I'm going to run it up so high that no one will ever beat it.'

In just five more fights, Archie Moore had the record and as he promised that night in Louisville, he ran it up so high that no other fighter has come close to beating it. When he quit the ring in 1963, his KO record stood at 141,143 or 145, depending which record book you look into. A few years ago, *The Ring* magazine listed Archie at number eight in their list of boxing's ten greatest punchers of all-time, Mike Silver writing, 'Moore's weapons were those of the master craftsman. His toolbox contained a vast array of punches and strategies from which to choose. The key to his success as a KO king was in his understanding of when and where to apply his weapons to achieve the most telling results. Moore was blessed with a strong body and unusually long arms. His legs were sturdy, but not built for speed. His entire torso, especially his huge shoulders, upper arms, back and forearms, bespoke power. Holder of a PhD. in professional boxing, this Methuselah of the prize ring completely understood the physics of dynamic punching.'

As one old-time fight manager said, 'The trouble was, everybody figured there was no percentage in fighting him. Champs like Freddie Steele, Ceferino Garcia and Al Hostak were avoiding him. So were

Tony Zale, Freddie Mills, Billy Conn and Gus Lesnevich. Jake LaMotta said no thanks, and so did Sugar Ray. It went right up to Joey Maxim. Moore could hurt you. He moved on good legs, like a middleweight, he had shoulders like a heavyweight, and he hit like Babe Ruth.'

In the early Forties, Turkey Thompson, a murderous-punching middleweight who once dropped heavyweight contender Bob Pastor six times in a single round, was offered the choice of Charley Burley, Cocoa Kid or Archie Moore as an opponent. Turkey thought for a moment, then said, 'Charley Burley's okay. So's the Cocoa Kid. But when it comes to Archie Moore, I say let's go slow. Fact is, I don't think I need a payday that bad!'

Oakland Billy Smith was a good fighter who had boxed a draw in the first of three fights with Moore, losing the other two, and he would say, 'Old Arch was the best. You should stand on your feet when you mention his name. He's so smart in there it's not fair to others.' They crossed gloves again in Portland in January 1951 and in the eighth round, Oakland Billy lifted the ropes apart, climbed out of the ring and headed for his dressing-room, muttering, 'There's no law says a man has to take that kind of punishment.' When pressed by reporters, Billy replied, 'Well, all I will say is that if my manager didn't know enough to quit, I did!'

In June 1948, Archie was knocked out in one round by Leonard Morrow in Oakland. He claimed he was tagged at a moment when he was extending his gloves in apology for an unintentional foul. It wasn't until December 1949 that Archie got Morrow back in the ring in Toledo. 'This fella isn't going to fight much after this,' he told manager Charley Johnston before going in and knocking out Morrow. The record shows that Morrow had only one fight in the next two-and-half years, and Johnston remembered, 'Two rounds running, Archie knocked him down right at the end of the session when he couldn't be counted out. Then he draped him over the ropes, just carrying him along instead of finishing him off. When he finally knocked him out, Morrow hit the floor so hard we had to hang around for a couple of hours to see that he was all right.'

Al Sheridan was a fighter before becoming a cop in Chicago, and he recalled Moore's two fights with Holman Williams in Baltimore in 1945. Williams was a good fighter and he took a decision off Archie in their first meeting, but a few weeks later Moore got him out of there in eleven rounds. 'Holman should have been a champion,' said Sheridan, 'you couldn't hardly hit that man at all. But Archie Moore did. Holman's wife told him if he fought Archie again, she was going to leave him. She didn't want to see her husband come home like that again, all cut and busted up.'

'I fought Ezzard Charles three times,' recalled Archie, 'and lost to him three times. Somehow, he had my number. I felt I beat him in our first fight but the record is there, it says he beat me. In our second, he was on his homeground and I really thought I was robbed. Sportswriters agreed with me, but the record says I lost in ten rounds. After the third fight, Charles told me he never wanted to fight me again.'

'Moore is completely different every time you fight him,' Charles said a few years after their last fight. 'You can never be sure what he'll do next. Frankly, I was lucky to beat him. The time I stopped him, I had almost been knocked out myself earlier in the fight.'

Ezzard Charles would become heavyweight champion of the world, but boxing experts always said he was one of the greatest light-heavyweights. He was ranked number one to champion Gus Lesnevich at the time of his third fight with Moore, in January 1948, with Archie at number three. It was one of the best fights seen in the Cleveland Arena in years, with Charles taking the first two rounds, Moore the next three, with Ezzard fighting his way back, and there was nothing between them when they came up for round eight. Both men set a terrific pace and midway in the round, Moore caught Charles with a tremendous left hook, another hook and a sizzling right cross. Charles was on the verge of being knocked out, eyes glassy, legs shaky, when he suddenly snapped out the fog to land a volley of left hooks ending in a perfect right that sent Moore tumbling to the canvas, where he was counted out.

Cleveland heavyweight Jimmy Bivins upset Archie in their first fight, in August 1945. 'We fought in Cleveland,' Moore told author Peter Heller in a 1970 interview. 'Bivins hooked me and I went down on one knee, and Bivins, mad at me, stood up over me and hit me when I was on my knees. He hit me with an uppercut on the left side of my face right underneath the cheekbone and knocked me head over heels, knocked me out. He had struck a nerve and all across my front gum, all the way across my mouth, was numb for two years. I despised Bivins. They gave me ten minutes' rest then made me continue the fight, and Bivins eventually knocked me out again. Finally, two years later, I got a rematch with him in Baltimore. We went in the Armory. Capacity was 12,000. They had 14,000 in there. It must have been ninety-five degrees that night. I knocked Bivins down in the fourth round, beat him unmercifully all through the fight, and then in the ninth round I caught him on the ropes, knocked him out. I finally had got Bivins.'

Moore beat Bivins three times after that 1947 fight, knocking him out twice. In those days, with Gus Lesnevich, Freddie Mills and Joey Maxim running the world championship, top black fighters like Moore, Bivins, Lloyd Marshall, Curtis Sheppard, Bert Lytell, Holman Williams, Charley Burley and Alabama Kid were virtually frozen out and had to fight each other to keep busy and make a few bucks. Moore beat Marshall twice in 1945, and he recalled the first fight for author Heller. 'Lloyd Marshall, rated number one in the light-heavyweights, dangerous puncher, break your head with a punch from either hand, shifty fighter. He knocked me down four times. I got up and I cut Lloyd dusty, knocked him down three times. I cut Lloyd seventeen times, over the eye, under the eye, around the nose, around the mouth, and he was a bloodied, bleeding hulk. I could have knocked him out in the tenth round. I hit him and he stumbled into the ropes and I stepped back. The crowd rose to its feet and said, "What a sportsman!" I didn't hit him hard no more. The fight ended and Marshall collapsed on his stool. He lost by decision.'

They called Curtis Sheppard 'Hatchet Man'. He once broke a man's collar bone with a right hand while trying to decapitate him, and he was the only fighter to stop Joey Maxim in 115 fights. Archie Moore fought Sheppard in Baltimore in 1946. 'In the opening round,' Moore recalled, 'the Hatchet Man hit me with one of the very best right-hand punches he ever threw. It was carelessness on my part. I happened to be standing where he'd been swinging all year. I hit the canvas like I'd fallen out of a tree, and you can bet I didn't feel much like getting up. I thought it all over and decided it would be safe to miss the ten count because I could probably get a return match. In the return, I'd be sure to settle his hash without getting knocked down again.' But Archie got up and won the fight.

The beginnings of this phenomenal fighter are somewhat obscure. In one account of his early life, his mother claimed he was born on 13 December 1913 in Benoit, Mississippi, while Archie would say he was born 13 December 1916, somewhere in Missouri, or perhaps in Illinois. 'My mother should know, she was there,' he conceded. 'But so was I. I have given this a lot of thought, and have decided that I must have been three when I was born! By the beard of the Prophet, I'm just a kid, yet everyone seems to want to age me faster than bathtub gin. Take my word for it, I was born on 13 December 1916.'

Henry Armstrong, the great triple champ, always said he recalled Archie as an amateur in 1930, while former welter and middleweight champion Mickey Walker remembered, 'When I was in training for Ace Hudkins back in 1929 in California, Archie happened to be my sparring partner. There's only one Archie. I couldn't ever mistake that man, even though his goatee is a little greyer now than it was then.'

He was born Archibald Lee Wright and when his parents separated, he and a sister were raised by an uncle, Cleveland Moore, in St Louis. So he became Archie Moore, and his name became known to the St Louis police once he started running with the street gangs. His half-brother Louis was no better. 'Louis was light-fingered by nature,' Archie recalled, 'and somehow a man's watch got tangled up in his hand, and the man sent the police to ask Louis what time it was.' Archie spent twenty-two months in the Missouri reformatory at Boonville for hooking coins from a streetcar motorman. 'I'm grateful for what it did for me,' he would say many years afterwards. 'It forced me to get eight to ten hours' sleep every night, it gave me an opportunity to have three hot meals a day, and it gave me a lesson in discipline I would never get at home.'

He was still a kid when his interest in boxing was aroused. 'I was coming home with a wagon full of chips from the ice house and I passed a fence. Behind the fence, people were screaming and yelling. I peeked through a hole and I saw two men slugging it out. The people screamed, the men punched, and I was thrilled. I almost fainted with ecstasy. I decided that I gotta be the champ. Someday, I gotta be the champion.'

'It is unlikely that any fighter has ever put more thought and effort into learning the boxing trade than Moore did,' wrote San Diego sports editor Jack Murphy. 'He was skinny as a boy, but he developed unusual strength with exercises of his own invention. One of his stunts was walking on his hands. He'd go upstairs and downstairs on his hands, and sometimes around the block, or around several blocks. The boy also developed his arms and shoulders by exercising phenomenally on a chinning bar. While still in his teens, he once chinned himself 255 times, and he used to shadow box hour after hour in front of a mirror. To develop his jab, he got the idea of practising before a mirror with a five-pound weight in each hand. He would wrap his hands around a pair of Aunt Willie's flatirons and spar for six minutes without a rest. Then he'd pause for breath and repeat the process.

'"If I could spar with five-pound weights," he explained, "the six-ounce gloves would feel as light as feathers. I'd never have to worry about becoming arm-weary." He credits his stinging jab to the flatirons. "I had the best jab in the business, Joe Louis notwith-standing," he said proudly.'

In his 1960 autobiography, Archie recalled his spell in the Civilian Conservation Corps, which he joined at seventeen. 'It took boys off the street, fed and sheltered them and permitted them to contribute to the support of their families. We earned thirty dollars a month and twenty-five of this was sent home, leaving us five dollars a month for high living. You could go to a dance and hear a fine band for fifty or seventy-five cents in those days. I didn't smoke or drink and didn't care much for girls who did, so I could go out with $2.50 and have a fine time.'

The beginning of Moore's professional career is, like his birth, a matter for debate. Nat Fleischer's *Ring Record Book* has him starting on 31 January 1936 with a two-round knockout over Poco Kid at Hot Springs, while *The Boxing Register* shows his first opponent as Murray Allen at Quincy, Illinois, on 14 July 1936, by which time Fleischer had credited Archie with fifteen fights. 'Moore's first professional fight,' wrote Jack Murphy, 'to the best of his recollection, was against Murray Allen in 1936 at Quincy, Illinois, and he won, breaking his right hand in the process. His share of the gate was three dollars, which was two dollars less than the sum required for a boxing licence.

"The commission was very generous," says Moore. "When they told me I'd have to take out a licence, they agreed to waive the other two dollars."'

By 1938, Archie was living and fighting in San Diego and building a reputation as a guy to stay away from. Around town, Johnny 'The Bandit' Romero was the box-office favourite, and his experience got him home in front of Archie in their first fight. A few weeks later, when they fought the main event at the newly-opened Coliseum, Moore caused a local sensation when he knocked Romero out in eight rounds. Running out of opponents, Archie took off for Australia, where he won seven fights, six by knockout. 'There was tough Ron Richards,' he recalled, 'who knocked me down three times before I was able to place a KO on him. I was in my twenties at the time and this win in Australia over their triple crown holder really gave my career a tremendous shot in the arm, as Richards was a great fighter, holding the heavyweight, light-heavyweight and middleweight titles at the time I beat him. I beat Richards again, but I didn't knock him out because I broke my left hand in the second round. After eight months in Australia, I returned home with a broken hand and 800 dollars.'

Eddie Borden had been in Australia with Gus Lesnevich prior to Moore's arrival, and he would recall years later, 'Lesnevich made a tremendous hit with the Australians, but when Moore came in he made an ever greater impression. In fact, he knocked out and won a decision over Ron Richards, who had beaten Lesnevich. They still talk about Archie Moore Down Under.'

In March 1941, Moore's future suddenly looked all behind him. He collapsed in the street in San Diego and was rushed unconscious to hospital, where he was diagnosed as having a perforated ulcer. An emergency operation was performed and newspapers reported that if he survived, which was doubtful, he would never fight again. Archie spent thirty-eight days in hospital and was still convalescing when he was rushed to hospital again, suffering from appendicitis. When he first entered the hospital, Archie Moore was the number four middleweight in the world. When he came out later that summer, he was a flyweight!

He took a job as a night-watchman in a trailer camp and, shortly after, Milt Kraft, his boss, investigating reports of strange activity around the camp, found Archie jogging among the trailers as he made his rounds. 'Here was Archie,' Kraft recalled, 'down on his luck, a physical wreck, the doctors telling him he would never fight again, yet he was positive in his own mind that he'd become a champion.' By January 1942 Moore was back in the ring, running off five straight knockouts, and in May 1943 he beat Jack Chase over fifteen rounds to become Californian middleweight champion.

Syndicated columnist Jimmy Cannon recalled those early years, writing, 'There didn't seem to be a place on earth, starting in 1936, that Archie didn't make across twenty impoverished years. It was Tasmania and North Adams, Massachusetts, and all the spots in between, from Flint, Michigan, to Panama. The money was always short. He toiled in a lunch wagon, flophouse, bus-jumping, empty-belly, charity-ward obscurity. He took them all, clown and cutie, banger and sticker, the runners and the holders, the cowards and the brave ones. Putting together what he learned from their different styles made Moore a great fighter. But you didn't see the greatness unless you caught him in the mean arenas in the bus-stop towns. The punches didn't hurt Archie much, and his scarless face tells you that. Some wounds never bleed. They penalized him because of his skills. They knew how good he was and they wanted no part of him. They shut him out of the big towns and protected the famous pugs. They angled him around until the ulcers began to punch his insides. They cut them out in 1941 and he laid off a year. There is a lumpy scar across his pot that traces the course of the knife. Seldom has a modern fighter endured as much.'

'By June 1944,' recalled Archie, 'I had grown into a 165-pound light-heavyweight and Linn Platner, who had gotten me some fights, told Al Weill about me. Weill wasn't interested – somehow that man never has been interested in me. Then I got a big break. Platner convinced Jimmy Johnston, the celebrated New York promoter and manager they called the 'Boy Bandit', that I was his kind of fighter. I met Johnson in his office at the Paramount Building. He put his feet up on his desk, tilted back the derby he always wore indoors and out, and kind of growled at me, "Platner says you've got everything, including ticker. If he's right, we'll make some money. I'm not in with Mike Jacobs and his Twentieth Century Crowd. So we'll start on the outskirts and build up. It won't be long before I have Jacobs begging me to use you."

'In five months and seven fights under Jimmy, I got farther than I had in the previous eight years. He was a gamecock and a supreme ballyhoo artist. He fought for his fighters. In May 1946, Jimmy called me in. "Archie," he said, "I'm going to create my own light-heavyweight champion. I'm going to promote fights at Ebbets Field. I'll put you in there with Freddie Mills, the British champion. When you beat him, we'll claim the world title and Jacobs will have to give you a fight with Lesnevich." I left Jimmy's office in high spirits. The next morning, I picked up a newspaper. I took one look at the sports page and was sick. A headline said Jimmy Johnston had died of a heart attack in the night. Jimmy's brother Charley inherited me. For the next three years I was back on the treadmill, no nearer a title shot than the day I got back from Australia.'

As the New Year, 1949, dawned, Archie was ready to quit. He was thirty-two and had been a pro for thirteen years but was resigned to his fate, saying, 'Let's face it, I was never going to get a shot at the title. I was never going to be a champion, except in my heart.' He took a fight with the Alabama Kid in Toledo because it was on the way home to San Diego. The fight was at the brand new Arena which could seat 8,500, but there were barely two thousand fans in the place when Archie faced the Kid across the ring. They had a good fight. 'The Kid was a cute old southpaw,' remembered Archie. 'Maybe I got a little careless, because he floored me in the first round. But I decked him three times in the third and in the fourth I finished him. The fight had the crowd screaming.'

Next day, Archie picked up his $300 purse and when he had paid his handlers and settled his expenses, he had a hundred bucks left to buy a second-hand car. At Bob Reese's showroom, Archie found his car and he found a friend. 'Everybody is talking about the fight,' said Reese. 'Why don't you stick around, have another fight? You could use the money.' Archie had to agree, so they fixed him up with Bob Satterfield, a bomber from Chicago. I remember an American trainer telling me Satterfield would belt you on the jaw and if you didn't fall down, he would walk around you to see what was holding you up!

The Toledo Arena was half-full this time and they saw another thriller. Moore decked his man in the second and again in the third, but Satterfield got up and really laid one on Moore, shaking him to his toenails. Archie fired back with a booming left hook that stretched Satterfield out like a rug. This time Archie's purse was $1,600 and when Bob Reese offered him a job if he stayed in town, he accepted. Toledo liked Archie Moore, and Archie liked the city where Dempsey had licked Willard. He started fighting regularly again and in four years put thirty-eight fights in the book, losing only two and racking up twenty-seven knockouts over men like Jimmy Bivins, Leonard Morrow, Phil Muscato, Billy Smith and Clint Bacon. Harold Johnson beat him by decision but he whipped the Philadelphian three times. And they rated him number one contender to Joey Maxim, who had taken the title from Freddie Mills. The time was coming.

Jack Doc Kearns was managing Maxim and in his autobiography,

*The Million Dollar Gate*, he told how old Archie Moore finally got his shot at the title. 'After Maxim's win over Ray Robinson, it became increasingly evident that the days in which we could avoid meeting Archie Moore were definitely limited . . . There were two major drawbacks. First of all, there wasn't much doubt in my mind that Moore had the punch, weight and experience to beat Maxim. Secondly, it was my personal opinion that the bout wouldn't draw peanuts at the gate.' Kearns went to see Charley Johnston in his New York office and laid his cards on the table. Charley didn't like the hand he had been dealt, but he knew that Doc held all the aces. 'First, naturally, I want a return-bout clause,' said Kearns, and Johnston breathed a little easier. 'Second,' Doc continued, 'I want a $100,000 guarantee.' As Charley started to protest, Doc came in with the clincher. 'And third,' he said, 'if you win the title, I want a piece of Moore.' When Doc walked out of Charley's office that day, his man Joey Maxim had his $100,000 guarantee for a title defence against Moore, and if Moore won, Kearns was in for ten per cent of the new champ.

'Doc Kearns couldn't put me off forever,' Archie would recall, 'so it was that on 17 December 1952, four days after my thirty-sixth birthday, I found myself in the ring at the St Louis Arena with Joey Maxim. After sixteen long, often weary years of fighting, I finally had reached a championship fight. St Louis was a fitting site. Here, I had spent my boyhood. Here, as a teenager, I had got into trouble for stealing and been sent to a reformatory. Here, I had begun fighting as an amateur in 1935 and as a pro a year later. Here, as a young middleweight, I had lost a ten-round decision to a former champion, Teddy Yarosz. Like Maxim, he was a defensive specialist, whose lessons were now to serve me well. I was ready. Joey Maxim is a clever fighter and a game one. He had to be to take what I handed him and last fifteen rounds. And then they were lifting my hand. The crowd was cheering. Man, I felt happy!'

Reporting the fight for *Boxing & Wrestling* magazine, Eddie Borden wrote, 'There was no questioning the verdict. Moore won by an overwhelmingly decisive margin, winning the last nine rounds successively. He waged an incessantly aggressive, non-stop type of fighting. He forced his way to the inside and began a barrage of left and right blows to the body, occasionally switching to right uppercuts and the infrequent occasions on which he jarred Maxim repeatedly with smashing right-handers to the head. Maxim was disfigured with bruises on both cheeks and he was cut around his left eye. He took a thorough body-beating and was in dire straits at the finish.'

The official scoring saw one judge give it to Moore thirteen rounds to one with one round even; the other judge gave it to Archie by nine rounds to two with four even. 'Now we come to referee Harry Kessler,' wrote Borden. 'He called it seven rounds for Moore, seven rounds for Maxim, with one even. His point system favoured Moore by a slim two points, 76-74. Mr Kessler has been called the Millionaire Referee who officiates for the sheer liking of the sport and donates his purses to charity. But he has done irreparable harm with his inefficient manner of scoring a fight and we have brought him to task on previous occasions. With all due respect to Mr Kessler and his business success, he is not a good referee.' Mr Moore and Mr Kessler would meet again.

'When I beat the tar out of Maxim and won the title,' Archie recalled later, 'my trainer run over to me and tried to pick me up in the air. I said, "Turn me loose! Don't do that. Just slip my robe on my shoulders. Be cool. Don't get excited. I should have won this thing twelve years ago. This is nothing new to me. Be cool."'

At long last, Archie Moore was light-heavyweight champion of the world. He was also broke, and had to borrow $10,000 from the International Boxing Club, who promoted the fight, to cover his training expenses. 'I borrowed it against my next fight,' he said, 'and finished up with just enough money to get out of town and buy Christmas presents for my relatives and friends.'

Moore was never beaten for the championship he had worked so hard for. He was champion for ten years and defended the title nine times before the boxing commissions finally took it away from him. He took care of Maxim in the return bout and gave him another shot in January 1954, in Miami. To make the weight, Archie starved himself for four days and ran four miles in a rubber suit on the morning of the fight to lose five more pounds. 'They said they'd have to carry him into the ring,' Maxim said later. 'They almost had to carry me out!'

On 11 August 1954, Archie Moore finally made it to the big time, a fight in Madison Square Garden. The main event, defending the championship against Harold Johnson, a guy he had beaten three times in four fights. In his *Newsweek* column, John Lardner wrote, 'Moore is a consummate ring craftsman, perhaps unmatched in our time for a union of style, subtlety, wisdom and power, except by Ray Robinson . . . When the bell rang to start the fight last week, Archie's robe was off and he no longer looked like a perfumed, bass-rhythm Emperor Jones. He didn't look much like a boxer, either, but he never has, round-bellied, listing to port at the hip, covering ground in skips, like a seal. I doubt if any fighter but Moore could have won a fight like this, in the circumstances. It was against the pattern. Every great pugilist meets in time, at some age like thirty-seven, a younger, fresher, faster, stronger, more eager man, of high ability, and he breaks stride, goes under, because it is inevitable.

'Moore has a talent that in this case cancelled the inevitable. Where he should have reached the end, it turned out that he had been pacing, feinting and setting in place, with quietly desperate wisdom, a different ending, historically wrong. When he hit young Johnson on the point of the jaw at almost the last moment, it was immediately over, except for details of broom work that Archie took care of in a few seconds. Then he was the Emperor Jones again, back in his satin robe, laughing happily.'

Moore knocked Johnson out in fourteen rounds to keep his title, but he had to haul himself off the canvas to do it. In one of his brilliant essays for *The New Yorker*, AJ Liebling, describing the knockdown, wrote, '. . . near the end of the tenth round, Moore was pressing in to get in one more combination of punches before the round ended, and Johnson hit him with a beautiful overhand right to the left side of the head and knocked him flat. It was as if Vladimir de Pachmann had been assaulted by a piano stool. It was an event so unexpected, so unprecedented, that even the referee, Ruby Goldstein, lost his head. Goldstein's first impulse must have been to help Moore to his feet and apologize on behalf of the management, but he checked it in time and began to count . . .' Moore was on his feet at three, and Goldstein, forgetting the compulsory eight count was waived in championship bouts, counted to five before the bell rang ending the round. Four rounds later, Moore was the winner and still champion.

Every kid who dreams of being a fighter, dreams of being the heavyweight champion of the world. Archie Moore was no kid in 1955 but that was still his dream. But before the dream, there would be the nightmare. Doc Kearns got him a fight with Nino Valdes in Las Vegas; win that one and you fight Rocky Marciano for the big one, the heavyweight championship. As a tune-up for Valdes, Archie lined up Frankie Daniels in San Diego, but in the course of the routine medical examination, the doctor discovered a problem with his heart and ordered Archie to bed. A heart specialist diagnosed the defect as organic, and said his fighting days were over. Anxious to get a second opinion, Doc Kearns obtained Moore's release and flew him to San Francisco. The diagnosis was confirmed. Then Kearns took his fighter to Chicago. Same thing. In desperation, Doc took Archie to the Ford Clinic in Detroit, said to have the finest heart specialists in the world.

It was their last gamble and it paid off. The problem wasn't organic: Moore had a fibrillation, an irregular heart rhythm, that was correctable with medication. Five days later, Archie Moore was out of the hospital and back in the fight business.

Now Archie set his sights on Rocky Marciano and the heavyweight championship. With a little help from his friends in Toledo, a campaign was begun to get Moore his chance. On 17 November 1954, some 427 letters were posted to leading sports editors throughout the United States, stating Moore's case for a shot at the title. Daily releases of letters, telegrams and cartoons were sent to every part of the communications media, to boxing promoters, to boxing commissions. Archie even had a 'Wanted' poster printed, stating, 'Reward for capture and delivery of Rocky Marciano to any ring in the world for the purpose of defending the heavyweight championship against the logical contender Archie Moore!' Author Budd Schulberg called Archie the 'All-time Communications Champ of Boxing'.

Marciano's manager Al Weill knew all about Mr Moore. He knew he was old, and getting older by the day. Keep him waiting long enough and maybe they'd have to bring him to the ring in a wheelchair. Weill tried to build a fight for Rocky with Nino Valdes, but Archie took the big Cuban and punched him full of holes under the Las Vegas desert sky. It was his first fight since the heart scare and he was fat, but he fought himself into condition over the fifteen rounds, cleverly keeping Nino facing the setting sun. 'By the eighth round the sun had gone down,' said Archie, 'but by then it didn't matter because I already had one of his eyes closed.'

Carl Bobo Olson was the world middleweight champion and he had just beaten former light-heavy champ Joey Maxim, so they put him in with Moore for his title at the Polo Grounds and Archie picked up his biggest purse to date, $81,668. 'It took me into the third round to set up Olson,' he recalled. 'Then I hit him with a couple of good rights to the head and he practically impaled himself on my left hook. The dispatch with which I handled Olson won me attention where long years of much more solid performances had failed. The huge television audience discovered me.'

Al Weill and the International Boxing Club, Marciano's promoters, had counted on Archie being put out of the picture by Olson after having to sweat off twenty-three pounds from the Valdes fight to the title bout with the Hawaiian. But controlling his weight was something the veteran was rather good at – he always said he learned the trick from an aborigine in Australia. 'One of the important parts of my diet is to thoroughly chew meat, then spit out the pulp,' he claimed. 'Chewing without swallowing is not easy. It's agony, in fact. It drives you crazy not to swallow a succulent hunk of meat, but my will to lose weight was even stronger than my taste buds.' Sportswriter Al Silverman scoffed, 'Secret diet, hell! As a cynical newspaperman once said, "Why in hell would an Australian bushman want to watch his weight?" Archie just stops eating. If he has to, he will subsist on raw eggs and fruit juice.'

So Archie Moore finally got his big chance, a shot at the heavy-weight title, and he could weigh what he wanted for this one. He actually hit the scales at 188 pounds, a mere four ounces lighter than the champion Marciano. The fight drew a crowd of 61,574 fans to Yankee Stadium that September night in 1955, with the gate just short of a million dollars. They got value for their money.

'When I stepped into the ring,' recalled Archie, 'I was confronted by Harry Kessler, who had been assigned as referee. Why my manager, Charley Johnston, didn't protest is a mystery to me. Here was the spectre of my childhood, and the man who almost spoiled my unanimous win over Maxim. I felt I now had to fight two men. How right I was. The first round was nothing. In the second round I spotted an opening. Rocky lunged in with a wide right hand. I pivoted away, and then came back with a half right uppercut. Though I was too far out to get the best leverage, he dropped like a pound of mashed potatoes on a tile floor. I went to the farthest neutral corner. Kessler began counting. One . . . two . . . Rocky was up, but Kessler went on, three . . . four. The mandatory count does not apply in championship bouts, but Kessler must have been excited, too. My seconds were screaming at me to finish him and I moved to do so, but Kessler got there ahead of me. He carefully wiped off Rocky's gloves, giving him another few seconds, and then as he released him gave him a sort of stiff jerk, which may have helped Rocky clear his head.

'When Rocky first got back on his feet, he had an elbow on the ropes and was staring out at the crowd. I know, I was there. I was so furious at Kessler I thought I better hit him first and get that obstacle out of the way. But, as it was, I turned to fight Rocky. I was blind and stupid with rage. And my rage wasn't directed at Marciano, because so far he was the only one co-operating with me! I began to slug toe-to-toe with Rocky. Even then he didn't catch up with me until the ninth round, when he fought me back into my own corner. I was still trying to keep my shell defence effective, but took a left hook to the body. From habit I covered for an expected right hand. Instead he threw another left hook and that one caught me on the head. I saw it coming but I was like a man in a trance. The punch knocked me down, and he had me . . . I must say that the cheer that went up when I decked Marciano was the most thrilling and inspiring sound I have ever heard. You cannot imagine what the roar of 60,000 people can do to your spine. You stand under the lights with a fallen champion at your feet and with one voice the crowd salutes you. I realize that when I was knocked out, the same crowd saluted Rocky, and that's as it should be. In sport, you have to face the fact that they cheer winners.'

'Three times the doctors went to Moore's corner and asked him how he felt,' observed Jimmy Cannon. 'He could have copped out, but this is a true fighter and he honours the chivalry of the dirty racket. Moore told the physician there were only two ways a pug is beaten. It goes the limit and he loses the decision or they count him out . . . He got his ten seconds in the ninth and he bought his dignity with pain.'

So Rocky Marciano took his unbeaten forty-nine fight record home to Brooklyn, Massachusetts, and announced his retirement. They gave Moore another shot, this time with Floyd Patterson in Chicago for the vacant title, but on that November night in 1956 the kid from Brooklyn had too much of everything. Archie had nothing, and twenty-one-year-old Patterson became boxing's youngest heavy-weight champion with a sweeping left hook in the fifth round. Archie somehow got to his feet only to be dropped again, and when he got up this time, they stopped it. George Herrick wrote in the *San Diego Tribune*, 'The brutal fact is that Archie probably never was cut out to win the heavyweight title. Fate had been kind to him at times, but when it comes to that heavy title business, Dame Fortune twice threw him snake eyes.'

So Archie Moore never did realize his dream of being heavyweight champion of the world, but he was a great light-heavyweight champion and he was never greater than on a freezing cold December night in a Montreal ice rink in 1958. In the other corner was Yvon Durelle, a tough fisherman from the New Brunswick community of Baie Sainte Anne, who had dragged a living from the sea and battered one from the ring. 'Don't let that first name fool you,' Doc Kearns said later. 'Durelle was tougher than a seventy-five cent steak, and for a while it appeared that we had lost the championship. Durelle hammered Archie to the floor three times in the first round, and if Moore hadn't been an all-the-way champion, he well could have sat out the dance from there on in and called it a night. But Archie got up, and up and up. Then in the fifth round Archie was down again, but he made it perpendicular somehow and weathered the round. "Don't sit down," I lashed out at him when he came back to the corner. "Wave to your wife."

'"What?" Archie asked, looking at me as if I had lost my mind. "Wave to her? I don't even know where she is."

'"Over there, beyond Durelle's corner," I pointed. So Archie waved briskly and, as I suspected, the watching Durelle's jaw dropped almost down to his chest. Never underestimate the power of pure psychology. He had just had Moore on the verge of a knockout and here was Archie waving at him with a rather puckish look on his face, Archie being rather bemused at the whole business. That was the end of Yvon right there. Archie's gesture took the heart out of him. Archie went out and took charge and in the eleventh round sent Yvon crashing to the canvas for what was to us a highly satisfactory finish.'

For that tremendous victory, Archie Moore was voted Fighter of the Year and presented with the Edward J Neill Memorial Trophy at a banquet in the Waldorf-Astoria hotel in New York. Before opening his speech, Archie asked Yvon Durelle to stand up, saying, 'It takes two to make a fight.' Few of the guests knew that Durelle was in the room, but Archie Moore knew, and he did the right thing.

He once said, 'I want to be remembered like Joe Gans or Jack Dempsey or Harry Greb or Stanley Ketchel. I don't want to be remembered as an ordinary champion. I want to be remembered as a great one!' He is.

# The Dead End Kid 12

Throughout ten years as a professional fighter, Rocky Graziano was trained by Whitey Bimstein, a professor of pugilism at that legendary college of hard knocks, Stillman's Gym on Eighth Avenue in New York City. They're all gone now. Stillman's was torn down in 1962, Whitey died in 1969, Rocky in 1990. Together, they made quite a story.

It was early 1942 and Rocky Bob Barbella had busted out of the Army and got back to the lower East Side, where his pal Terry Young was glad to see him and didn't ask too many questions. Terry was a pro fighter, a lightweight, and he was always on at Rocky to come up to Stillman's and see his manager, a nice little guy named Irving Cohen. Terry found Rocky an old suit and a sweatshirt and a pork-pie hat, and as Rocky would recall in his autobiography, *Somebody Up There Likes Me*, '. . . that is how I look when I first walk into Stillman's Gym. Stillman's Gym don't look no better to me than I do to Stillman's. If this joint was down on the East Side, it would be condemned, and if it was condemned, it wouldn't be worth our trouble stripping out the lead pipe.'

Terry Young introduced Rocky to Cohen, who was not too impressed with the look of him. 'He put his hand on my shoulder,' recalled Graziano in his book. '"Kid," he said, "you don't want to be a fighter, do you? A good looking kid like you?"

'"I tell you the truth, Mr Cohen," I said. "Terry said I could make fifty dollars a fight, that's the only reason."

'He smiled and shook his head slowly. "Just forget there's any easy dough in fighting. And remember what a favour I'm doing you by telling you this."

'"Mr Cohen," I said, "I give it a chance. Get me a fight and I'll take the chance."'

The manager finally agreed to have a look at Rocky. Terry fixed him up with some trunks and gloves and a mouthpiece and they put him in the ring with a South American middleweight. The guy boxed Rocky's head off and had him floundering all over the ring. Then Rocky pinned him in a corner and hammered him senseless, leaving him slumped against the ring post, and suddenly Irving Cohen was yelling for Whitey Bimstein, saying, 'Whitey, you got to teach this guy!'

'The trouble was, Rocky didn't want to be taught,' remembered Cohen when I met him many years later in Miami Beach. 'I tried to reason with him as he got dressed, but all I got was, "That's the way I do it, Mr Cohen. If you don't like it, I'm sorry. If you do like it, then I'd like to fight somebody. Get me a fifty-dollar bout and Terry will let me know." As he headed out of the gym I stopped him and, against my better judgement, shoved ten bucks in his hand. He muttered something and shot down the stairs on to Eighth Avenue, and I didn't expect to see him again. Or my ten bucks!'

Before he could even think of going back to the gym, however,

Rocky Bob Barbella was picked up by the cops and handed over to the Military Police, who took him to the Fort Jay guardhouse on Governors Island. A date was fixed for his court martial and he was given a train ticket and told to report to Fort Dix. But he decided to go via the East Side and he bumped into his old pals. Terry thought he was out of the Army and he took him back to Stillman's where everybody was glad to see him, especially Irving Cohen and Whitey Bimstein. 'I felt so good,' said Rocky, 'I hung around a couple of hours and did some exercises that Whitey showed me and punched the light bag a little. But I think Whitey got more exercise than me, all the time running up and taking cigarettes away from me and stamping them out. Finally he give up on me, slaps me on the can, tells me to take a shower, then go home and eat a big dinner and get some meat on my bones.'

A week later Cohen gets Rocky up to the gym and tells him he is fighting Curtis Hightower at the Fort Hamilton Arena in Brooklyn. An Army post! Rocky's mouth is still hanging open when Irving asks him his full name for the programme. 'All I can think of now is, who's out of circulation who won't know the difference if I used their name?' recalled Rocky. 'Tommy, and Dominick Graziano. "Tommy Graziano," I told Irving. "That's my real name." Why they call you Rocky? he says. "Well, Tommy Rocky Graziano, that's what it really is." Irving writes it down. And that was how Rocky Graziano was born.'

Rocco Barbella was born on New Year's Day 1921 in a cold-water tenement flat on Rivington Street on the lower East Side of New York City, the fifth child born to Nick and Ida Barbella but only the second one to live longer than a few months, the other being Rocco's brother Joe, three years older. Nick had been a so-so fighter and he would have his pals round and they would drink wine, and when they had drunk enough Nick would make the boys put the gloves on. He would show Joe how to punch and knock Rocco down, and little Rocco would get up crying, throw the gloves at his father and run out into the street and take his anger and frustration out on the first kid he saw.

'When I was six years old,' Rocky would recall, 'I was already a little lone wolf, running wild all over the streets of Brooklyn. When my father was not looking for work, he was looking for me.' His mother couldn't do anything with him and packed him off to his grand-mother's on the East Side. He found a soulmate, a kid called Houdini, and they would break open penny gum machines on the subway and jump on the back of passing trucks, throw stuff out the back, then jump off at the next corner. The cops caught them one day and Rocky's grandmother had to come to Children's Court to get him out. Watching them walk out the door, a detective growled, 'Well, there goes another little Guinea on his way. Look in his eyes, you see the devil himself. Ten years from now, the Death House at Sing Sing.'

By the time he was twelve, Rocky Bob (short for Barbella) had already done a year in the Catholic Protectory. He learned how to pick locks and jemmy windows and steal a car without a key, and which cops could be bought and which fagins gave you a fair price for the stuff you robbed. 'But I will say this for the place,' he put in his book, 'because I was there, I went a whole year without missing very many classes. Otherwise I would be illiterate today, like so many of my old friends who can neither read nor write. So maybe the joint done me some good.'

At a local boys' club he got to know Terry Young, 'a tough little guy from Eleventh Street, an Italian kid. He was there for hours every day, working at the punching bag, shadow-boxing, skipping rope. He was the hardest, the quickest little guy I ever seen, and we become good friends right away. Terry sparred with me a little, and the first time I knocked him down he got up with his mouth wide open. "Jesus, Rocky," he said, "you're a fighter, a real fighter!" From that day, Terry never stopped his campaign to make a fighter out of me. "Rocky, I

ain't just kidding," he would say. "You got a punch like nobody I ever
seen. You could be a professional inside a year. You could make
money, big money. You could have all the broads you wanted, a car,
your own house. Rocky, I'm telling you!"'

But the streets kept calling him back and by the time Rocky was
nineteen he had done time in the state prison at Coxackie and six
months in the notorious Tombs, plus a spell in the New York
Reformatory. Then Terry and his pals talked him into entering the city
amateur tournament and the bomb in his right fist brought him the
Metropolitan AAU welterweight championship. They handed him a
gold medal which he sold for six bucks and gave the money to his Ma.
Then a neighbourhood guy called Lupo the Wolf started getting him
amateur fights where they gave you a watch you could sell for ten,
fifteen dollars. The stag fights were a cash deal – ten, fifteen bucks a
fight.

'I fought in the Waldorf and in bingo parlours and parish houses
and lodge halls,' he recalled. 'I fought for business clubs and racket
mobs and church societies and Elks and Mooses and firemen and
policemen. Every fight was the same. I just come out to kill the
bastard facing me. If he hit me, I got wild like an animal. I'm going to
break him in two. Knee in his crotch, thumb in his eyes. Grab him by
the back of the neck and smash him with a right. Man, I was winging
along at a wonderful clip. Fighting two, three times a week and picking
up thirty, forty-five, sixty bucks. I played plenty of pool, I kept a rented
car and paid for the gas instead of syphoning it on the street.'

Rocky was waiting to be picked up by Lupo one day when Big Sal
drives up and takes him to see Eddie Coco, saying, 'He's an important
guy and he's going to get you some matches.' Coco got him two
fights for thirty-five bucks apiece as Robert Barber, before the cops
got him for violation of parole and he went back to the New York City
Reformatory for a spell. Released, he found more trouble and this

time they put him in the New York City Penitentiary on Rikers Island, six miles up the Hudson River and a million miles from his beloved East Side. He was free in October 1941, but not for long. In January 1942, Rocco Barbella was drafted into the US Army. This was something different, something he didn't like, guys he couldn't understand giving him orders, and he slugged a corporal and a captain, walked out of camp and didn't stop until he was back in the East Side and knocking on Terry Young's door. So Terry took him up to Stillman's Gym, and Irving and Whitey got him eight pro fights before the Army found him again and gave him his court martial, a dishonourable discharge and a year in the Army prison at Leavenworth, Kansas.

He still couldn't take orders and spent more time in The Hole on bread and water. He belted out the toughest guy in the place to become top dog in the prison yard, and they finally let him on the boxing squad. Rocky served nine months and when they let him go, he was in the best shape of his life from eating and sleeping regularly and boxing on the prison team. Something else happened to Rocky in Leavenworth. He had a lot of time to think about his life, and he didn't like it. He reckoned he had spent six years of the last ten in some prison or other, and had sent his mother to the hospital sick with worry. He made up his mind he was going straight.

Back in New York, he went up to Stillman's and Irving and Whitey got him started on the road to the championship of the world. 'Graziano's another Dempsey,' Whitey would say. 'Just walks in there and starts to punch and when he lands, brother, something's going to fall. Only thing, Rocky was tough getting into the gym. When I got him in there he would work hard, but getting him in was tough. But once he started to make money, I had no trouble getting Graziano to work. Rocky can be very serious about money.'

When they got him started back in the ring, in June 1943, Rocky was already serious about money. He was going to get married. His kid sister Yolanda had introduced him to a pretty Jewish girl named Norma Unger. 'She used to go to see him fight,' wrote WC Heinz, 'but that was at first. One day, while they were still just going together, he asked her to walk over to the gym with him to watch him train . . . Then he always wanted her to go with him when he fought, to Fort Hamilton and the Broadway Arena and the Ridgewood Grove. Less and less she liked it, and the first Frankie Terry fight was the last she saw. It was such a bad thing to watch, because they were cursing and even kicking. It was a real free-for-all, and after that she wouldn't go anymore.'

Graziano was rated number nine welterweight by *The Ring* when he tangled with Frankie Terry in June 1944 at Dexter Park, a semi-pro baseball ground in Queens. There was no love lost between these two and from the opening bell Terry abused Rocky with his tongue as well as his fists. The kid from the East Side blew his top and at the bell ending the first round their handlers had to jump in the ring and help referee Pete Hartley pull them apart. In the second round, Rocky shoved Frankie into a corner and waved for him to come out fighting. Graziano was in charge through the third, but in the fourth Rocky lunged in with a right, missed and was sent to the canvas by Frankie's right-hander. He jumped straight up and stormed at Terry, only for the referee to stop him so he could wipe his gloves off. That was when Frankie leaped over Hartley's shoulders to get at Rocky, who promptly smashed Terry in the face with a couple of right-hand shots. In the fifth, Rocky crashed the right to the jaw and Terry went down for four, up on his feet but not for long, another right-hand bomb exploding in his face to send him down for nine. The bell saved Frankie but nothing could save him in the sixth as he was dumped for counts of nine, two and nine before Pete Hartley had seen enough.

Rocky had three fights in Washington that year: three knockouts, and he remembered the third one, with Tommy Mollis. 'I don't just

flatten Mollis. I destroyed him. I caught Mollis one of the hardest
rights I ever landed, in the street, in the can, in the ring, anywhere. It
was a shot to the side of his mouth. It felt like I threw my fist into a
110-volt socket. It zinged down to my toes. His head snapped around
and threw off a shower of white blobs, mouthpiece, drops of sweat
and his front teeth. It was like you took a knife to a row of corn on the
cob.'

Irving got Rocky his first main event in Madison Square Garden in
November 1944. It was not his first fight in the Garden – he had
boxed Ted Apostoli for four rounds in August the previous year, and
that was when Eddie Coco came back into the picture. As Rocky came
down out of the ring, Coco got out of his ringside seat and stopped
him. 'Ain't you Rocky Bob?' he said.

'Yeah,' says Rocky. 'Come on back.'

Back in the dressing-room, Irving Cohen learns he has a partner in
Graziano's management. 'Me and this boy had an agreement that I
handle him over a year ago,' Eddie says to Cohen. The next day
Cohen and Coco and Jack Healy, who is with Rocky all along, have a
pow-wow at Stillman's and agree to share the manager's one-third
portion of Rocky's purses.

In his 1981 book *Only The Ring Was Square*, Teddy Brenner, who
would become famous as matchmaker at the Garden, wrote of Irving
Cohen, 'Dan Parker used to write that "butter wouldn't melt" in Irving
Cohen's mouth. Parker was the sports editor of the *Daily Mirror* in
New York . . . When he was writing, he was a real knocker. He kept
boxing people on their toes, because he had more spies than the CIA.
Irving was a problem for Parker. What can you say about a man who
ran a lingerie shop and had a good family and spoke so softly you had
to listen carefully to get his words? Though he had to deal with at least
one gangster in boxing, Irving kept his name clean. Not even Parker
went after him when it became public that he was associated with

Eddie Coco in the management of Rocky Graziano. Coco was a small man with a big reputation in the mob. He had a police record as long as your income tax form, and some years ago he was convicted in Florida of shooting a man to death. Before Coco was sentenced to prison for a long term, Al Weill, who was Rocky Marciano's manager, wrote to the judge and said, "I've known Eddie Coco for twenty-five years and I've always found him to be a straight shooter." Could be the judge didn't have a sense of humour. He threw the book at Coco.'

Harold Green was a cagey pro with a good left hook who boxed Rocky silly and spoiled his main event debut in the Garden, dropping Graziano in the fourth and coming out with the decision. A few weeks later they went back in the big Eighth Avenue arena and again Green came out a winner over ten rounds. 'I figure to kill this Green,' recalled Rocky, 'but it seems he don't aim to get killed, especially by me. He grabs me so tight I don't get a good shot at him until there's less than ten seconds to go. By the time the referee counts up to six, the fight is over and I'm a loser on a decision all over again. Sure, Green don't appreciate he's won, on account of it takes three men to scrape him off the floor and hold up his flipper as the winner.'

Early in 1945, a black kid from Philadelphia had everybody steamed up and the writers were calling him another Joe Louis even though he was only a middleweight. His name was Billy Arnold and he lost only one of thirty-three fights and he knocked out twenty-eight guys, and Rocky Graziano told Irving that if he didn't get Arnold for him he would quit fighting. 'Get me that bum,' he would plead when Irving came into Stillman's. 'I'll knock his brains out. He's mine. I'll give him to ya for a present!' He finally wore Irving down. As Cohen would recall, 'Both Whitey and I thought Arnold would win, but we also figured that as long as Graziano was losing fights for $4,000, he might as well lose a fight worth $10,000 to him.'

Irving made the match for the Garden and the bookies made Rocky a ten-to-one shot. Even co-manager Jack Healy, Rocky's pal since he was a kid running wild on the East Side, tried to jump ship. He tried to sell his share of the Rock for $2,200 to Jack Blumen and Lou Schiro. The pair laughed at Healy. 'And just what are we supposed to do with the guy when Arnold gets done with him?' they asked. 'Get him a job on the docks?'

Just over 14,000 fans were in the Garden that March night to see Rocky go against the new sensation. In his autobiography, Rocky wrote, 'This is it. This is all of them wrapped into one. This is the big one for the wise guys at the poolroom and every other son of a bitch who didn't believe me and made me ten-to-one underdog . . . for all the cops and the judges and the wardens and the guards who seen the devil in me and who seen the writing on the wall. It's my hand doing the writing tonight, my right hand. Look out, world, because here comes Rocky Graziano!'

Don Dunphy broadcast over 2,000 fights on radio and television over forty-five years, and in his book *Don Dunphy at Ringside* he listed his ten greatest fights. Graziano-Arnold was number four on his list. 'Arnold, a terrific hitter, tore into Graziano in the first round and battered him from pillar to post,' wrote Dunphy. 'Rocky took more punishment in that one round than he had in all his previous forty-six bouts. It was amazing that he didn't go down. It was unbelievable. Apparently, Arnold didn't believe it either. The bell saved Rocky, but I can remember it as though it were happening right now. At the end of the round, Arnold went back to his corner, but before he sat down he stood there for a long moment looking over at Graziano. He seemed to be wondering what was keeping Rocky on his feet. The second round was not quite as violent, but it was all Arnold. Rocky still took a battering. But he didn't go down. The third round began much the same way, with Arnold on the attack. All of a sudden, as if from nowhere, Rocky fired a right to the jaw. It caught Arnold flush. He staggered. The crowd came to its feet roaring. Rocky tore into Arnold. And now the wild Rocky, who hadn't landed a good punch in the previous two rounds, became Rocky the sharpshooter. He measured Arnold again and again and pounded him with both hands. Arnold went down and was counted out, clear out into obscurity.'

Of that dramatic third round, Rocky would recall, 'At the bell I roared out after him. Before I could get set he hit me a combination. Then he hauled back to lob a left hook at me. This was the split-second I been waiting for this whole fight. I let my right hand go like a thunderbolt. I got him solid on the chin. His mouthpiece sailed out on to the canvas. He stood there with his arms halfway down to his side. He was hurt. I felt my blood get hot and my breath come faster and this funny, hungry-thirsty feeling rise up in my throat that I always get when a guy stood helpless there, and I begun to kill him off . . . I caved him in with lefts and rights and I shook his head around on his neck again and I caught him with another looping right that was like crashing a brick on his chin. He went sprawling through the ropes on to the apron . . . He made it to his feet before the ten count and stood there by the ropes, wobbling, waiting to be killed. His eyes were open but he wasn't seeing very much when the referee stepped away and let me have him. This was it. He was mine. I don't remember anything I done. They told me later I grabbed him by the throat with my left hand and hammered his head with my right like it was a punching bag. He slid down into a neutral corner, got up again, and I fired my right fist once again and it exploded in his face and he went down for the last time.

'Irving and Whitey reach me and started to hug me. I didn't know it, but right down below me this former boxing writer named Damon Runyon passed a note along to the writer next to him that said, "There's your new Stanley Ketchel." And another columnist was writing, ". . . the deadliest killer in the ring since Jack Dempsey."

Everybody and his brother is squeezing into the dressing-room after the fight. One guy they bring in, they introduce to me as the Vice-President. I don't know Harry Truman from a keg of beer. One month later, in April 1945, President Roosevelt dies and this guy Truman becomes President. When Truman left the dressing-room, I jump in the shower. While I'm soaping myself, Sonja Henie, who's a big star then, runs in all excited from the fight and tries to jump into the shower with all her clothes on. She's trying to grab me, getting all wet and fighting and scratching at the same time, while he's trying to pull her out of the shower. It was like that from then on during my fighting career, people wanting to touch me after I just almost killed some guy in the ring.'

A couple of months later, Mike Jacobs had Rocky back in the Garden against Al Bummy Davis, a tough guy from the streets like Graziano – in fact, they were once in jail together. Davis was a Jewish kid who had flattened the great Tony Canzoneri at the end of his career, and everyone was telling Rocky, 'Ya gotta flatten this Davis, Rock, for what he done to our Canzoneri. Ya gotta kill the bum, Rock!' Rocky was so confused by all the advice coming at him from all sides, he was in a spin when he walked out to face Davis. There were nearly 17,000 fans in the Garden that night and they were all yelling for Rocky. But in that first round, Bummy hit Rocky with his pet left hook and sat him on his backside. Rocky was so mad he jumped up and was still hitting Bummy after the bell. In the fourth round he flattened Davis to send his fans home happy.

Jacobs put him in with welterweight champion Freddie Red Cochrane a month later. The New Jersey veteran had just come out of the Navy, and was a clever boxer who could make you look bad. He made Rocky look terrible for nine rounds, but Graziano belted him out in the tenth. Cochrane thought he could do better next time and Jacobs had 18,071 fans in the Garden to see it, with just over a hundred grand in the box office. Once again the welter champ made a game stand, for eight rounds, but he was giving Rocky nine pounds and it was too much. Midway in the ninth round, Graziano smashed a left hook to Cochrane's jaw and he dropped flat on his back. On his feet at nine, he walked into a right-hand bomb that blew his legs from under him and he took another nine count. The bell gave him a minute's respite but it wasn't enough. Rocky hammered him to the floor three times for nine counts. From the corner, Freddie's manager Willie Gilzenberg signalled only a minute to go, but his champ couldn't make it. Rocky smashed another big right on Red's chin and stretched him out like a rug. Referee Benny Leonard stopped the fight with twenty-three seconds left on the clock.

Harold Green was next. The Brooklyn boxer, still undefeated after twenty-two bouts, figured here was Graziano, the hottest fighter in town, and he had licked him twice. Bring him on! So it was Green v Graziano, chapter three, but this was just a short story and there was no happy ending for Harold Green. He outboxed Rocky over the first two rounds, but the right hand caught Harold in the third and he dropped. He was sitting up at eight but his legs weren't working and he was counted out. Back on his feet, however, Green was still full of fight and he went after Rocky, closely followed by cornerman Charles Duke. When things calmed down, Green drew a $1,000 fine and suspension, while Duke had his licence revoked by the Commission. Many years later, Green would claim he had been told to take a dive by Duke, who was alleged to have underworld ties.

Marty Servo was a good little fighter who lost only to Sugar Ray Robinson in forty-eight bouts before joining the US Coast Guard in 1942. But Marty had no luck after that. Out of the service, he knocked out Freddie Cochrane to become welterweight champion, but manager Al Weill had to guarantee Cochrane $50,000 to get the title shot so Marty made no money. To get out of hock, he took a big money bout with Graziano in the Garden. It was over the weight so his title at least would be safe. A crowd of 19,088 paid their way into the Garden, the biggest crowd in two years, and the $173,163 gate was the best since Louis v Buddy Baer in 1942.

'I was favourite because of my size and my hard punch,' recalled Rocky in his book, 'but just before ringtime, Eddie Coco came running in all worked up. "There's something fishy going on," he says, "they got Rocky a ten-to-one underdog. All the dough is suddenly on Servo. It looks like somebody bought off the officials, that's how I got it figured. Get Colonel Eagan."'

Someone brought Colonel Eddie Eagan, the Chairman of the New York Commission, from ringside, and Coco told him what he had heard and said he wanted the fight called off. But before Eagan could act, Graziano stopped him, saying, 'I'm going out there to fight. I got my own officials.' He held up his fists, the Colonel got the message and the fight was back on. But not for long.

Columnist Red Smith would write, '. . . Marty has his back to the ropes on the Eighth Avenue side of Madison Square Garden and a maniacal Rocky Graziano is holding him by the throat with a gloved left fist and smashing Servo's blank face again and again with dreadful rights. Marty had been champion for fifty-six days. When he woke up he was still champion, but he was through as a fighter. Rocky had hammered his nose permanently askew – a deviated septum, doctors called it – and Servo never again would breathe without difficulty.'

'Servo seemed so child-like,' wrote WC Heinz, 'trying to sink to the canvas with Graziano holding him and beating him in a kind of frenzy, that it was a frightening knockout.' The welterweight champion found giving seven pounds to a puncher like Rocky was too much, and he was decked three times before referee Arthur Donovan stopped it at one minute fifty-two seconds of the second round.

Rocky Graziano had slugged his way from the East Side slums to become King of New York City. 'When Graziano fought,' wrote Heinz in *The Ring*, 'you could breathe the tension. When he fought in the Garden, you could feel it over on Broadway, and the night he fought Zale for the first time you could sense it two hours before the fight, between the cars jammed along Grand Concourse, half a mile from Yankee Stadium.'

Tony Zale was middleweight champion of the world. He came out of Gary, Indiana, which was a big steel town. 'I hated the steel mills,' he would recall. 'I hated getting up at six in the morning and breathing the burnt air, catching the hot rivets that could burn a hole right through you if you missed. I wanted out so bad that it was all I could dream about when I flopped into bed exhausted every night. So when I went to the gym one Saturday to watch my older brother box, the sweat around the punching bags and in the ring smelled like Chanel No 5 to me. I knew then that the ring was the way out for Tony Zale.'

The Polish-American kid started fighting in the clubs at fifteen but after a year he had lost six of his last ten fights, his manager lost interest and Tony was back in the mills. He stuck it for three months before giving boxing another shot. He signed with Sam Pian and Art Winch in Chicago and he was on his way. He recalled, 'When I got my chance at NBA middleweight champion Al Hostak in 1940, I was ready. It took me six rounds to get one good right smash below his ribs, but he fell apart after that. I figure it took me ten years to throw that one punch!'

Now it was 1946 and on a chill September evening, Tony Zale had come into New York to give Graziano a shot at his title. Nearly 40,000 fans jammed into Yankee Stadium to see if the thirty-three-year-old champion could stand up to the twenty-four-year-old slugger from the East Side. The bookies had Rocky odds-on, but they and The Rock got a shock in round one when Zale smashed a left hook to Rocky's jaw

229

and dumped him on the canvas. Up at four, Graziano was hammered across the ring and a sizzling uppercut almost tore his head off. Body punches slammed into Rocky, but he kept throwing leather and suddenly a tremendous right caught the champion and he was in trouble. A mighty roar split the night air as Rocky's fans jumped to their feet, but the bell stopped him doing any more damage. Tony tries to box his man in the second but he has to fight to stay alive with this guy and a savage right drops the champ by the ropes. His head is hanging over the edge of the ring and Graziano is standing over him, with Ruby Goldstein trying to pull him away to pick up the count. Then the bell cuts through the crowd frenzy and Whitey is in the ring pulling Rocky back to the corner. When they get Zale back to his stool, he tells Art Winch his right thumb is broken.

Graziano mugged the veteran in round three like he was in an alley on the East Side and the guy had just insulted his mother, and Tony was lucky to see out the three minutes. Yet this incredible champion fought back in the fourth session to win the round, and the fans were as limp as the fighters when the bell rang. The fight swung back to Rocky in a tremendous fifth. He smashed the Chicago veteran bloody with those rocks he called fists and as Zale reeled to his corner at the bell, Goldstein followed him to say, 'You'll have to start doing better this round, Tony.' Around the ring the bookies were laying odds of three to one that Zale wouldn't come out for round six.

He came out. He was a champion. He didn't have to go looking for Rocky, the kid was right there in his face, and a big right hand sent Tony reeling across the canvas. Graziano followed him to smash both hands to the body, then another big right under the heart and you had to wonder what was holding the old guy up. Then as Rocky came at him again, Zale put everything he had into a pile-driving right that sunk wrist-deep in Rocky's belly, and as the challenger hung there, the breath gone from his body, Zale's left hook crashed against his jaw and he was down. The crowd was going crazy, jumping out of their seats yelling and screaming, and Rocky Graziano was trying to get up off the canvas.

'It was like the ground exploded up and hit me in my stomach,' Rocky would recall. 'The lights spin in a fast circle, then dim down to a little spot like through the wrong end of a telescope. I try to yell out and I can't make a sound. I am deaf again, in the middle of Yankee Stadium. I am deaf and I can't talk and I can't lift my right hand or my left hand and I am falling.' When Rocky got the feeling back in his limbs and jumped to his feet, it was too late. Tony Zale was the winner and still champion of the world.

Trainer Whitey Bimstein said later, 'From the first round to the sixth we couldn't believe how Zale was living under the punishment. But all of a sudden, Zale threw a punch six inches above Rocky's waistband. I sensed trouble . . . Rocky sat down with a funny expression on his face, not going forward, but sorta like an Indian chief at a council fire. He got up but he was counted out. He blew it.'

'Up in Sing Sing,' Rocky would say later, 'Terry Young busted two windows and got thrown in the Hole for trying to start a riot when they told him that Zale knocked me out. It was a tough night for Norma. When I come home, she was hysterical and I couldn't stop her sobbing.' Rocky took the family to Florida for a few weeks but he didn't like it and he was glad when Irving called him back to New York to get ready for a fight with Cowboy Ruben Shank. But they called the fight off after Rocky wrenched his back in the gym. Then he was in trouble again. Picked up by detectives, he was grilled for eighteen hours by the District Attorney over an alleged $100,000 bribe offer to throw the Shank fight. It was common knowledge in the city that Rocky was made a scapegoat in a political battle. A Manhattan politician had been murdered and the case was front page news for weeks. Then it was off the front page and Rocky Graziano was on there instead.

Columnist Red Smith wrote in the *Herald Tribune*, '. . . it was never proven that Graziano has ever dumped a fight. There never was any supportable evidence that he had entertained a thought of selling out. He was hounded back to the edge of the slums from which he sprang by headline-hunting prosecutors who could not make their willowy charges stand up.' And Bill Corum wrote, 'If I lived to be a hundred and nothing more came out in the matter than has come out up to now, I still would never understand what anybody could possibly have gained by attempting to fix a Graziano-Shank fight. It would be about as silly to try to bribe Joe Louis to go into the tank for Mickey Rooney.'

The Grand Jury told Rocky to go home and forget about it, but Commissioner Eagan hit Rocky below the belt when he suspended his New York licence for failing to report an attempted bribe offer. But he had a friend in Abe J Greene, Commissioner of the National Boxing Association, who gave his blessing to Rocky's rematch with Zale for Chicago. It was July 1947 and the city was wilting in a heatwave, yet a crowd of 18,547 paid a record indoor gate of $422,918 to sit in the cauldron that was the Chicago Stadium. It was 105 degrees under the lights when Zale and Graziano climbed through the ropes to fight once again for the world middleweight championship.

Sportswriter Jimmy Cannon reported, 'The first round was Zale's and the crowd muttered with sadistic excitement as the champion moved with a brutal smugness, the calmness of him menacing and contemptuous . . . The second round belonged to Rocky. Zale left-jabbed at Rocky's bleeding eye with a taunting impatience as he searched for the big punch. But two rights and a left made Zale do a small wandering dance and he strolled to the wrong corner as the round closed. Zale had evaded the dream which Rocky's punches had beckoned him into, and in the third round he jabbed at Rocky's eyes, one blurred by the running blood, the other pinched by the bruised and swelling flesh. Zale waited and then hit Graziano with a right which knocked Rocky down. Rocky was up before the crowd had completed their cry of surprise.

'If you ever doubted the courage of Graziano as a prizefighter, this round makes you wrong. Rocky, hit hard in the belly, misjudged the distance to the ropes and fell backwards into them, heavily and dreadfully slow, the blood on his body now resembling a ragged scarlet cloak. He must have known he was on the edge of disaster, but he flung off insensibility as though it was an overcoat which bothered him in the heat . . . The fourth was the end of Zale as Graziano's master . . . the energy was gone from Zale's flat-muscled white body and Rocky was like a man who has climbed many flights of stairs and now gets his breath back on a landing . . . Zale was jabbing in the sixth, but he was an exhausted man. The right Rocky let go hit Zale on the chin. The punch had allies in the heat and the years. Zale was suddenly worthless as a pugilist . . . Rocky went at him and I counted the punches. Thirty-six times Rocky hit Zale, and they were every punch any fighter ever threw. Zale walked backwards in slow retreat, a man backing up into insensibility, and you could see him going as the punches changed his angular face into a flat-featured, bloody mess. He leaned back through the ropes and Rocky was still hitting him, Rocky on top of the middleweight champion, hitting him short punches the way a man hits nails with a hammer. They were both leaning out across the ropes in a writhing embrace when the referee pulled Rocky back. The round had gone two minutes and ten seconds and Rocky Graziano was the middleweight champion of the world.'

'Rocky,' Lester Bromberg of the New York *World Telegram & Sun* asked him in the dressing room, 'how do you feel about winning the title while you're still suspended in New York?' Graziano put his hands up in a preacher's gesture. 'Tell them, 'he said, 'tell the people of New York the black sheep becom' the champ.'

# Sweet As Sugar 13

Ernest Hemingway once wrote, 'If you fight a good left hooker, sooner or later he will knock you on your deletion. He will get the left out where you can't see it, and in it comes like a brick. Life is the greatest left hooker so far, although many say it was Charley White of Chicago.'

Sugar Ray Robinson wasn't far behind. One American sportswriter reckoned, '. . . the single left hook with which Sugar Ray Robinson KO'd Gene Fullmer in their return bout in 1957 should be preserved somehow in a glass museum case. It was as perfect a punch as was ever thrown.' A photograph of Robinson landing that punch found its way into the *World Book Encyclopedia* as an example of the ideal left hook.

'I always thought that was a heck of a way to get my picture in the *World Book Encyclopedia*,' joked Fullmer later. 'People tell me it was a great left hook, but I wouldn't know. I never saw it.' His manager

Marv Jensen recalled, 'When I got to Gene, his eyes weren't focusing, but he looked towards me and said, "Why'd they stop it?" I held Gene up and told him, "Because the referee counted to ten. They'll generally stop it when they do that."'

Madison Square Garden matchmaker Teddy Brenner recalled, 'Sugar Ray was the greatest one-puncher hitter we've ever had. Was there ever a tougher fellow than Gene Fullmer? I don't think so. Ray got him out of there with one left hook, and that was a guy who'd seldom been off his feet before, let alone knocked out. Steve Belloise took a good punch, Sugar Costner looked like a coming champ, and if you think Bobo Olson wasn't a good fighter, look at his record when he was young. Well, Ray took them all out with just one shot. Many a guy was around at the finish of a fight with Robinson just because Ray felt like sharpening up his boxing that particular evening.'

In October 1961, when Robinson fought Denny Moyer for the first time at the Garden, his finest hour was long gone and the clock was ticking towards midnight, but the posters outside the arena still described Ray as 'The All-Time Great Champion of Champions'. When Milton Gross, sports columnist for the *New York Post*, queried the billing, the Garden's boxing director Harry Markson defended the claim, saying, 'During the height of his career, Sugar Ray didn't lack a single attribute which the great fighters need. He had a left hook, a right cross, defensive skill, the will to win, ring generalship, speed of hand and foot, courage, a sense of pacing, a variety of punches, the ability to size up an opponent after a round or two, split second reflexes, magnificent legs and the ability to reach superior heights when the situation required it.'

That's why they still call Sugar Ray Robinson the greatest fighter, pound-for-pound, in the history of the fight game. The record book tells you some of it. From 1940 through 1965 he had 202 fights and won 175 of them, a staggering 109 inside the distance, proof of the dynamite packed in his gloves. As recorded in *The Ring* a few years ago, 'During his prime (1941 to 1949) Robinson fought 100 bouts. His weight varied between 142 and 150 pounds, but he was so good he often challenged middleweights who outweighed him by five to fifteen pounds. Of the seventy-six welterweights he faced, he knocked out fifty. Of the twenty-four middleweights, he KO'd eleven . . . Robinson's boxing brain was razor-sharp. An opponent could not afford to make a single mistake, or run the risk of being knocked out. No puncher ever performed with such grace, flair and class.'

Holly Mims was a good middleweight who boxed Ray ten rounds in Miami in 1951. 'I knew I had to stay close to the man and punch inside if I was going to stay alive,' he recalled. 'But what made Robinson such a great fighter was that he could punch like the devil backing up.'

Tommy Bell came out of Youngstown, Ohio, and in December 1946 he boxed Robinson for the vacant world welterweight title. Tommy knew what to expect – he had been in with Sugar Ray almost two years before, in Cleveland. He told columnist Red Smith about that first meeting. 'He was knocking out everybody, see? I figure if he hits me, I'm gone, so I was extra careful. Then in the tenth he catches me coming out of my corner and hits me a right and a left hook to the chin. I didn't go down, and I couldn't believe it. But then he moved back and I tried to move away and my legs kind of wouldn't work and I fell on my head. But I got up and it was a hell of a round after that.'

British newspaperman Harold Mayes remembered a night in Liège, Belgium. 'It was Ray's penultimate contest before he met and lost to Randy Turpin in London in 1951. He met a French-Pole by name of Jean Walzach, and because of the approach of my deadline, I was rather anxious to see the fight over quickly. A French newspaper colleague seated next to me at ringside was equally anxious – he wanted to see a real Robinson right hand, a one-punch knockout. At the end of the fifth round, I tapped Robinson on the heel as he sat on his stool in the corner, and said, "Come on, get it over." He turned and said, "You want it over, he (pointing to the Frenchman) wants to see a right hand? So watch." He walked out, feinted a left hand, and knocked Walzach spark out with one right-hand punch!'

In October of 1965, Dick Tiger was training for the fight in which he would regain the middleweight title from Joey Giardello. Watching the workout was the former lightweight champion Ike Williams. 'You were the best lightweight I ever seen,' a guy said to Ike. The former champ looked at the man for a long moment, then said, 'I hear people say I was the best, Joe Louis was the best, Archie Moore was the best. We were good fighters. There was only one fighter in our time who was great. I hate the s.o.b. but Sugar Ray was the greatest.'

Ironically, the name he made world famous was not his own. He was born Walker Smith Jnr in Detroit on 3 May 1921, just after the family moved there from Georgia. Marie was four and Evelyn was two when Junior came into their world and that was what everyone called him, nobody called him Walker. And when his parents split up and his mother took the family and moved to New York's Harlem, the kids he ran with called him Smitty. One of the kids was named Warren Jones and he was a boxer at the Salem-Crescent gym which was in the basement of the Salem Methodist Church at 129th Street and Seventh Avenue. The trainer there was Warren's uncle, a man called George Gainford. Smitty fancied himself with the gloves on and had boxed a few amateur fights, but big George wasn't impressed when he first saw him. 'Too skinny,' he said. 'Smitty, you better go home and tell your momma to buy you more milk.'

But Warren had told Smitty of fighting on the bootleg circuit where they gave you a watch you sold back to the guy for eight, ten dollars. Just fifteen years old and weighing 110 pounds, Smitty thought of those ten-dollar fights and he told Mr Gainford he really wanted to be a fighter. So the big fellow let the kid work out and he gave him some gloves and shoes and trunks and a protector. But a couple of nights later, Smitty had a change of heart about being a fighter when Joe Louis was knocked out by Max Schmeling up there in Yankee Stadium. Back in Detroit, Smitty had gotten to know Joe when he was boxing amateur as Joe Barrow, and would carry his bag to the Brewster Gym. 'If my man Joe could be knocked out,' Sugar Ray would write in his autobiography, 'a skinny kid like me had no chance. Instead of returning to the Salem-Crescent gym, I hocked the boxing equipment Gainford had given me. I got three dollars for it.'

Joe Louis went back to the gym after that crushing defeat by Schmeling and went on to become one of boxing's greatest champions. Smitty went back to the gym a few weeks later and big George Gainford agreed to give him another chance. This time the kid stuck with it, training every night, but Gainford didn't let him fight, not yet. Then one night George took a team up to Kingston, New York, and Smitty went along for the ride. The promoter was stuck for a flyweight and Gainford looked at Smitty, then said, 'Here's my flyweight.'

'Where's his card?' asked the promoter. Amateur boxers needed an Amateur Athletic Union card to certify they were not professionals.

Gainford pulled a handful of cards from his pocket, shuffled through them, then handed one to the promoter. 'Here's his card, Ray Robinson,' he said. Robinson was another kid from the gym who hadn't boxed for a while, so that night Walker Smith Jnr became Ray Robinson. It was his first proper amateur contest and he won a three-rounds decision. He kept the name because he didn't want his mother to know he was a boxer.

Not long after that, Ray was boxing on a card at Watertown, up near the Canadian border, and he knocked the other kid out. As he came out of the ring, Jack Case, sports editor on the local paper, said to Gainford, 'That's a sweet fighter you've got there.'

'As sweet as sugar,' a lady at ringside added. In his paper the next day, Jack Case wrote about Sugar Ray Robinson and a legend was born.

'The mix-up over my name was a blessing,' Ray said. 'Sugar Walker Smith doesn't have the same ring. Sugar Ray Robinson is different.' It was a name he guarded jealously. George Costner was a welterweight out of Cincinnati who called himself Sugar. Robinson caught up to him in Chicago one night in 1945 and after the referee's instructions, Sugar Ray glared at Costner. 'We better touch gloves now, because this is the only round,' he said. 'Your name ain't Sugar, mine is.' The fight lasted two minutes, fifty-five seconds, and Robinson said later, 'By then, Costner didn't look so sweet!' And just to make his point, Sugar Ray did it again five years later and six seconds quicker.

As an amateur, Sugar Ray Robinson blazed his way to an amazing unbeaten string of eighty-five bouts, sixty-nine by knockout, forty inside the first round. He won the National Golden Gloves feather-weight title in 1939 and the same championship as lightweight in 1940. 'The greatest thrill I ever got,' he would say years later, 'was when I won the Golden Gloves and they streamed that light down on me in the Garden and said, "The Golden Gloves featherweight champion, Sugar Ray Robinson!" I bought all the papers, I read about it over and over. It was more of a thrill than when I won the welterweight championship of the world.'

With that second Golden Gloves title in 1940, George Gainford knew he had something special in Sugar Ray Robinson. It was time to go after the real money, as a professional. At the time, Ray was training at Grupp's Gym along with Buddy Moore, the Golden Gloves heavyweight champion. Moore had a sponsor in Kurt Horrmann, wealthy son of the brewing family, and Gainford worked out a deal with Horrmann to handle Sugar Ray. The boxer would get a regular salary, his mother would get a weekly allowance and Gainford would stay on as trainer. The columnists gave it a big play in their papers and there was more than a little interest in the kid's pro debut, which of course was in Madison Square Garden. Ray topped the story off nicely with a second-round knockout of Joe Echeverria. The main event that night, 4 October 1940, saw Fritzie Zivic challenge Henry Armstrong for the welterweight title, and young Ray sat ringside and watched his idol badly beaten by the rough, tough Pittsburgh fighter. Armstrong's defeat took the shine off Ray's victory, but the kid swore vengeance that night. He would make Zivic pay, sometime, somewhere.

It took Sugar Ray just twelve months and twenty-five winning fights, twenty by knockout, before he was ready for Zivic. Promoter Mike Jacobs arranged for Ray to have a non-title bout with Freddie Cochrane, who had outpointed Zivic for the world title, and Sugar was already training at Greenwood Lake when Cochrane pulled out. Jacobs offered ex-champ Zivic, but Gainford wouldn't hear of it. Not yet. But Ray was starting to think for himself – he insisted the fight go on and big George knew it was useless to protest. At the weigh-in, Zivic's manager Luke Carney said to Horrmann, 'You're making a mistake. Your boy's an amateur.'

'During the first round I fought like one,' recalled Ray in his autobiography. 'Zivic was a slender little guy with pale white skin and a pushed-in nose. And he was clever. His style was to move in close to you. When he did, he liked to hook his hand behind my head in a clinch and he would hold me high on the neck and yank me towards him. The way he did it, I was butting myself! When the bell rang ending the first round, I turned and walked back to my corner and I wanted to hide. For the first time as a pro I had no idea what I was doing. "Don't let him get close," said George. "Keep him away with the jab." I did, and even though he jolted me with a right hand in the sixth, I loosened up and caught him with some good left hooks. I got a unanimous decision, and Horrmann said to Luke Carney, "Is it okay if we turn pro now?"

The Pittsburgh veteran came out of the fight with his first black eye and told reporters, 'The kid's great. He can hit and he can box. He'll beat Cochrane easy.' Boxing writer Bill Heinz recalled that fight. 'Young Otto, who boxed the best lightweights in the business over two decades, refereed the fight. One day in Stillman's, I asked him about it. "In the sixth round," he said, "Robinson said to me, 'He's sticking his thumbs in my eyes.' I said, 'You ain't no cripple.' After that he gave it back to Zivic better than Zivic was givin' it to him. I said to myself then, 'This kid is gonna be a great fighter.'"'

'The bout was so fast,' remembered Don Dunphy, 'that I had trouble keeping up with the punches in my blow-by-blow description. The return bout with Zivic a few months later attested to Robinson's greatness. In the ninth round of a close bout, Zivic caught Robinson coming in, with a powerful solar-plexus punch. It landed flush in the mid-section. I saw that Robinson was hurt. His mouth flew open and his mouthpiece went flying. But a split second later, Robinson landed a whipping right to Zivic's jaw. Zivic went down, face-first into the canvas. Before or since, I have never seen a fighter who went down face-first. Zivic staggered up, chalk-white from the rosin dust. Referee Arthur Donovan had to stop the fight temporarily. He took out his handkerchief and wiped off Zivic's face to keep the dust from getting in his eyes. The temporary respite was not enough for Zivic. Robinson now easily KO'd him. The Sugar Man had arrived.'

'I first saw him when he was only a year and a dozen fights out of the amateurs,' recalled Budd Schulberg. 'But he was one of those naturals, like Joe DiMaggio and Ernest Hemingway. He had speed and grace and cleverness and power and endurance and passion. Sugar Ray was a picture fighter in those early forties. He had the long, slender, rippling-muscled legs of a dancer. If you wanted to box he outboxed you, and if you wanted to fight he outfought you. There was not a welterweight in the world could touch him then; perhaps there never was. They wouldn't let him fight for the title, because it was the personal property of the boys in the back room.'

Mike Jacobs was frank about it, telling Ray, 'I can't let you be welterweight champion. You're too good and you'd kill the class. I gotta have two or three guys fighting for the title. If you win it, I can't make any money out of it.'

So Sugar Ray went after middleweights, and they didn't come any tougher than Jake LaMotta, the Raging Bull from the Bronx. In October 1942, they hooked up for the first time in the New York Garden and a big crowd saw a thrilling ten rounds, with Ray copping the decision. In a blazing seventh round, Robinson set up a tremendous attack, only for Jake to come fighting back at the bell. 'This was my first main bout in the Garden,' recalled Jake. 'I was tense, and while I chased him all over the ring, I didn't throw any punches. You can't win unless you punch.'

A few months later they met at the Detroit Olympia before 18,930 fans, most of them rooting for LaMotta, a big favourite in the Motor City. Jake fought like a man possessed, charging in to hammer the body while Ray used his flashing combinations. In the eighth round, Jake bulled Ray across the ring and a right to the body and a savage left to the head sent Robinson out through the ropes on to the ring apron. He just beat the count and tried to get on top over the final two rounds, but at the bell Jake had the decision and Sugar Ray had his first defeat, after 125 amateur and bootleg bouts and forty professional fights.

Jake had fifteen pounds on Ray in that one, which helped. 'Our second fight,' recalled LaMotta, 'was in the winter and it was below zero, but I was out every morning running on the icy pavements. You have to be in superb condition if you're going to beat Robinson. I was in condition and I chased him again. Only this time I stayed on top of him. I didn't give him punching room. I pounded his body with both hands. In the eighth round, Ray went down. He got up at nine and finished the fight, but I received the decision. It was the first time he was beaten, amateur and pro.'

Incredibly, Ray went back in with LaMotta in Detroit just three weeks later, and he had beaten Jackie Wilson in the Garden in between. There was a reason for his industry. He was to be called into the US Army within a few weeks, and the $50-a-week pay didn't look too attractive to the Sugar Man. He had become used to good living. He beat LaMotta to make it two out of three with the Bull, but he had to get off the floor again to cop the decision.

A few days later, Sugar Ray Robinson, professional prizefighter, became Private Walker Smith Jnr, US Army. Ray travelled with Joe Louis and his troupe giving exhibition bouts at Army posts all over the United States, but when they sailed for Europe, Ray was in a hospital. He had fallen downstairs in the barracks, and when he woke up it was almost a week later and he was suffering from amnesia. Two months later, in June 1944, Robinson received an honourable discharge as a sergeant.

Back on the fight beat, Ray found LaMotta waiting for him and a near capacity crowd of 18,060 jammed Madison Square Garden to see them battle for the fourth time. It was action-packed all the way with Sugar Ray several times having Jake staggering, but you needed ether or a two-by-four to knock out the Bronx Bull and he was still there at the finish as Ray moved to three-one in the series. They took the show on the road and in Comiskey Park, Chicago, Ray again emerged triumphant, this time over twelve rounds.

By this time Freddie Cochrane was out of the Navy, but Marty Servo beat Robinson to a title bout and knocked out Cochrane in four rounds. Ray had whipped Marty twice – Servo's only defeats – but before they could get together, Servo ran into the heavy hands of Rocky Graziano. Marty got a big purse and a damaged nose that prevented him keeping his date with Robinson. The New York Commission vacated the title and nominated Ray to box Tommy Bell for the championship. At long last, after seventy-five pro fights over five years, with only that one defeat to middleweight LaMotta, Sugar Ray was to get his shot at the title. He and Bell were matched for 20 December 1946 in the Garden.

Six weeks before his date with Bell, Ray was in the Cleveland Arena meeting Artie Levine, a rough, tough, hard-punching middleweight from Brooklyn, and for the best part of ten rounds it was the second LaMotta fight all over again. Levine had a 9½lb pull in the weights and although he had won his last seven fights by KO, he was a five-to-one shot in the betting. Robinson went all out from the opening bell but Artie came blazing back in rounds two and three to punish Ray with savage left hooks. In the fourth round, one of those hooks sent Robinson to the canvas and he only just beat the count. That night Ray Robinson proved he could take it as well as dish it out. He fought his way back into the fight and in the tenth round crashed a thudding right to Levine's jaw to send him down by the ropes, where he was counted out with just sixteen seconds left in the fight.

After a short rest, Ray went into training for the Bell fight and he was in superb condition that night in the Garden. It was just as well, for Tommy Bell had come to fight. He wanted that title, too. Sugar was sweet in the opening round as he outboxed his man but he received a rude shock in the second when Bell hit him a whistling left hook on the jaw and down he went. Badly hurt, he was on one knee at seven and when he stood up, Bell did his best to knock him down again. Ray made it through the round and boxed his way back over the next two but near the end of the fourth he was staggered again. Tommy tagged him with another rocket in the fifth, but Robinson was firing on all cylinders now and in the eighth he dropped Bell for an eight count. At the final bell, Sugar Ray Robinson was champion of the world.

He lived like a champion. He had his own training camp, he had an entourage with him wherever he went, he had a beautiful wife, Edna Mae, who had been a nightclub dancer when she was knocked out by the handsome boxer with the flashing smile. Although he never got past junior high school, Ray was self-educated and well-versed on many subjects. He had property in Harlem, on Seventh Avenue, and his new cafe-bar opened just in time for the Bell fight. Drinks were on the house that night. Standing at the kerb would be his fuchsia-coloured Cadillac convertible. 'I had a fuchsia-coloured tie,' he said, 'and Edna Mae, my wife, says why don't you get a car that colour? So I did.'

John Condon, publicist for the Garden, would recall, 'Ray would leave that Cadillac anywhere, even in the middle of Times Square, for hours on end, and no one would touch it. Sometimes he would park it right in front of the Garden and come upstairs to negotiate a deal. When he would go down, three or four hours later, he would find the police guarding the car for him. Nobody would ever think of giving Sugar Ray a ticket!'

Six months after winning the championship, it rained on Ray's parade. Defending the title against Jimmy Doyle in Cleveland, he knocked his man out in the eighth round and Jimmy never regained consciousness, dying the next afternoon. Strangely enough, Ray had dreamed the night before the fight that he knocked a man out and he died in the ring. Gainford brushed it aside when Ray told him about it on the morning of the title bout. 'Big fight nerves,' he said. But the dream became reality. At the inquest, when the coroner said, 'Mr Robinson, couldn't you see that Doyle was badly hurt and was groggy?' Ray answered, truthfully, if not too sensitively, 'Mister, that's what my business is, to hurt people.' The fighter was deeply troubled by the tragedy and later set up a $10,000 trust fund for Doyle's mother.

Robinson defended the welterweight title against Chuck Hunter, Bernard Docusen and Kid Gavilan. 'Nobody took a punch on the chin like Kid Gavilan,' recalled Ray. 'The second time I fought the Cuban in Philly, in one of the early rounds I nailed him with as good a right hand as I ever hit anybody. It was right on the button and I stepped back and waited for him to fall. But he just shook all over and got right back in there. So I say, "To hell with this, I'm boxin' this guy from here on." Gavilan never was knocked out in his whole career.'

By the time he faced Charley Fusari in the summer of 1950, Ray could no longer make the welterweight limit. He was giving his purse for this title defence to the Damon Runyon Cancer Fund, taking only $5,000 for training expenses. Abe Greene was the National Boxing Association Commissioner and he allowed Sugar to weigh in privately, with his weight being announced as 147 pounds on the button! Robinson won an easy decision and one boxing writer put in his paper that Sugar Ray Robinson was the best carrier since Mother Dionne.

It was time to go after the middleweight title. The champion was Ray's old sparring partner Jake LaMotta, who had beaten Marcel Cerdan. Ray set the scene with a brilliant performance against another tough Bronx middleweight, Steve Belloise, stopping him inside seven rounds at Yankee Stadium. 'I was content to outbox Belloise,' said Ray afterwards. 'I was surprised when I knocked him out.' So was Steve. In the seventh round he threw a left hook just as Ray fired his own hook. Belloise missed. Ray didn't. He caught the Bronx veteran flush on the chin and Steve reeled back into the ropes, sitting down with a thud. He was still there when the bell rang and his handlers had to drag him back to his stool. Manager Eddie Walker took one look at his tiger and told the referee it was over.

Nat Fleischer, editor and publisher of *The Ring* magazine, wrote, 'Ray displayed a brand of all-around fistic perfection that was amazing. It was a revelation to see this speed king box and punch. He always has been recognized as a great fighter, but against Belloise he was superlative. A truly great fighter is Sugar Ray Robinson.'

In 1950, while LaMotta made some money staking his title against Tiberio Mitri and Laurent Dauthuille, Ray won recognition as middleweight champion in Pennsylvania by whipping Robert Villemain over fifteen rounds after the chunky Frenchman had licked LaMotta in a non-title bout. Robinson defended his claim by knocking out Jose Basora and Bobo Olson before taking off for Europe for a barnstorming tour that saw him rack up four knockouts in five fights in four weeks in four different countries.

Back home, it was time for Jake LaMotta, fight number six, the one that would define Sugar Ray Robinson's charismatic career. It took place in Chicago on 14 February 1951 and they called it the St Valentine's Day Massacre. That's what it had become in round thirteen when referee Frank Sikora finally called a halt to the punishment that LaMotta was soaking up as he lay against the ropes. Up to then, Jake had fought like never before, but this was Sugar Ray's night. He was middleweight champion of the world, and for the first time in his career Jake LaMotta failed to finish a fight. He could still boast that nobody had knocked him down, but against Robinson that night he did some funny things standing up as the leather bullets thudded home. They never fought each other again.

Ray had enjoyed his month in Europe. They had loved him in Paris, where he found no colour prejudice such as he had encountered in various parts of his own country. The Robinson circus packed their bags, even Ray's Cadillac. In one of his columns, veteran Los Angeles sportswriter Jim Murray wrote, 'Sugar Ray put the word entourage on the sports page. When he arrived in Paris, someone said that the last time so many Americans arrived in a body in the City of Light they were riding in tanks.'

Ray was a riot whenever he appeared, crowds following his Cadillac through the streets of Paris, Zurich, Antwerp, Liège, Berlin and Turin. Seeing the sights, living it up and fighting once a week to pay the bills.

And at the Hotel Claridge in Paris there was British promoter Jack Solomons dangling a five-figure purse in front of Robinson and Gainford for a London fight with Randy Turpin. The Americans even signed blank contracts before packing for London. The fight would be on 10 July 1951 at Earls Court Stadium.

Just nine days before he was due to meet Turpin, Robinson fought Cyrille Delannoit in Turin. Peter Wilson was there for the *Daily Express*, writing, 'Sugar blitzed Belgium's Cyrille Delannoit into the state of gangling incomprehension, a resident of cloud-cuckoo land, which is the normal consequence of sharing a twenty-foot ring with this savage slayer in sepia.' The British champion was given little chance against the American superstar, who brought to the ring a record of only one defeat in 132 pro fights, with eighty-four KOs. Yet the coolest man in the huge arena, packed with 18,000 eager fans, was Randy Turpin. One of three fighting brothers, Randy was British and European champion with only two defeats in forty-three fights, with twenty-nine KOs. Robinson was just another fighter to him.

And that's just how he handled the Harlem Hot Shot, a strong left jab thudding into Ray's handsome face, Turpin's awkward cleverness giving Ray problems, his solid punches hurting him. Turpin took the first three rounds, Ray shaded the fourth, Randy was back to outfight the champ in the fifth. Concern in the American corner, rising hope in the hearts of 18,000 fans, now daring to hope that Turpin might win if he keeps this up, but Ray shows his stuff in a blazing sixth round and Randy is glad it lasts only three minutes. In the seventh a fearful clash of heads brings blood from Robinson's left eyebrow. He fights desperately but it is Turpin's round – he is a brown puzzle that Ray can't quite solve. Sugar is sweet again in rounds ten and eleven but this night belongs to Randy Turpin and he wins the last four rounds and the decision of referee Eugene Henderson, which triggers a roar that almost takes the roof off the place.

Back home in New York, they couldn't believe the news. Jack Doc Kearns gave his verdict, which had some truth in it: 'Ray still had Paris in his legs.' Robinson had one thing on his mind when he returned to New York: revenge. There would be a rematch in September and he would be ready. He was, but Turpin still gave him a helluva fight for nine rounds when they clashed at the Polo Grounds in New York before a crowd of 61,730 who had paid $767,626, a record gate for a non-heavyweight fight. In the tenth round, Sugar Ray, blood again streaming from a gash over his left eye, turned loose a blistering barrage of punches after knocking Turpin down and Ruby Goldstein jumped in to stop the fight.

Robinson had regained the title but it had been hard going, and he rested for six months before beating Bobo Olson over fifteen and knocking out Rocky Graziano in three rounds. 'That night against Rocky,' Ray would recall, 'I saw the opening and then I threw the punch. Six years ago, I would have seen the opening and thrown the punch right at the same time . . . I'm getting to be an old man and I don't like it.'

It was 1952, Ray was thirty-one, and thinking of retiring. But he had this dream of winning a third world title, at light-heavyweight. The champion was Joey Maxim, a good boxer with a good chin, and he would have fifteen pounds on Ray. It was an intriguing match and speculation was rife among the critics, so the fight was made for Yankee Stadium. But it was the hottest 25 June in the history of the New York City weather bureau, and it was the heat and humidity that finally knocked out Sugar Ray when he was unable to come out for the fourteenth round. Trailing on points, Joey Maxim was still the light-heavyweight champion. It was the only time Robinson failed to go the distance in 202 fights. 'I was incoherent all night from the heat prostration,' he recalled. 'I passed out. But I went longer than the referee. Referee Goldstein passed out before I did. He passed out in the tenth round.' Ruby Goldstein had collapsed and had to be replaced by Ray Miller.

A few months later, Sugar Ray Robinson announced his retirement. He was swapping the arc lights for the footlights, going into show business as a dancer – $15,000 a week and no blood! It was good for a while. But as a dancer, Ray was a good fighter. The money dropped off, the engagements dried up. There was more trouble back home in Harlem. Ray's business manager had managed the business from the rails at Belmont Race Track! 'Ray had six businesses going,' said Joe Glaser who had booked his nightclub act, 'and not one of them was making any money. The books were in a mess, but they did show that there was at least $250,000 missing!'

'By the time I found out, the man died,' said Ray. 'There was no way to get back the money.' There was one way, though. In January 1955, Sugar Ray Robinson knocked out Joe Rindone in six rounds at Boston. He was back in the ring, and twelve months later he knocked out Bobo Olson to win the world middleweight title for the third time. And this phenomenal fighter still had a couple of miracles left in his locker. Gene Fullmer, a rugged Mormon from Utah, made the pilgrimage to New York to fight Ray for the title in the Garden ring. He climbed all over Robinson, knocked him through the ropes and came out with the title. Of course, Ray's iron-clad contract had a return bout clause and when they met again in Chicago a few months later, Ray exploded the left hook on Gene's chin to become champ again.

Then he tangled with the welterweight champion, Carmen Basilio, a teak-tough little gnome of a fighter who hammered his way to victory in a tremendous fight they still talk about in New York. So Ray got him back again, in Chicago, and closed Carmen's left eye and at the final bell he was champion yet again, for the fifth time. By this time it was 1958 and he was running out of miracles. And when Paul Pender took the title away in Boston, Ray couldn't beat him in the rematch. He was a champion no more. He tried, in two shots at Gene Fullmer's NBA title, but the best he could do was draw in one of them.

He was still hoping on a November night in 1965. Jesse Abramson wrote in the *New York Herald Tribune*, 'Tonight in Pittsburgh, this ghost out of the past faces Joey Archer, young, fast, skilful, who is next in line for a shot at Dick Tiger's world middleweight title. As humble now as he once was arrogant and commanded forty-five per cent and gave promoters ulcers, Robinson will earn maybe $5,000. "I want to win the middleweight title just once more and then I'll quit for good," he said. "I will beat Archer and then I'll fight Tiger."'

'Archer knocked Robinson down,' wrote Pete Hamill. 'The old champion got up slowly, dusting off his white trunks, looking humiliated. A few seats away from me was Miles Davis, the great trumpet player, who used to work out with Robinson at Harry Wiley's gym in Harlem. Miles is a tough, laconic man, but as he rose, looking into the ring at his stricken friend, tears moved down his cheek. Later, we were all in the dressing-room, and Robinson looked tired and old. He had lost a ten-round decision. His left hand was jammed in an ice bucket. And Miles started whispering, in his deep croaking voice, that it was over, that it was time to pack it in. Robinson nodded agreement. Slowly he got up off the rubbing table. "I never wanted to hurt anybody," he said to me. "If you write it up, put that in. I never wanted to hurt anyone." Sugar Ray had never looked sweeter.'

In Ray's later years he suffered from Alzheimer's disease and he was sixty-eight when he took the final count in April 1989. Among the tributes which came from all over the world was this one from Muhammad Ali: 'He was the greatest fighter of all time. He's the only one who was better than me.'

# The Brockton Blockbuster 14

Rocky Marciano's secret of success was best summed up in his own words, shortly after becoming heavyweight champion of the world. 'If anyone wants my title,' he told a reporter, 'they have to figure on chopping me in two halves. Even then, it would be pretty tough, because I figure both those halves would get up fighting!'

Sportswriter Jimmy Cannon wrote, 'Originally, the fight mob claimed he couldn't survive. He took too many punches. But they were wrong because Marciano out-toughed all the rough guys and broke up the cute ones. The ferocity of his style was glorious in its persistent recklessness. He had a jawbone that rejected the heaviest punches, and his body seemed to be a granite monument to himself. He was a glad slave in the bondage of his body.'

Trainer Freddie Brown, who often worked Rocky's corner, said, 'You will never find a more conscientious worker than Marciano. He was dedicated to getting into physical perfection.' Those words were echoed by veteran manager Charley Rose. 'In over fifty years of experience in the boxing game,' said Charley, 'I never met a more industrious gymnasium worker.'

That work in the gym and on the roads paid off in the ring. Following Rocky's untimely death in a plane crash in 1969, columnist Red Smith wrote, 'The records make Rocky the best. In forty-nine fights, nobody ever held him to a draw and only six opponents finished on their feet. Rocky Marciano couldn't box like Tunney and probably couldn't hit like Louis, but in one respect he had no challenger. He was the toughest, strongest, most completely dedicated fighter who ever wore gloves. Fear wasn't in his vocabulary and pain had no meaning.'

Yet this was a kid who never wanted to be a fighter. As a boy growing up in Brockton, a town of some 60,000 people twenty miles south of Boston, Rocco Francis Marchegiano dreamed of making it to the big leagues as a football or baseball player. At Brockton High, he was a centre-linebacker, a tremendous tackler, impervious to injury, his strength and courage an asset for any college team. Had he stayed in high school, an athletic scholarship would probably have been there for him at Boston College, Holy Cross or Fordham. But his grades were poor, he thought of little else but sports and he knew he would soon have to leave school anyhow to get a job and help out at home. So his dream of college football died.

Baseball was Rocco's other love and he showed even more promise on the diamond. He starred as a catcher, his arm was powerful, he had good baseball sense and was a right-handed hitter who slammed a tremendously long ball. But he hurt his arm pitching in a service game while in the US Army, at Swansea, in Wales. Out of uniform, he tried out on a farm team of the Chicago Cubs, but his arm was gone, along with his dream of big-league baseball.

When he left school, Rocco worked all sorts of menial jobs. He washed dishes in a diner, delivered beer for a brewery, worked in the winter shovelling snow and in the summer as a landscape gardener's helper. He did try the shoe factory where his father Pierino laboured all his life, but had to leave when the smell of the leather made him sick. In March 1943, the US Army took him. 'They must have looked at my thick neck,' he would recall, 'and said, "Here's a guy we can work," because right away I was in a brand new Combat Engineers outfit, the 150th. You know, the guys who used to be there to shake hands with the first wave on an assault landing.'

Rocco Marchegiano served three years in the Army, including a year in Britain. 'I started to fight a lot out at Fort Lewis in Oregon. The first one I fought was a decision, but most of the others were knock-outs. The boys got a big kick out of seeing me drop 'em, and I guess I did, too.' He didn't knock them all out, however. In fact he took a belting from one guy in an Army tournament in the Pacific North West. 'The man who did it came from up around Boston way, too,' said Rocco. 'He was a great boxer, and I didn't know whether I was coming or going while I was in the ring with him. I believe his name was DeAngelis, or something like that. He developed some physical trouble afterwards and never fought professionally. Who knows, maybe if he had, everything might have been different and it could have been him instead of me who made it.'

Rocco suffered some damage himself in one of those service bouts. He hit an opponent so hard he badly hurt his knuckles. Despite a warning from the doctor, he further damaged the knuckles by fighting on, losing out in the final. An Army surgeon performed an intricate operation on Rocco's hand which earned the medic a promotion and gave the fight game one of its most devastating punchers.

Out of the Army, Rocco worked on a road gang for the Brockton Gas Company and, egged on by his bosom pal Allie Colombo, he started boxing in the amateurs. In about thirty bouts he lost three, one of them to Coley Wallace, a black kid out of Harlem who had seventeen first-round knockouts. Rocco waded in with both hands as Wallace jabbed and moved, and at the final bell, much to Marchegiano's disgust, Wallace got the decision. The Brockton boy won the New England tournament and was looking forward to fighting Wallace again, but a broken thumb started him thinking about turning professional.

But it wasn't easy getting started. Boston promoter Sam Silverman had seen Rocco in the amateur championships but took no interest. The kid was a clumsy novice – he either nailed his man with a knockout right hand or fell down trying. Another well-known figure around Boston was Johnny Buckley, who had handled Jack Sharkey. One day Rocco went to Buckley's tavern, but as he was walking in one door, Buckley was walking out the other, heading for the racetrack. Then there was Peter Fuller, a Harvard man who was the son of Alvin T Fuller, former governor of Massachusetts. Fuller had the chance to buy half of Rocco's contract for $500, but turned it down. Fuller had seen Rocco fight in the amateurs and even figured he could beat the guy himself. Trainer Joe Cirelli told Rocco, 'Forget it. You're too old to be starting out. You're not tall enough. Your arms are too short and your legs are too thick. Forget boxing. You'll get killed in the pros.'

But Colombo's enthusiasm was enough for both of them. He wrote to Al Weill in New York City and the veteran manager invited them to the big town. Weill didn't send the fare, so Rocco and Allie made the seven-hour journey on a vegetable truck, arriving looking like a couple of hoboes. Rocco was not much more impressive when they stuck him in the ring at the CYO Gym on Seventeenth Street. Little Charley Goldman, who trained Weill's fighters, remembered, 'His head was way up in the air and he was off balance every time he swung. And that jab! His left arm was turned palm up and bent over to his left. This guy we tried him with backed him into the ropes and began belting the kid to the body. So he covered his head with his hands and just let the guy punch him. When I asked him what he was doing, he tells me, "The fellow who taught me to fight says when I got against the ropes I should put my hands over my face and let him hit me in the belly until he got tired, and then I should clout him on top of the head and knock him out." So help me, those were Rocky's own words. I had to walk to the other end of the gym and back when I heard that.'

But Charley and Weill saw enough in the gym that day to realize this strong kid had something. 'When I called time again,' said Charley, 'Rocky hit the other guy with a right hand which nearly put a hole in the guy's head. If I hadn't called time right away, he would have killed him for sure!'

'I seen right then Rocky had the beginning of it,' Weill told Joe Liebling of *The New Yorker*. 'So I sent him up to Manny Almeida, a friend of mine who promotes in Providence, which is near where he is out of Brockton, but Brockton is too small to have fights. And I asked Manny to put him in with the same kind he was, but no set-ups. Because you got a guy knocking over set-ups, you don't know what you got.'

Al Buck, boxing writer for the *New York Post*, recalled, 'I first saw him in the CYO Gym in New York where I had gone to watch Tony Zale, the middleweight champion, train. Charley Goldman, the veteran trainer, asked me to look at the young heavyweight whom he was teaching. This was Marciano. He was chunky, short-armed, heavy-legged, no more than 5ft 11in tall. He appeared to have two left feet, and I dismissed him with a word: "Impossible!" But Goldman knew what he was doing. He didn't try to make his pupil a fancy dan. He put him in a crouch, taught him to hook short with his left and follow through with a right cross.'

Fighting as Rocky Mack, Marchegiano had stopped Lee Epperson in three rounds in March of 1947, but his first fight for Weill and Goldman was in July 1948 against Harry Bilazarian in Providence.

'The first time he knocked me down,' recalled Harry, 'he broke my tooth. When I got up I was afraid I'd swallow it. Then he knocked me down again. Then I don't remember anything.' It took Rocky two right hands and ninety-two seconds and he was on his way. That first year, Rocky knocked out eleven guys and Weill didn't cut in on any of his purses. After he beat Eddie Ross, Al sent Goldman to be in Rocky's corner for the first time. Ross was a Canadian who had won twenty-five fights, twenty-one by KO. Rocky dropped him like a pole-axed steer. Weill wanted Charley to see Rocky against a fighter they knew could move around and handle himself a bit, so he got a heavyweight working out in Stillman's Gym named Jimmy Weeks. With Charley down there in the corner, Rocky knocked Weeks out with his first punch of the fight, a straight right inside a left hook lead. 'I knew after that fight,' said matchmaker Manny Almeida, 'that Rocky would go all the way.'

After another couple of knockouts in the Providence ring, Rocky fought Gil Cardione in Washington, DC. It was the first time Al Weill saw Rocky fight. Scheduled for outdoors, the fight was put back two days because of rain and finally moved indoors to the Uline Arena. In those few days, Rocky got friendly with the sad-faced Puerto Rican he would be fighting. Cardione told Rocky about how he needed the money – he was fighting and working at the same time so he could support his family, and if he was injured in the fight it would be hard paying the bills. 'Gee, I felt sorry for him,' said Rocky at the time. 'He had a tough life.' What happened in the fight? a reporter asked him. 'Oh, that?' said Rocky. 'I hit him a left hook in the first round and knocked him out. It was my quickest knockout.' As Cardione came in, Rocky hit him a left uppercut that jerked his head back and dropped him to the canvas just thirty-six seconds into the opening round. He was out for almost ten minutes.

Marty Weill was Al's stepson, and he remembered Manny Almeida calling his father one day early in Rocky's career. '"Hey, Al," says Manny, "we got to do something about your guy's name. It's too long for me to get on my show cards. Can't we shorten it a little?"

'"I'd prefer to keep an Italian flavour, Mr Weill," Rocky said. Then we discovered that the H-E-G in the middle of his name were hardly used when the name was pronounced quickly. By simply deleting those three letters and leaving the name Marciano, Rocky had the Italian flavour. He liked it fine, and that was how this swarthy, muscular young man became known to the world as Rocky Marciano.

'After sixteen straight knockouts, we wanted to see what Rocky would do with an opponent he couldn't knock out. We came up with Don Mogard, a tough, young heavyweight from Paterson, New Jersey, who had won fifteen of his first sixteen fights but had lost seven in a row, all on decisions and two of them to Roland LaStarza. The biggest of Marciano's forty-nine fights was against this Don Mogard, because until after this fight, we really weren't certain of what we had. Marciano nailed Mogard with two sweet right-hand shots to the face, a little high but good punches. Mogard did not go down. Instead, he countered with a right to Marciano's jaw, a real good punch. A startled look flashed across Marciano's face. When Rocky returned to the corner, he asked Charley, "What do I do now?"

'"You do what we've been teaching you to do," Charley hissed in Rocky's ear. "You think every guy you hit is going to go down?" Marciano nodded grimly. He moved a little more cautiously when the second round began. But then, as he was about to throw his left, he dropped his right a little and Mogard shot over a terrific right to Rocky's face. The punch shook Rocky more than he ever had been in his young boxing life. "This is it, Charley," I yelled. "We are gonna find out now."

'Marciano took the punch and kept his composure. He retaliated with a stiff left jab that found Mogard's nose. Rocky started keeping

his right hand up where it belonged. He asked no more questions for
the remainder of the fight . . . Late in the fourth, Marciano began to
take control. He had Mogard figured out now. He knew what to do.
For the first time in his boxing life, Rocky Marciano was fighting with
his head as well as his fists.

'The fight developed into one of the most sensational ever seen in
Providence. The arena was bedlam as they flashed punches at each
other. Black-haired Marciano, tongue flicking in and out of his mouth
in that strange manner, was passing his tests with A's in every
subject. When the fight ended, there was our boy Rocky standing in
mid-ring, arm raised aloft in victory. Seconds later the famous
Brockton charge to the ring was launched as wild-eyed fans of the boy
leaped over the ropes and carried him around the ring in triumph. The
sight of the confusion was too much for me. I slipped quietly out of
the ring. I was too choked with happiness. I worked my way through
the crowd and outside into the street. The fresh spring air felt good. I
lit a cigarette and inhaled deeply. Above me the sky was filled with a
thousand stars. As I stared up at that dazzling galaxy, I could have
sworn that in the middle a bright, new star was shining that night.'

Five months and three knockouts later, Rocky was taken the ten
rounds for the second time in twenty-one fights when Tiger Ted Lowry
stuck it out to the final bell. The New Haven veteran had lost ten of
his last eleven fights when he squared off with Rocky at the Rhode
Island Auditorium in Providence that October night in 1949, but he
hammered the unbeaten Marciano through the first four rounds
before becoming discouraged at Rocky's inhuman capacity for
punishment. Marciano kept pounding away at whatever part of Tiger
Ted's anatomy he could see and came out with the decision.

In September 1949, Al Weill was appointed matchmaker for the
International Boxing Club in Madison Square Garden. Under the rules
of the New York State Athletic Commission, he could not be a

manager while acting as matchmaker, so Al turned his tiger over to Marty, his stepson. Earlier that year, Rocky would recall, 'I was training at the CYO Gym for a Providence fight when I got a phone call. It was Weill, and he said to come straight up to the office. When I walked into Al's office there were three other fighters there, the only ones he had outside of me at the time. Weill sent them out as soon as I got there. "I'm the new IBC matchmaker," he said. "I just released those three guys. I'm not managing them anymore." He opened a drawer and pulled out a paper and passed it to me. "Sign it," he said. I didn't even read it. I signed it and Al put it away. Then he says, "That's a private agreement between you and me. But if anybody asks you who your manager is, tell them Marty." After Al and me signed this agreement, Marty was around for all my fights, but he was never my manager. We weren't fooling anybody.'

Five days after Christmas 1949, Rocky Marciano was in Madison Square Garden to go ten rounds with Carmine Vingo, another young heavyweight reaching for the stars. The day before the fight, Carmine was twenty, just eligible to fight ten rounds under the Commission rules. He fought six – and he doesn't remember any of them.

'At eight o'clock I was in my dressing-room,' Vingo recalled later. 'I was excited, but not nervous. You could hear the noise of the crowd echoing through the corridor. Whitey Bimstein taped my hands and I shot a few punches, and then he put on the gloves. I dance up and down a little. "Show him who's boss right away," Jackie was saying (Jackie Levine was Carmine's manager). Then there was a loud roar and I knew the fight going on was over. Whitey tied the cord to my robe. I blessed myself twice before the call came. I walked out, Jackie and Whitey and Freddie Brown, my other handler, in back. The corridor, and then six big steps up, the blur of faces all around. And that is all I remember. I try hard to remember the walk down that aisle and the fight itself, but my memory stops at those steps. The punches that knocked me out, or possibly my head hitting the canvas, wiped out all those details . . . I had a blood clot and there was a concussion and a small tear on the brain. They didn't think I had much chance to live. In fact, that first night a priest gave me the last rites. For the next ten days I was in and out of a coma. They say sometimes I'd scream, "Where am I?" and that I kept re-fighting the bout with my one good arm. Then it was the eleventh day and my mother's face was looking into mine and I was fully conscious at last. I was in hospital six weeks altogether. When I left, I was able to walk slowly and had got back some of the use of my arm. The doctors said it was a miracle I was even alive, let alone walking.'

Rocky would recall, 'I went back to the dressing-room and showered up. The newspaper guys came in, and finally some guy says, "That Vingo boy is in bad shape, Rocky, they think you better go to the hospital. They got him in St Clare's Hospital. Dr Nardiello's over there." Dr Vincent Nardiello was the Garden doctor. Allie and Charley and me went right to the hospital. There was this woman sitting there. She was sobbing so hard she had a handkerchief in her mouth, and I knew she was Carmine's mother. I just stood there and looked at her and said, "I'm sorry." She didn't say anything.'

The fight Carmine Vingo couldn't remember will never be forgotten by the big crowd that thrilled to it in the Garden, a savage Pier Six brawl that ended in the sixth round with Carmine sitting on the canvas and Dr Nardiello calling for a stretcher. A smashing right to the jaw felled Vingo for a nine count in the first round. He got up and was fighting back at the bell. Carmine was dumped again in round two for another nine count, but the more he was hurt the harder he fought and Rocky was surprised at his toughness. In the third, Vingo smashed Rocky across the ring with a stunning left hook and the 10,000 crowd was going crazy. Goldman advised Rocky to pace himself for a couple of rounds and the change threw Carmine off his game. He became frustrated, he wanted a punch-up!

Coming out for round six, he tore across the ring but Rocky stood his ground and met Carmine with a savage left hook, right cross combination that dropped the Bronx boy in a heap. The referee stopped his count at three and waved Dr Nardiello into the ring. If Carmine Vingo had died, Rocky Marciano was ready to hang up his gloves. He lived, and they became great friends. Rocky paid $2,000 hospital bills for Carmine and gave him $500 to add to the $500 he got from the Garden insurance policy.

When Carmine married Kitty in March 1950, Rocky wanted to go to the wedding, but he was training for his next fight against unbeaten Roland LaStarza in the Garden. He spoke to Carmine on the telephone on the day of the wedding and wished him luck, and Vingo asked him to beat LaStarza for him. 'That Carmine is a swell boy,' said Rocky, 'and he's got a swell bunch of friends. I beat LaStarza for him, but not so good. You see, LaStarza doesn't make a good fight for the fans. When you fight a guy like him, you've got to make the fight, come to him the whole way. When I fought him, I didn't have any experience with real clever boxers like him. So I get going with him, and I was pretty anxious to please all my friends from Brockton, down to see me in this big one. I tried too hard. He's a good boxer, but the whole time I'm leaving myself open, coming to him, trying to do something, trying to make a fight of it.'

A college-educated New Yorker, Roland LaStarza was as clever inside the ring as he was out of it. He had gone through thirty-seven bouts without defeat and a lot of people in the Garden that night thought he won this fight, too. One of them was Nat Fleischer. 'Marciano can hit,' he wrote, 'but that's as far as his knowledge of boxing goes. He is wide open and swings like a gate, and would be a target for any fighter who possesses courage and skill. My points score favoured LaStarza, seven to six, and my round-by-round tally showed Roland leading five to four with one even. Had not Marciano scored a seven-count knockdown in the fourth round, the count of the officials would not have been in his favour, because he missed frequently. In the infighting, at which it was figured he would shine, he was outscored by his opponent. Now that Marciano has hurdled LaStarza, even though by a hair's breadth, there'll be no further clash. Weill will see to that. Rocky in one round missed eight attempts to land on his moving target, yet one looping overhand right felled LaStarza in the fourth round and caused referee Jack Watson to give Rocky the points that earned him the decision.'

It had been too close for comfort. One judge saw it for Rocky, one for LaStarza. The referee gave them five rounds each, with his points tally nine to three in favour of Marciano. LaStarza's manager screamed for a rematch but Al Weill was out to lunch. Sure, the boys could meet later. Three-and-a-half years later! The Weills sent Rocky back home for a year and he fought around Providence, Hartford and Boston, winning nine more fights. But Tiger Ted Lowry again defied him for ten rounds, and so did Red Applegate.

Syndicated sports columnist Jimmy Cannon had little time for Al Weill, writing, 'There are few in the fight racket who know the angles as well as Marciano's manager. Deceit is his confederate. Stinginess is one of his characteristics. I would consider him an authority on the hoodlums who push in on fighters . . . Back as far as Red Applegate, Marciano was lacerated and bruised. Only last week, Weill narrated the cruelty of his cunning. The cut that gaped in the flesh over Marciano's eye in the Applegate fight appeared to gasp as a mouth does, so deep was it and so wide. It was Weill who described this with brutal pride. The gash, Weill told me, was so big he could have laid his forefinger in it. But how smart Weill is, how cunning he is . . . If the fight had been promoted in Boston, Weill explained, compassion would have compelled the referee to stop it. He made the match for

Providence, where, according to Weill's version, pugs are allowed to be terribly torn without a referee's interference.'

Just over two months later, Weill brought Rocky back to Madison Square Garden to face Rex Layne. The Utah strong boy had come into New York as a ten-to-one chance and whipped old Jersey Joe Walcott in a thriller, despite a badly gashed eye that took ten stitches. Layne had just hammered out a sensational victory over Chicago puncher Bob Satterfield in the Garden, but in between he had looked terrible against South American spoiler Cesar Brion, winning the decision but little else. Now he was back to face Marciano and he opened as an eleven to five favourite, with the smart money on him to beat Rocky.

For the first time, Weill sent Rocky to a training camp, at Greenwood Lake, upstate from the city. Marciano was in camp six weeks and when he came into New York for the fight he was in the best shape of his career. Something else had put him in a good mood. Some time after he started doing well as a pro, Rocky was sued by a Brockton bus mechanic named Gene Caggiano, who claimed Marciano had signed a document with him as an amateur stating that Caggiano would be his manager. The case dragged on for months and ended up in the Massachusetts Supreme Court. Ten days before Rocky was due in the ring with Layne, the court ruled in his favour. Bring on Rex Layne!

'Layne is a big, slow farmer sent to you from heaven,' advised Charley Goldman. 'Just keep pounding him in the body and when he starts slowing down, give him some hard raps on the chin. You can't miss knocking him out.' In that first round, the crowd was already on its feet as Rex and Rocky hammered punches at each other, Marciano heeding Charley's words and jamming savage lefts and rights to the body. By the end of the second round Layne was missing a tooth and his eye was already bleeding. Round three, and Goldman told Rocky to lay back a bit, '. . . tease him with left hooks, then follow up with the old Mary Ann.' Layne opened up more as Rocky gave him space, but he was now wide open to those overhand rights and in the fourth round a smashing shot to the chin dumped Layne on the canvas. But the Mormon was up straight away and fighting back at the bell. The fifth was a bad round for Layne as Marciano was now ploughing forward like a bulldozer clearing a site, bobbing, weaving, crowding and punching, all the time punching. It couldn't go on. In the sixth, Rex tried a left hook to the head but Rocky beat him to the punch with that devastating right hand he called 'Suzy Q'. As the blow crashed against Layne's head, he pitched forward to his hands and knees, his head hitting the floor, then rolled over on his side and it was all over. Back in his dressing-room, Layne said, 'I heard the count from one to ten and I kept telling myself to get up, but I couldn't move. It was strange and horrible, like being chained there.'

Rocky considered this fight with Layne his finest. 'Layne had never been knocked off his feet going into that bout,' he said. 'He was at his peak and so was I. He was dead game and Charley Goldman called it my perfect fight. He always said, "I never had to tell you a single thing to do in that fight." That was a lie, as you know, but I agree with Charley wholeheartedly. I really felt like a champion for the first time in that fight and I was pretty sure after it that I would win the title if I got a chance at it.'

Rocky's mother Pasqualena never wanted him to become a fighter, but she didn't stand in his way. She never saw him fight, not even on television, preferring to pray for her first son and his opponent. But there came a night when she decided to check out this fight game. Joe Louis, who had just announced his retirement, boxed an exhibition with Bill Weinberg in Providence. Mama Marchegiano went and watched, and when she got home she went straight to Rocky's room. 'Rocco, promise me one thing,' she said. 'Promise me you'll never fight this Joe Louis. He's a big strong man. He's like a big monster. His hands were going like machines in the shoe factory! Promise, *figlio mio*?'

On a Friday night in October 1951, Rocky Marciano walked to the centre of the ring in Madison Square Garden and looked up into the impassive face of Joe Louis as referee Ruby Goldstein gave them last-minute instructions. Rocky at 5ft 11in to Joe's 6ft 2in, 187 pounds to 212 for Louis, twenty-eight-years old with the old champ now thirty-seven, the glory days long behind him, fighting now to try and square his tax bill with Uncle Sam.

That Boswell of boxing, Joe Liebling, was in the Garden that night covering the fight for one of his fine essays in *The New Yorker* magazine. 'Near the end of the first round,' observed Liebling, 'Marciano threw one of those rights and it landed, it seemed to me, just under Louis's left ear . . . This was the kind of punch that addles a man's brains, and if it had happened thirty seconds earlier and Marciano had pressed his advantage, he might have knocked Louis out in the first round. I think that punch was the one that made Joe feel old . . . In the eighth round, Marciano, the right-hand specialist, knocked Louis down with a left hook that Goldman had not previously publicized. When Louis got up, Marciano hit him with two more left hooks, which set him up for the right and the pitiful finish. Right after Marciano knocked Louis down the first time, Sugar Ray Robinson started working his way toward the ring, as if drawn by some horrible fascination, and by the time Rocky threw the final right, Robinson's hand was on the lowest rope of the ring, as if he meant to jump in. The punch knocked Joe through the ropes and he lay on the ring apron, only one leg inside.'

'When I beat Joe Louis in the fight that really put me in the big time,' recalled Rocky, 'I got even more of a kick out of what Joe told me sometime afterward than I did out of winning the fight. "Man," he said, "you really pour it on in the ring." He asked me if I ever was a southpaw.

'"I've never been anything but a right-hander, Joe," I said. "Everybody always said all I got is a right hand."

'"They told me that, too, Rock," Joe said, "and they don't know how wrong they all was. You did all the hurting with that left hand of yours."'

By this time, Jersey Joe Walcott was the heavyweight champion. He was the target for the Rock, and Marciano cleared the way on a humid summer night in 1952 when he blasted Harry Matthews out of the picture inside two rounds in Yankee Stadium. The veteran Matthews should have been fighting Joey Maxim for the light-heavyweight title, but the backroom boys at the IBC figured the clever Seattle boxer to be too much of a threat. Offer him a heavyweight eliminator with Rocky! Good. Round two. Three wild haymakers came over and each time Harry leaned to his right. When he did it again, a Marciano left-handed pile-driver smacked him on the jaw and the following punch drove him into the canvas. He was still trying to stand up when the ten count was called. 'Matthews did an amateur trick,' lamented manager Jack Hurley. 'He pulled back into a Marciano left hook.'

A crowd of some 40,379 fans sat spellbound in Philadelphia's vast Municipal Stadium on 23 September 1952 to see Rocky Marciano fight Walcott for the world heavyweight title. Round one, and a shock for the Rock. Halfway through the round, the champ smashed home a left hook to the jaw and Marciano was down for the first time in his professional career. His fists were still clenched as he landed, and as he looked up at the old man standing over in the neutral corner, he said to himself, 'You s.o.b., I got to get you.' He did, but it took him another twelve rounds to do it, and for three of those rounds he was fighting blindness, caused by something on Walcott's gloves and shoulders.

When Rocky's life story was serialized in the old *Saturday Evening Post* in 1956, the former champion revealed how a Philadelphia policeman discovered that capsicum Vaseline had been smeared on Walcott's gloves and upper body by manager Felix Bocchicchio. Capsicum Vaseline is a heat-producing medicine, '. . . hot stuff, almost like menthol,' said Rocky's second, Allie Colombo, 'but you never take it to the corner or use it during a fight.'

'From the sixth round through the eighth,' recalled Rocky, 'every time Walcott jabbed me and his glove came in contact with my eyes, or every time I clinched with him, my eyes would smart. I'm sure Jersey Joe had nothing to do with this. He was a helluva fighter that night, even without any extra help. By the end of the sixth round my eyes were burning. They burnt so bad during the seventh and eighth rounds I could hardly hold them open . . . For those three rounds I fought Walcott on instinct . . . If I hadn't stopped him in the thirteenth round he would have got the decision and kept the title. The policeman said there were rumours around town that it was being rigged for Walcott to get the decision anyway.'

'Practically everybody after the fight said age finally caught up with Walcott,' said old-time manager 'Dumb' Dan Morgan. 'That is because it figured to, but Jersey Joe returned to his corner as straight as a soldier at the end of the twelfth after chopping Rocky to ribbons. The fact is that the law of averages caught up with the old man after a magnificent stand. Anybody who throws as many punches as Marciano has to land one now and then. And when Rocky hits them, they stay hit.'

Veteran broadcaster Don Dunphy remembered it this way. 'Walcott, a great fighter that night, was successfully defending his crown against the undefeated brawler from Brockton. In the twelfth he gave Marciano an awesome going over and seemed to have the fight won as the thirteenth opened. As I remarked in the blow-by-blow description, Walcott's ageless legs seemed to carry him out of trouble whenever he got into it. Now Jersey Joe backed to the ropes. Rocky crashed over a right hand that landed flush on the jaw. Walcott crumpled and sagged downward. The minute that punch landed, I knew it was over and that there was a new champion. The referee counted over Walcott but it wasn't necessary. It took five minutes to revive him. That single right-hand punch by Marciano was the most devastating I ever saw.'

One sportswriter, describing the knockout, said, 'You could see his body quiver with the shock. His lips, cheeks, nose and eyes all seemed to shake loose and run together like blobs of wet mud. Then he sank slowly, painfully, pathetically. When he fluttered to the canvas, he had no more life than a rag doll.'

That championship wallop was measured shortly after the fight by the United States Testing Company in a stunt arranged by Ben Lee Inc., makers of sporting equipment. After Rocky threw over a hundred punches at a specially designed punching bag, the Testing Company announced that, 'Marciano's knockout blow packs more explosive energy than an armour-piercing bullet and represents as much energy as would be required to spot lift 1,000lb one foot off the ground.' They could have just asked Jersey Joe Walcott. 'Soon as it landed,' said old Joe, 'all the lights went out.'

According to boxing writer Barney Nagler, 'Walcott had a contract for a return bout and promoter Jim Norris was eager to put it on because the first fight had been so exciting. At this point, Frankie Carbo moved into focus. Carbo was the underworld's overlord of boxing. Marciano insisted that he did not know Carbo and actually had spoken to him only once, during a chance meeting in front of Stillman's Gym in New York. Yet Carbo actually had a piece of Marciano. Or, to put it another way, he had a piece of Weill's piece . . . And he was friendly with Walcott's manager, Felix Bocchicchio, who was like Carbo, a man with a wide and personal familiarity with the penal code in various jurisdictions. Together, Carbo and Bocchicchio put the squeeze on the promoter. They convinced Norris that the former champion would not fight Marciano again for less than $250,000, though he received only $188,070 the night he lost to him. The fight was a travesty, over in the first round. Walcott took his $250,000 and went home to New Jersey. Marciano's purse came to $166,030. The champion had been short-changed.'

By this time, Al Weill had stepped down as matchmaker for the Garden and assumed full control of the heavyweight champion. Rocky explained what that control meant to him. 'He told me when to go to bed, when to get up, what to drink, what to read, who to talk to, where to go, who to do favours for. My family was nothing. He decided when I could get married to Barbara, when I could see her, when we could talk to each other on the phone, when we could write to each other, when we could raise a family. "What are you?" Al would say. "You're just the fighter. Without me, you're nothing!"'

Rocky would defend his title six times in three years, blowing Walcott away inside one round, hammering Roland LaStarza in eleven and beating Ezzard Charles twice, the former champion taking Rocky the distance for only the sixth time in forty-nine pro fights before being knocked out in the rematch a few months later. Gutsy British champion Don Cockell stood up for the best part of nine rounds in a brutal beating, and light-heavyweight champ Archie Moore put Rocky on the canvas before being swamped in an avalanche of leather in round nine.

By this time it was September 1955 and Rocky Marciano had had enough of prizefighting. He had had enough of Al Weill, too. In the Louis fight, Rocky had been forced to accept fifteen per cent against forty-five per cent of the take demanded by the old Brown Bomber . . . Walcott made far more than Rocky in their two fights, and it would come to light that Weill had received a $10,000 'under-the-table' payment in the Cockell fight. Finally, in the Moore fight, as related by Rocky's uncle Mike Piccento, 'Rocky was burned up about the $10,000 from the Cockell fight. He and Weill had split up almost half a million from the Moore fight, and Rocky had worked out a deal to have the money spread out over three years. Then he heard Weill had scalped thousands of dollars of tickets on the fight. Rocky wanted his cut but Weill wouldn't give him anything.'

'Rocky had plenty of money,' wrote biographer Everett M Skehan. 'The undefeated heavyweight champion's forty-nine fights had earned over $4 million. Rocky himself had made more than $2 million including purses, television, radio, films and personal appearances. He had not squandered it like many champions. He had hidden it, buried it, put it in banks and invested it. But he had spent very little.'

In a 1989 article in *Boxing Illustrated* magazine, Mike Marley wrote, 'Marciano was a notorious miser known to have hidden money in such odd locations as inside a toilet bowl tank and in curtain rods. "The mystery goes on," said Marciano's brother, Brockton business-man Peter Marciano. "I guess the figure is about two million. It's all buried somewhere, wherever Rocky hid it . . . he wouldn't tell anybody where it was. He took the secret to his grave."'

Maybe Al Weill had created his own financial Frankenstein's monster. 'The dollar is his God,' Weill told Joe Liebling when Rocky was fighting his way up. 'He is a poor Italian boy from a large, poor family and he appreciates the buck more than almost anybody else. He only got two halfway decent purses, with LaStarza and Layne, and it was like a tiger tasting blood!'

When the world was stunned by news of Marciano's death on 31 August 1969, Barney Nagler wrote, 'He had been moving around, picking up loose change for personal appearances of one kind or another, and he was in Chicago when friends in Des Moines asked him to come to their home for a birthday celebration the next day, 1 September. Instead of flying to Des Moines on a commercial plane, Marciano accepted the offer of a free ride on a Cessna 147 owned by a building contractor who also doubled as the pilot. Their destination was Newport Airport, twenty-five miles from Des Moines. A few minutes out of Newton, the pilot communicated with the airport asking for landing instructions. That was the last word. Some time later, the smashed aircraft was found by searchers. A free ride had cost Marciano his life. His death contained an absolutely essential element of true tragedy. Marciano could have reached Des Moines one way, but picked another path instead.'

# Bibliography

**Books**

Anderson, Dave, *Sugar Ray Robinson, An Autobiography*, Robson Books, London, 1996

Armstrong, Henry, *Gloves, Glory, and God*, Peter Davies, London, 1957

Bak, Richard, *Joe Louis, The Great Black Hope*, Taylor Publishing, Texas, 1996

Brenner, Teddy, with Barney Nagler, *Only The Ring Was Square*, Prentice Hall Inc., New Jersey, 1981

Bromberg, Lester, *Boxing's Unforgettable Fights*, Ronald Press, New York, 1962

Corri, Eugene, *Refereeing 1000 Fights*, C Arthur Pearson, London 1919

Cutter, Bob, *The Rocky Marciano Story*, Twayne Publishers, New York, 1954

Dempsey, Jack, with Bob Considine and Bill Slocum, *Massacre in the Sun*, Heinemann, London, 1960

Dempsey, Jack, with Myron M Stearns, *Round By Round, An Autobiography*, McGraw-Hill Book Co., New York, 1940

Doughty, Jack, *The Rochdale Thunderbolt*, Pentamen Press Ltd, Stockport, 1991

Douroux, Marilyn G, *Archie Moore, The Ole Mongoose*, Branden Publishing, Boston, 1991

Dunphy, Don, *Don Dunphy At Ringside*, Henry Holt, New York, 1988

Fleischer, Nat, and Sam Andre, *A Pictorial History of Boxing*, Citadel Press, New York, 1959

Fleischer, Nat, *Black Dynamite, Vols II to V*, The Ring, New York, 1938-1947

Fleischer, Nat, *Jack Dempsey, The Idol of Fistiana*, The Ring, New York, 1936

Fleischer, Nat, *Max Baer, Glamour Boy of the Ring*, The Ring, New York, 1942

Fleischer, Nat, *Terrible Terry, The Brooklyn Terror*, The Ring, New York, 1943

Fleischer, Nat, *The Michigan Assassin, Saga of Stanley Ketchel*, New York, 1946

Fleischer, Nat, *50 Years at Ringside*, Fleet Publishing, New York, 1958

Fleischer, Nat, *The Louis Legend*, The Ring, New York, 1956

Fleischer, Nat, *Nat Fleischer's Ring Record Book 1952*, The Ring, New York, 1952

Fleischer, Nat, *Nat Fleischer's Ring Record Book 1957*, The Ring, New York, 1957

Fried, Ronald K, *Corner Men*, Four Walls Eight Windows, New York, 1991

Graziano, Rocky, with Rowland Barber, *Somebody Up There Likes Me*,

Hammond, Hammond, London, 1956

Graziano, Rocky, with Ralph Corsel, *Somebody Down Here Likes Me Too*, Stein & Day, New York, 1981

Grombach, John V, *The Saga of Sock*, A S Barnes, New York, 1977

Harding, James, *Cochran, A Biography*, Methuen, London, 1988

Heinz, W C, (Editor) *The Fireside Book of Boxing*, Simon & Schuster, New York, 1961

Heinz, W C, *Once They Heard The Cheers*, Doubleday, New York, 1979

Heller, Peter, *In This Corner*, Robson Books, London, 1975

Henderson, Eugene, *Box On*, Stanley Paul, London, 1957

Hurst, Norman, *Big Fight Thrills*, Withy Grove Press, London & Manchester, 1948

Jakoubek, Robert, *Joe Louis, Heavyweight Champion*, Chelsea House, New York, 1990

Kahn, Roger, (Editor) *The World of John Lardner*, Simon & Schuster, New York, 1961

Kearns, Jack (Doc), with Oscar Fraley, *The Million Dollar Gate*, Macmillan, New York, 1966

Liebling, A J, *The Sweet Science*, Victor Gollancz, London, 1956

Mitchell, Ray, *Fight For Your Life*, Scripts Pty Ltd, Sydney, 1967

Moore, Archie, *The Archie Moore Story*, Nicholas Kaye, London, 1960

Morgan, Dan, with John McCallum, *Dumb Dan*, Tedson Publishing, New York, 1953

Odd, Gilbert, *Ring Battles of the Century*, Nicholson & Watson, London, 1948

Odd, Gilbert, *The Woman In The Corner*, Pelham Books, London, 1978

Pep, Willie, with Robert Sacchi, *Friday's Heroes – Willie Pep Remembers*, Friday's Heroes Inc., New York, 1973

Rice, Grantland, *The Tumult and the Shouting*, A S Barnes, New York, 1954

Roberts J B, and Skutt, A G, *The Boxing Register*, Robson Books, London, 1998

Schmeling, Max, Translated by George Von Der Lippe, *An Autobiography*, Bonus Books, Chicago, 1998

Schoor, Gene, *Sugar Ray Robinson*, Greenberg, New York, 1951

Schulberg, Budd, *Sparring With Hemingway*, Ivan R Dee, Chicago, 1995

Skehan, Everett M, *Rocky Marciano, Biography of a First Son*, Houghton Mifflin, Boston, 1977

Sugar, Bert Randolph, *The Ring 1981 Record Book & Boxing Encyclopedia*, The Ring, New York, 1981

Wilde, Jimmy, *The Art of Boxing*, Foulshams, London, 1927

Wilde, Jimmy, *Fighting Was My Business*, Robson Books, London, 1990

Wilson, Peter, *Ringside Seat*, Rich & Cowan, London, 1949

**Magazines, Newspapers**

*Boxing, Boxing News, The Ring, Boxing & Wrestling, Boxing Illustrated, KO, Boxing Pictorial, True Boxing Yearbook, Time, Life, Look, Saturday Evening Post*

# Index

Gross, Milton 236

Grossingers, New York State
143, 186

Grosvenor, Walter 2

Grupp's Gym, 116th Street,
New York City 77, 240

Gutteridge, Reg 97

Guy's Hospital, London 102

Hague, William Ian, 'Iron' 49-
50, 53

Haley, Patsy 6, 9, 12

Hamill, Pete 252

Harper, Al 127

Harringay Arena, London 131,
149

Harris, Sam 4, 5, 9, 11-20

Harrison, Tommy 63

Hartley, Pete 141, 221

Harvey, Charley 60

Harvey, Len 101-102, 111

Hatry, Clarence 67

Healy, Jack 222, 224

Heeney, Tom 118, 120

Heinz, W C (Bill) 167, 173,
180, 182-183, 187-189,
221, 228, 229, 242

Heller, Peter 179-180, 182,
186, 197

Hemingway, Ernest 155, 235,
242

Henderson, Eugene 249

Henie, Sonja 169, 226

Herford, Al 17, 18

Herman, Pete 62, 71-72

Herrera, Aurelio 18, 19, 177

Herrick, George 212

Hightower, Curtis 217

Hitler, Adolf 133, 169

Hoffman, Ancil 116, 118, 123,
125-126, 128, 130

Holborn Stadium 67

Horne, Lena 169

Horrmann, Kurt 240-241

Hostak, Al 194, 229

Hotel Claridge, Paris 249

Houseman, Lou 11, 12

Howard Athletic Club, New York
City 8

Howard University 164

Hoxton Baths 66

Hudkins, Ace 199

Hughes, David 71

Hughes, Johnny 63, 66

Humphreys, Joe 13, 17, 19

Hunter, Chuck 246

Hurley, Jack 183, 268

Hurst, Norman 100, 104-106,
107

Hurst, Tim 35-36

Hurst, Tom 111

Huston, Walter 125